# Up
# Against
# the Clock

# UP
# AGAINST
# THE CLOCK
## Career Women Speak on the
## Choice to Have Children

**MARILYN FABE** and **NORMA WIKLER**

Random House
New York

Library of Congress Cataloging in Publication Data

Fabe, Marilyn.
    Up against the clock.

    1. Motherhood. 2. Mothers—Employment—United
States. 3. Mothers—Interviews. 4. Single
parents—United States. I. Wikler, Norma, joint
author. II. Title.
HQ759.F16      301.42'7      78-21805
ISBN 0-394-50221-3

Manufactured in the United States of America
9 8 7 6 5 4 3 2
First Edition

FOR ALL THE WOMEN
WHO GENEROUSLY SHARED WITH US THEIR THOUGHTS
AND EXPERIENCES ON THE CHOICE OF MOTHERHOOD

# ACKNOWLEDGMENTS

The most important contributors to this book are the ten women whose personal accounts appear in it. We are truly grateful to them.

We wish to thank as well the seventy-five other women whom we interviewed. Their descriptions of their life situations and their attitudes and perspectives on the choice to have children were enormously helpful to us in formulating our ideas.

A number of health professionals and academicians shared with us their expert knowledge. We want to particularly thank Barbara Artson, Ph.D.; Christine Bachrach, Ph.D.; Alexandra Botwin, Ph.D.; Pat Bourne, Ph.D.; Judith Ellis, Ph.D.; Robert Glass, M.D.; Mitchell Golbus, M.D.; Sadja Goldsmith, M.D.; Judy Goldstein, M.D.; Patricia Kelly, Ph.D.; Ms. Esther Levine; Robert Neff, M.D.; Ms. Leah Potts; Nancy Rosser, M.D.; Arthur Salisbury, M.D.; Maida Taylor, M.D.

We wish to thank Ilana Bar-Din, our exceptionally capable research assistant, and Marcy McGaugh and Jana Reiser, who transcribed the interviews and typed the numerous drafts of the manuscript. We would especially like to thank Lillian Fabe for generously donating typing time and for her encouraging response to our material.

We are indebted to Carol Cosman, Jane Jordan, Marcia Millman, Ph. D., and Alan Sable, Ph. D. We also benefited greatly from the superb editorial skills of Moira Roth, Ph. D.

Finally, the men in our lives deserve special acknowledgment. Lars Lerup offered solid and sustaining support for the book and kept Norma well cared for and well fed. Tom Schmidt gave our book valuable organizational suggestions and gave Marilyn patient and loving support throughout the project.

Norma Wikler was supported during parts of this project by Faculty Research Funds granted by the University of California, Santa Cruz.

# CONTENTS

# Introduction

# WHAT ARE WE
# WAITING FOR?

What are the nearly one million childless American women now in their thirties going to decide about motherhood? As they approach their biological deadline for having children and find themselves "up against the clock," will they suddenly start to have babies to make up for lost time? Or, after having waited so long, will they find themselves unwilling or unable to have children?

Population demographers disagree: some predict that a mini baby boom will be produced by these women who have deferred childbearing. Other experts argue that though some of these women will become mothers, many more will continue to defer until their time on the clock runs out. The fact that no one really knows what these women are going to do does not surprise us—two childless women in our thirties. If the difficulty we have had deciding whether or not to have children is any indication of what other women are going through, no wonder the experts are confused.

We have written *Up Against the Clock* to help the undecided women in our generation, and the generations of women who follow, make up their minds about motherhood. The motherhood dilemma is rooted in a morass of ill-defined and amorphous issues, which we began to untangle by asking a question the population experts haven't fully considered: What are these women waiting for? We begin by telling why we were undecided for so long.

# Marilyn Fabe's Story

When I was in the seventh grade, my English class was asked to write a paper entitled "My Three Wishes." I remember now, with some embarrassment, that my number-one wish then was to get married and have children. Today I am thirty-five and have been married for five years. Yet children are still not a part of my life.

What am I waiting for? To answer that question it is necessary to go back about fifteen years, to the period shortly after I graduated from college. I was engaged, and marriage and children seemed right around the bend. But somehow that goal no longer had the same appeal it did in the seventh grade. In college I had developed a serious interest in English literature and decided to pursue an academic career. Before committing myself to marriage and children, I wanted to get a Ph.D. first. That decision broke up the relationship with my fiancé, and I set off for graduate school in English at the University of California at Berkeley.

The atmosphere of Berkeley in the sixties, with the Free Speech Movement, People's Park, and the civil rights and antiwar movements, was not conducive to the single-minded pursuit of a doctorate or, for that matter, to marriage and children. In the chaos of Berkeley's cultural upheaval I began to question everything from the kind of relationship I wanted with a man to the relevance of English literature to society. Time flew by. I didn't get married until I was thirty, and it took three years after that for me to earn my doctoral degree. Even then it still didn't seem a good time to have children because my position as a lecturer in film at Berkeley was not secure. To establish a reputation as a scholar and to find a regular academic teaching position, I felt I needed to give undivided time and energy to my work. I was late in starting my career as it was. How could I possibly take any time out now to start a family?

But my husband and I want children. We are happily married and see children as the natural extension of that happiness. The problem is: How can we work it out? My husband had been planning to quit his nine-to-five job as manager of a film company and set up a business in our home so that when we had children he could share equally in child care. But recently he has accepted a demanding administrative position at the university and I can no longer count on his day-to-day support.

Sometimes I found myself thinking, Why have children? Our life is happy and fulfilling as it is. Maybe deferring so long means that unconsciously we're ambivalent about having children. But whenever my husband and I were with friends who have children, we always felt that they had something special that we also wanted to have in our lives. But the more I pondered, the more confused I felt. At thirty-five and very much up against the clock, I knew I had to come to a decision soon.

## Norma Wikler's Story

When I was growing up, my mother would often remark, "It's best to have children early on in life. If you wait too long, you become interested in doing other things. Women who wait often end up never having children." While this could have been interpreted as a liberating statement—there are more interesting things in life to do than having kids—I knew it was meant as a warning: "If you don't have children, you'll regret it for the rest of your life."

I married at age twenty-four and felt pressure from my husband and his family to start having children right away. But I insisted on deferring having a child until at least I got my Ph.D. in sociology at Berkeley and landed a good academic teaching job. By the time that happened my marriage had broken up, and I was twenty-nine years old. Caught up in my job as an assistant professor of sociology at the University of California at Santa Cruz, and involved in a number of political movements, I didn't think about the subject of having children again for some time. It was not until I approached my mid-thirties and began to hear the biological clock ticking away that I was forced to confront that difficult question: Was I going to become a mother or not?

I had always enjoyed children and had become close friends with my neighbor's four-year-old child. But, I wondered, did the pleasure I got from his visits mean that I wanted to become a mother myself? I wasn't at all sure. If I did decide to have a child, I anticipated a particular problem. For several years I have been involved in a relationship with a man who is not at all interested in having children. He is a university professor and a productive artist as well. So much of his time is taken up with his work that he cannot see how children would possibly fit into his life. If I were to go ahead and have a child, I realized it would be "my baby" quite literally. Most, if not all, of the child-care responsibilities would fall on me. With my commitment to my career as well as the principle of equality between men and women, I knew that this would create serious tension and strain. And why risk such a good relationship for the uncertain rewards of a child, especially since I really felt no strong desire to have one?

The more involved I became with this man, the less I found myself thinking about having a child. But periodically the fact that I had stopped thinking about having children became a concern in and of itself. At those moments I would recall what my mother had said, and realize that I had done exactly what I had been told not to do. I had waited too long and now would probably never have children. What about my mother's implicit warning? Would I regret not having children for the rest of my life?

Although one of us was leaning in the direction of not having children, while the other thought she probably would, until quite recently neither of us was ready to make a final commitment one way or the other. In this regard we knew we were not alone. Countless of our friends and acquaintances shared our dilemma about motherhood. In the fall of 1977 we decided to write a book to help ourselves and other women understand the complexities of the issues and, we hoped, make up our minds. Because of our different academic backgrounds—one, a psychoanalytically trained literary critic, and the other, a sociologist—we believed that our collaboration would be especially fruitful.

In the first phase of our research, we met with many other undecided women in their thirties to find out what particular conflicts were preventing them from making their choice. After several months of such investigation, we were able to divide the women into three groups, on the basis of their primary set of concerns. The first group of women wanted mainly to know what effect a child would have on their careers—and vice versa. For the women in the second group, the only way they could have a child would be as a single mother, and they were concerned about the consequences of that option for themselves and their children. The third group were the women who doubted that they wanted a child at all but worried about what they would be giving up. The stories of the three women which follow each illustrate, in turn, a particular set of concerns.

## Gail Gordon's Story

Gail Gordon, a thirty-two-year-old corporate lawyer in a large Los Angeles firm, has been married to a fellow lawyer, Howard, for six years. When the couple got married, they looked forward to starting a family after they had completed law school and had their careers under way. Howard is still eager for parenthood, but now Gail finds herself in a quandary. It's not that she likes children any less than before; it is just that she likes her work more. Having plunged into an exciting career, she can't bring herself to cut back on her work in order to have a baby. Her dilemma is compounded because of the kind of mother she wants to be: "I think that children need their mothers around most of the time for the first few years. If I had a child, I would certainly want to do it right. But in my kind of practice, the law is constantly changing, and if you disappeared for a few years, you'd be totally out of it when you came back." Even if Gail wanted to take the risk and drop out of practice for a while, it is doubtful that she could, since her law firm has a policy of granting only a six-week paid maternity leave and discourages extended leaves of absence. Her only option, she feels, would be to hire enough day care to let her combine motherhood with her work. But that is easier said than done.

One of Gail's female colleagues recently had a baby, and even though she used day care eight hours a day, the effect on her career was disastrous. Lawyers in her firm work very long hours and are available to their clients around the clock. Because she had to get home to relieve the baby-sitter promptly at the end of the day, she lost the respect of the other lawyers in the office. They felt that if she wanted to be a lawyer, she should be available at all times as are the other lawyers in the firm. Never again was she assigned an important case. Gail read the warning signals clearly: if she were to opt for a child, her career might be similarly affected. And this would be an intolerable compromise for her, since she did not go to law school to end up doing boring and routine things. She loves challenging and exciting work, and is frankly ambitious.

But for Gail, giving up motherhood is not so easy. She has always loved being with children and would hate to miss the experience of having one of her own. On top of that, Howard wants a child, and her parents are pressing for grandchildren. So Gail keeps going back and forth on the issue. "Sometimes I think I want a child, but the timing is off; other times I think maybe I don't want a child. Perhaps after I've been in practice longer, I'll feel confident enough in my work to risk having a child. If I thought I could have a child without wrecking my career or wrecking my child, I might go ahead today. But I may not feel that secure for five or ten years. By then I may be too old to have a baby."

# Beverly Tolman's Story

Beverly Tolman is a staff writer on a national magazine. Her career is going very well, and she knows that she wants children. But at thirty-four she is still childless because she has not yet found a man she wanted to marry or live with. Beverly had a number of relationships with men during her twenties, but none of them became serious. "All of my energies back then went into building a career as a television reporter. That was a very demanding profession. Often I'd have to work fourteen hours and when I'd come home at night, I'd be totally worn out from the pressure I'd been under all day. I didn't have time to establish close relationships with men or women."

But even with a less hectic schedule, Beverly doubts that she was psychologically equipped at the time to sustain a deeply intimate relationship. She started in television at a time when women weren't in the business, and in order to compete in a tough, male-dominated world she had to adopt a certain kind of hard-nosed posture, and learn to separate her feelings from what she did or how she acted. The mask she wore was fine for her professional life, but it didn't help her relationships with men. In her job it would never have done to show weakness or to cry when deeply upset. But in a personal relationship she felt one needs to be able to do both those things. Having denied many of her feelings because of her work, she couldn't show them when she wanted to, they just weren't there.

Just after she turned thirty, however, her life began to change. She quit her job in television and began to work as a reporter on a magazine. Free from the pressures and furious pace of her former way of life, she began to relax and get in touch with the part of herself she had previously cut off: her repressed feelings began to emerge and she became more sensitive to her own needs and the needs of other people as well. Turning thirty also made Beverly aware that she very much wanted to have a child before it was too late. She went to a psychologist to find out why she was having such trouble finding a man. Her therapist's answer was simple—it was sociology: "She told me I was a very healthy woman with a tremendous capacity to love and be loved. Unfortunately, many intelligent men tend to shy away from independent, successful women. Even at the university, where my therapist teaches part time, she has noticed that most smart men are invariably married to women who are not nearly as bright and talented as they are." This explanation was reassuring, but didn't make her feel any more confident that her future would include marriage. If she was going to have a child, it looked as if she would have to have it on her own. At age thirty-three she began to consider becoming a single mother.

In many ways Beverly is confident that she can manage with a child on her own. Her present job gives her flexibility, excellent career options and high enough pay so that she can afford good child care. But she has many reservations to counterbalance her confidence. One of her biggest problems is to find a father for a child. She has cautiously asked several of her male friends if they would impregnate her, with the understanding that they would have no further obligations, but so far the men she has asked have been adamantly opposed. If she went ahead and got pregnant without the man's knowledge or consent, that would pose a difficult moral dilemma: she'd be using his body in the same exploitative way in which women's bodies have been used over the years. The idea of using a sperm bank was unappealing because there was no way of knowing what is really in that test tube. Even if she could figure out a way to get pregnant, she would still have a big worry. What would she tell the child about his or her father? "I read somewhere that by the time children are two years old, they know they're 'supposed' to have a father. So what do you tell them? If somebody could give me a crystal ball and say: 'Look, your child won't need a father on the scene to turn out all right, and you'll be a terrific mother,' I would say 'Fine' and find a way to become pregnant. But where am I going to get the crystal ball?"

# Pat Barker's Story

Pat Barker, thirty-four and a psychiatric social worker, has been struggling with the motherhood decision for the past several years. Her husband, Peter, is also ambivalent about having children, and in spite of endless talks they have made no headway on a decision.

Whenever she thinks of a good reason not to be a mother, a counterthought immediately pops up. "I really don't feel I like children very much, but several of my friends have said they didn't like kids either until they had their own. Perhaps I'd be the same way. Then I think to myself, kids aren't really that bad, it's the *role* of motherhood I don't like. All I'd ever think about would be how to make good child-care arrangements so I could escape from my child to do other things. But then I think, How can I be so sure I'd want to run away? I often resist new experiences and then discover that I enjoy them tremendously after I try them out. Perhaps motherhood would be the same."

Pat's most serious concern is that perhaps she is not psychologically equipped to be a good mother. She didn't get very good mothering herself and she worries that may show up in the kind of mother she would be. Her therapist feels that her fear is ungrounded. She tells Pat that if she chose to devote enough time and energy to doing it well, she would have the emotional resources to be a good mother. But that brings up another problem. Pat's standards are incredibly high. For her to "do well" as a mother could mean sacrificing everything to her children.

For all her ambivalence, Pat knows she is moving in the direction of a decision not to have children. What is keeping her from closing the case is a feeling of family obligation. Pressure from her family began soon after her marriage and has not let up since. On top of that, Pat feels the pressure from the people in her community, a small college town where everyone who is married has kids. The people she knows seem obsessed about whether and when she is going to have children. When she wears an Empire dress, everyone asks if she is pregnant. When she says no, they ask when she is going to become pregnant. Having noticed an interesting pattern, Pat takes some of this pressure with a grain of salt. The women who are happy being mothers never tell her what she should do. Only the ones who seem dissatisfied themselves put pressure on her to conform.

Another worry for Pat is that someday Peter might change his mind and feel strongly that he does want a family after she is past her childbearing age. So Pat remains in a state of indecision and pays a price for not being able to make up her mind. She is anxious a lot of the time, and is aware that her indecision drains her energy.

The stories of the three undecided women, and also our own, suggest the many conflicts women have over whether to bear children or not. More than ever before in history, motherhood is a matter for scrutiny and debate. Why? The social movements set in motion in the sixties created new options for the seventies. The awareness of the world population explosion and the environmentalists' critique made people question the assumption that having children was really for the "social good." Advances in medical technology and legalized abortion gave women who did not want to have children the contraceptive potential for total control of their fertility. And most important, the women's movement emerged. In 1963 Betty Friedan exposed the Feminine Mystique. Later, other writers questioned the inevitability or the desirability of women becoming mothers. The Women's Movement pushed and pushed and finally succeeded in opening up new jobs for women in higher levels of employment, and thus the way was paved for them to compete with men for interesting and well-paying work. All these factors together have created a social climate in which motherhood has become more of a choice and less of a mandate.

The new choice of motherhood is liberating, most women would agree, but it has also created new dilemmas which are very hard and painful to resolve. One fifty-year-old college professor, the mother of three grown daughters, commented on what she saw her children and their friends going through: "I think it's terrific that women have the choice today. But with it they've had to take on an awesome responsibility. It's hard to know how to choose, or how to know if what you think you want today is what you will want in the future. And the decision whether or not to have a child is the most irrevocable of all: If you go ahead and have one, you can't take it back. If you don't, and you pass a certain age and you want to, you're out of luck."

This brief statement sums up the most common features of the motherhood dilemma which we heard over and over again. It is hard to know how to choose, partly because the choice is so new that we don't know what questions to ask ourselves. For example, what feelings should we take as indicators that we would or would not enjoy being a mother? It is also difficult to know if what we want today is what we will want in the future. One major reason for this is that the new choice of motherhood takes us into uncharted territory where there are few precedents to follow or formulas to apply. Because the experience of women in our mothers' generation was so different, we do not have the accumulated wisdom to guide us when assessing the consequences of the current choices. Finally, there is the issue of the biological deadline for childbearing. The more complicated the choice of motherhood becomes, the more trouble women have in making up their minds, and the longer they *defer* a decision. The deferral itself raises new and complicated issues. Women wonder: How long can I wait? What are the biological risks of having children late in life? What are the psychological and social ramifications of being an "old" new mother?

All the women we interviewed who are contemplating motherhood were confronted by these three general issues: What questions are relevant to making a choice; how can one assess what it will be like living with the choice; what are the consequences of deferral? In addition to the above concerns, each group of undecided women we identified—those in conflict between children and career; those thinking about becoming single mothers; and those leaning toward the choice to remain childless—had to deal with a host of other specific issues.

Let's first consider those women who are primarily concerned with how to combine children with career. As we all know, many women with children have always worked, so that in itself is not new. But having a career is different. It involves a sustained investment of intellectual and emotional energy and commitment over a long period of time. And most careers, especially those previously dominated by men, are structured in a particular way. The vital years of career building are during one's twenties and early thirties. If you haven't established yourself by then, the chances are you never will. These years, of course, overlap with what is generally considered to be the ideal reproductive period for women. Not surprisingly, conflicts occur.

The women we spoke to in this group had a number of different worries on their minds. Almost everyone wondered if she could be a good mother and maintain a successful career too. How much child care could she relegate to others? How would her colleagues react to her pregnancy, and more important, how might her being a mother affect the way her professional competence was perceived and evaluated? She was also interested in knowing how having both a career and a child would affect the relationship with her mate.

The second group of women were also involved in their work, but potential career conflicts were of less importance to them than their worries about the consequences of being a single mother. Recent statistics show that the number of children born to unmarried women in the United States is steadily rising. There are no figures to tell us just how many of these women deliberately chose to become single mothers because they were up against the clock, but social scientists following this trend suggest that in the major urban centers, especially on either coast, more and more older single women who want children are taking this step. Still, choosing single motherhood is not an easy path to follow. There is much criticism of single motherhood, which undecided women are well aware of, regarding the possible negative consequences for the child, and also for the woman herself. And clearly, there is a special set of practical difficulties when there is only one parent to shoulder all the child-rearing responsibilities. In addition, there are a number of other thorny problems, such as how to go about getting pregnant and what to tell the child about its father.

Through our talks with women in the third group—those leaning toward the choice to remain childless—we came to realize that few women can relinquish without conflict and doubt what has been celebrated throughout history as the most fulfilling experience in a woman's life. Despite a more tolerant social climate, and the increasing number of career women who are choosing to be childless, women who do not want to be mothers must still cope with considerable social pressure and pronatalist propaganda. Negative stereotypes of the childless woman—selfish, immature, frivolous, unhappy —persist in the general culture. And many mental-health professionals *still* believe that a woman who does not want to have children is abnormal. Family, friends and even casual acquaintances not infrequently pressure childless women to start a family. The undecided women we spoke to said these external pressures made their motherhood choice more difficult. A compounding factor was their own questioning of the extent to which the unfavorable judgments of childless women might be true. Also, they wondered what they would be missing by giving up the unique experiences of childbearing and child rearing—what the consequences of their choice would be now and at a later age.

Once we had identified the major questions and concerns of each of these three groups, the first phase of our research was concluded. It was apparent by now that the resources available to most undecided women were inadequate to give them the answers they needed. Some women had talked about their dilemma with others who were undecided, but they had gained little clarification of the issues because their friends were in the same boat. Other women set off for the library. But there again, they found little help. The literature on the subject is surprisingly sparse, and most of what exists is either too theoretical, too simplistic or too biased by a distinct ideology to be palatable to most women. All this confirmed our original conviction that the most important source of information and advice had not yet been adequately tapped: the thoughts and experiences of other women of our generation who *had* made a decision for or against motherhood when they were in their thirties.

The second phase of our research was devoted to finding and interviewing these "Voices of Experience."

## THE VOICES OF EXPERIENCE

It was tempting to go back to find women who had made their decision in the previous generation—whose children, if they had them, were already grown—because they would have been able to discuss the consequences of their choice from a longer look back. But clearly, their circumstances and options were so different from our own that their experiences would not have been germane to the special concerns of this book. In that era very few women combined children with a demanding career, and few were childless by choice. Virtually no women deliberately became single mothers.

The women whose experiences would be of most help were those who made their choice in the seventies, in the context of the new social conditions we have described. With one exception, it was from this group of women that we selected the personal accounts to present to our readers. We were very fortunate in finding many highly articulate and candid women eager to share their experiences with others, and able to address themselves directly to the concerns of the undecided. These accounts, it is important to point out, come from well-educated, middle- and upper-middle-class women whose jobs offer the potential for high pay, the rewards of doing interesting work, and in general more flexibility and control over their lives than most other American women (or men). Though they are in no sense representative of working women in general, they are typical of the new wave of career women who are deferring the decision of motherhood into their thirties. And for this reason we have focused on their experience in this book.

We were the first to benefit from the experiences of the women we interviewed. Their accounts served as "sounding boards" and helped us clarify our own thoughts and feelings. Equally important, we greatly expanded our vision as to what each choice entailed and what other viable alternatives exist.

Gradually we began to think about our decisions with greater clarity and less anxiety. As the months went by, we found ourselves gaining deeper insight into our personal motivations about having children and more awareness of our needs and desires. Without knowing quite how it happened, we each found that the issue had been resolved. Norma came to a firm choice to remain childless, and Marilyn decided to have a child.

Even if this book does not resolve the motherhood dilemma the way it did for us, it will have served its purpose if it raises new questions, answers some of the old, brings ambiguous issues into focus, and suggests new ways of approaching problems and resolving conflicts.

# Voices of
Experience

# COMBINING CHILDREN AND CAREER

## Marlene Heldmann

Marlene Heldmann, thirty-six years old, is professor of history at an Eastern university. Her husband, Peter Sullivan, teaches in a different department in the same institution. They have a four-year-old daughter, Jennifer. Marlene told us she has always been committed to having a full-time profession, and this she attributes to her unusual background. She was born in Eastern Europe toward the end of World War II. Her father died when she was still an infant, and her mother had to go to work to support herself and her child. "Because she wasn't prepared for the kind of work her brains and energy suited her to," Marlene explained to us, "she always thought that I should prepare myself for a profession that would make full use of my talents." An only child, Marlene grew up during Europe's postwar recovery. "Everybody was working then, men and women alike. I had a woman doctor, and I saw women lawyers and judges coming to my uncle's house. So I always thought that women worked, that it was 'natural.'" Although Marlene always felt more strongly about having a career than a family, nevertheless, without giving the matter much thought, she and Peter decided to have a child. With unusual frankness she told us that she deeply regrets her decision.

*You said you felt more strongly about a career than a family. What were some of the reasons why you decided to have a child?*

For me it was almost an unspoken understanding that if you were happily married and felt that your marriage would hold together, and if you were reasonably healthy and well off so that you could afford a child, you had one. I didn't question it. I always felt that there wasn't anything I couldn't do, and of course one of the things I would do would be to have one or two children. Maybe I had the superwoman syndrome, but I didn't see any reason why I couldn't have a child and also have my career.

*Did you discuss combining career and children with other women who were working mothers?*

No. At that time I didn't know any women in my profession who had children. The three or four other women in my department were single. Before I met Peter, I was married to a lawyer, and most of the women we knew were lawyers' wives who had three or four children and didn't work.

*Were there any other influences on your decision to have a child?*

Not really. Mainly I had a child because I never expected not to do it. Of course, my mother was always interested in my having a child, and my husband wanted one. Peter is very sentimental about children—more than I am. He has a child by his first marriage, but his wife got custody. They live on the West Coast, so he doesn't see them often. Peter had seen me with my aunts and uncles and thought that I was a very affectionate and family-minded person. Judging by that, he felt that having a child would be a wonderful thing for me. Several times I expressed to him that I wasn't that interested in having children, but he thought that was natural because I hadn't tried it.

*It sounds as if you had some doubts about being a mother from the start. Why was that?*

I felt there was so much in my life that was already so gratifying—mostly books and ideas, even teaching. And my relationship with Peter was close. There was no great gap to fill. And frankly, I was never that interested in children. I'm interested in adults and in old people. Children have never attracted me intellectually or emotionally.

*At what point did you actually decide to have a child?*

When I was thirty. The way people talk about it, you shouldn't wait much later than that. It becomes statistically more dangerous for the mother and the baby. Looking back, I think it's possible that if I had waited longer, I might not have had a child. But it happened that a "perfect" year came along and I decided to go ahead with it. My book had just come out, and that gave me some leverage for keeping my job at the university.

Also, I had applied for and gotten a National Endowment of the Humanities grant, which meant I would be taking off the year anyway. I thought I could have my child and meanwhile be working on my project. I wouldn't have taken a year off without pay. All that played into my decision to try to have the child at that time. I got pregnant right on schedule.

*What was your reaction when you learned you were pregnant?*

For a long time I just didn't want to think about it. It had happened and both Peter and I knew it, but it wasn't something I told people for a long time. In fact, I looked very pregnant before I told anyone—except my family. It took me quite a while to get used to the idea that I really was going to have a child.

*What was the reaction of your colleagues and students?*

As I said, I didn't talk about it much and I wore loose dresses and capes, so not very many people knew I was pregnant. I do remember when my dissertation adviser found out I had had a baby he said he hadn't realized I was pregnant and that he didn't think of me as the mother type. I don't know how he intended that remark. I guess he thought I was very work-oriented and therefore wouldn't have a child. I think he divides women into two classes: mothers who stay at home and women who work. But most people at the university seemed impressed with me: "She does all this and that, too!"

*Did your pregnancy interfere with your work?*

I had been worried that it would. But physically I didn't have any problems at all. Toward the end I experienced shooting pains when the fetus pressed on nerves, but basically I was quite healthy and continued doing everything as usual up to the last day. I wasn't in a hurry to deliver. In fact, I felt that the later I had it, the better. I knew that once I did, everything would change. I had a sense of urgency and began to prepare for what I feared would be a change for the worse. I organized everything—my books, my notes—as if I were getting ready for a siege. I was reading almost up until the minute the baby was born. Even in the labor room.

*What about childbirth—how was that experience for you?*

I wanted to do it right, which for me meant natural childbirth, but I didn't want to go to the classes and huff and puff on the floor with a lot of other women. I'm a great believer in the word. I thought that if you read about it, there was no reason you shouldn't be able to do it. But it turned out that wasn't the case. It was the worst pain I've ever felt in my life. I had caudal anaesthesia, which was fine because I was awake when the baby was born. A lot of women feel guilty if they have to have anaesthesia, but I didn't. Apparently the intensity of the pain one experiences in childbirth is inherited. There are studies that confirm that. My mother, too, thought birth pains were excruciating. On the other hand, a close friend of mine who's terrified of any sort of pain had natural childbirth and it didn't hurt at all, even though she didn't practice much.

*Once you had the baby, did your fears that you would be in a state of siege materialize?*

In a way, yes. I had been used to spending whole days doing research in the library, but after I had Jennifer I had to be back home every two hours. I was breast-feeding, which I believe in because it is healthier for the baby and it gives you a nice feeling of closeness with the child. But when you're breast-feeding, you are tied to that house and tied to that baby.

*Were there other ways in which the baby interfered with your work?*

The baby completely upset my schedule. The kind of scholarship I do needs unbroken stretches of time taken when I need it. If I become inspired and my work is going well, I need to be able to stay up all night, and not have to worry about getting up with a child at six-thirty or seven the next morning. I discovered that that's the sort of time you rarely have once you have a child, even if you have a husband, as I do, who is willing to do fifty percent of everything and more when the pinch comes. The problem is, there are constant pinches. If you are a night person like me, there are times when you'll want to stay up practically every night, but if you do, you find that you have no time to spend with your child. If you're not there in the morning to see him off to day care, you won't see him until five that afternoon. By that time you are already gearing up for work and are preoccupied and not able to be as sympathetic or playful as the child would expect who has been away all day.

*What about working during the day?*

When I'm not teaching, of course, I try to work at home. But the days are so short. And once you have a child, your time is completely consumed. The number of things that children need is astounding. They're not big consumers, but they outgrow their shoes every month. They have ballet at Jennifer's day care, so I have to go out and get her a leotard. When that runs, I have to get her another leotard. Children are always invited to birthday parties, so I have to go to a toy store and buy her a birthday present. When I take her to a party I realize that all the other mothers are still there, so I have to stay because otherwise she's going to feel motherless.

Often I'm too tired to do my most creative thinking during the day. I was completely unprepared for what it physically means to have a child in terms of my work schedule. Like a lot of other people, we happen to have a child who is not a good sleeper. She has never slept for very long stretches. Even now she wakes up almost every night, so of course we wake up too. Peter and I take turns going to her, but as a result, I've gotten to be a light sleeper. I used to sleep like a log. But since I had her I wake up at the slightest noise and that certainly cuts into the amount of energy I have for work the next day.

*Some people think the academic life is more compatible with having children than most other professional work because of the flexible hours. Do you agree?*

I think it's just the opposite. Even teaching at a university like this, where I don't teach all that many hours a week, the students are very demanding and used to having me constantly available. Even when I'm home—and we have an unlisted number—the students are still on my mind. I'm reading their dissertations, or they're asking me for extensions or letters of recommendation. You know, between September and January I have to write between twenty and twenty-five letters of recommendation. Then there are the committees which often meet when no one is teaching, but that's the time when I should be picking up my child—at four-thirty or five. And of course, the evenings aren't free either. I do busy work, grade papers or think about what I'm going to teach the next day. People think our summers are free, but we're expected to publish during the summer. The worst thing about an academic job is that you're never off and you're always behind. The responsibilities of having a child make it that much worse.

*Would you go so far as to say that your child threatens your career?*

Yes. I'm not all that success-oriented, so I don't feel that I need to have my name well known or get invited to fly all over the country giving lectures. But I do worry about keeping my job. It's very difficult for me now to get a lot of writing done and that is going to be crucial when I come up for my tenure review.

I think Jennifer also poses another kind of threat to my career. Sometimes I find myself thinking, Well, if I lost my job, my husband could support me. It would be best, anyway, to stay home and take care of my child.

*Do you believe that children serve as a "way out" for many career-oriented women?*

That is a real danger. Women have not been brought up with a strong enough sense of themselves as professional people. It is very easy if one hits a snag in one's career to say, "I'm going to do something more important; I'm going to have a baby" or "I don't have to take this. My job is ruining my home life and making a wreck out of my child. I'm quitting." But if you do quit, you are minimizing your chances of ever doing important or interesting work. And I don't know if it's true for all women, but I know that for me it would never be satisfying to spend the whole day with one or two children. It's very tedious. It would drive me crazy.

*To what extent does your husband share in taking care of your child?*

Peter is very fair-minded and believes in the principle of sharing equally, but in some areas I know I have to work on him more. For example, Peter doesn't like to talk to people on the phone. Now, I don't love that either, but I can do it. So I'm always the one who has to get on the phone whenever we need a baby-sitter. Baby-sitters can be hard to find and I spend endless hours calling around trying to make arrangements.

In many ways, though, Peter does more than I do. That's partly because of our career stages. He feels that I need more time because I'm coming up for tenure soon and he already has tenure. So he'll be the one who puts Jennifer to bed so I can get started earlier in the evening on my work, and if I'm in a crisis, he'll take over on weekends. But I don't see how he can give any more time in the day than he does without sacrificing his own career.

*Do other women you know have husbands who share in child care?*

Men may be doing more than they used to, but not nearly half. Of all our friends, I think I have the only husband who really shares equally. In most cases, even when men are married to women who are at least their equal in promise and intelligence, the women still make most of the household arrangements. Whether this is due to the circumstances of their jobs or partly to our inner compulsions, I don't know.

But from what I see, most husbands are only too happy to accept it and get on with their work.

From my experience, dual-career families just don't work out. Women who want a career—and not just a job—and also children should find men who aren't so interested in having a career themselves. This is happening more and more. Women who are serious about their work are choosing men who are their opposites, who somehow complement their own drives.

Personally I know of three such cases. The women—and they all have children—divorced their well-established and well-off husbands because they were tired of being relegated to the position of housewife and of not having their work ambitions taken seriously. These women went out, got jobs, worked very hard and became quite successful. Now they live with younger men who don't have jobs or who have jobs that are undemanding—occasional carpentry or some such thing. The men do just enough so that they don't feel they are doing nothing, but it's understood that the person whose time is important is the woman. I doubt that these men would want a woman who wasn't working. They still value the Protestant ethic of hard work and achievement, I think, but *they* don't want to do it; they want to be associated with someone who wants to do it.

When you have two people like Peter and me who are both ambitious and career-oriented, it is almost impossible to also have a child or children because who's going to take care of them?

*It sounds as if you use plenty of day care for Jennifer. How do you feel about the arrangements you've made?*

I have no feelings of guilt at all about hiring people to take care of my child, and indeed, have done that all along. We figured out that with both our salaries we could afford a lot of child care and we've had it from the time she was born.

When she was too young to go out for day care, for instance, people would come in and take care of her.

Of course, we weren't always satisfied with the people we hired. They were reasonably affectionate people, but often kind of slack or lazy and not as interested in her welfare as we were. When she was old enough to go out, we found some nice enough places, but we didn't really like everything they were doing. In one place we knew they watched too much television. In another place a woman had the thermometer up to ninety-nine degrees every day during the winter. At another place they gave them junk food—crackers and pink lemonade for snacks.

Now, I don't feel I need to control everything that my child does. I'm a strong believer in her becoming independent. But there are certain habits, dietetic and emotional, that I would like her to acquire. In essence, when you relegate your child to others, you do give up some control over what happens to your child. The only suitable place we found was a cooperative day-care center where everything—food, activities—was a matter of joint policy with the parents. But that didn't work out for us either.

*What were the problems with the cooperative day-care center?*

It was an incredible amount of work for us. We worked there once a week, from nine to two o'clock, taking care of five to ten kids. We were exhausted when we came home. Another two hours a different day of the week was a meeting of the parents, but some parents met every evening. Then there were all sorts of extras—fund-raising events, picnics—that we had to go to because all the other parents were going to them. There were all kinds of little coercions. Children are so conventional. They want to do exactly what the other children are doing, and they feel they're missing out on something if you don't go. So we stopped sending her to the co-op.

I'm sorry. It was a nice place for her. The place she goes

to now costs twice as much and it's rather conventional and square, with too much emphasis on clothing, which I don't like. The little girls dress up. There's too much sex-stereotyping. But all the commercial places have that. The co-ops don't, but the co-ops, I think, are just too hard for working women to manage.

*If more quality child care were available, do you think that would solve some of your problems?*

No. Because quality child care is not really the issue. The most important thing to realize about hiring people or sending your child out is that it usually doesn't work for most children. No matter how nice that person is who's taking care of them, children have to spend a lot of time with *you*. If they don't, they will start feeling unloved, and if they are articulate and expressive, which we encourage our daughter to be, they will let you know that they want to be with you more. We see it in Jennifer. She becomes whiny, overdependent, and tells us she thinks she's ugly and that we don't love her.

So it's not so much a question of money or finding people competent to take care of your child. Once you have a child and you are a feeling and compassionate person, you know that child needs you in many cases more than your career will allow.

*Does the conflict between your career and your child make you feel guilty?*

It's very easy to feel guilt, to feel that your child isn't managing at all because you are spending too much time working and not enough time with your child. On the other hand, various friends of mine who do stay home all day with their kids say that their children have the same kinds of problems I see in Jennifer. That's important to realize, because if you're working, you tend to idealize what you would do if you were home.

*You told us that your mother worked long hours away from home almost from the time you were born. Do you feel that her absences have in any way damaged you emotionally?*

I don't think so because I didn't rely on my mother as the sole source of affection. I had two aunts I was very close to—one was a childless widow—who would take care of me when my mother was working. In essence, my mother had me only two or three evenings a week. Every weekend and every summer I spent with an aunt who had a big house in the country. I was especially close to her. Essentially I grew up in an extended family, but here it's just Peter, Jennifer and I without a large family for support.

*If you lived in an extended family situation now, do you think that would make it easier for you to combine motherhood with a career?*

It would take a lot of pressure off us, but I'm not sure it would be good for our marriage. My cousins in Europe have an extended family, but living with those old people is hard on them. They all work and have children, and the old people help to take care of the children, but they also make demands on them. When they come home from work they have to talk to their grandmothers as well as to their children. As it is now, it's hard enough for me to find time alone with my husband.

*Would you tell us something about the effect of your child on your relationship with your husband?*

Having a child drives a wedge between you and the person you're living with. There's no question about it. Peter and I have continued to be very attached to each other, but we don't have much time to be together anymore. During the day when Jennifer's away, we are teaching or trying to get some work done. Sometimes we go out for lunch together. But whenever Jennifer is home, all our attention must be focused on her. She never lets us talk to each other, and she's quite right. She doesn't want to feel left out.

Vacations used to be the time when we would get closer after we had been working hard all year. We would take four or five weeks in Europe and really be together. Now that we have a child, traveling has become a completely different experience and to my mind is greatly diminished by her presence. For example, when we used to visit my family in Europe we would take our books and plan to read and spend time talking with my aunts and uncles. Sometimes we would sightsee, but mostly we wanted to be alone and read or talk to people about politics. Now Jennifer is always there. She won't let us sit and read, and she won't let us talk to other adults.

We've remained quite close to each other, but having a child hasn't made us feel closer. Just the opposite. The things we have in common we have less time to talk about. There's always somebody there when you're having dinner. And the way we spend our free time and whom we spend it with have totally changed.

*Could you elaborate on the way your child has affected your recreation and social life?*

Our weekends used to be times when we would read or relax or go to museums. But now, whenever there is a Saturday stretching before us and Jennifer isn't going to day care, we ask ourselves what we could do that would give us reasonable satisfaction and won't bore the child too much either. So we go to all sorts of places—the beach or the zoo—places that we would ordinarily never visit and that are not much fun for us, but that we go to for the sake of our child. She needs the fresh air or she needs to see some animals. I don't mean to imply that these activities are horrible and we're biting our nails until we're released from the ordeal. There's admittedly a certain pleasure in seeing Jennifer running around on the beach or looking at animals for the first time. But if we were on our own, we wouldn't choose to go to these places.

There's another thing about children. They're really quite compulsive. They want you to read the same book to them twenty times, or see the same places over and over. I'm sure we were like that too, and somebody had to put up with us. But it really is very nerve-racking.

Our social life has completely changed. We used to have people over in the evenings a great deal, but now with Jennifer our conversations are constantly interrupted. She's always coming downstairs, asking me to go upstairs and put her to bed, all of which is very distracting. We've even changed the people we socialize with. Many of the people we meet whose children are friendly with our daughter are nice people, but they aren't necessarily the people we want to spend a great deal of time with. But when they bring their children over, or bring Jennifer home, they sit down and stay around. Because we're so pressed for time, we find that these are the people we see instead of the friends we were close to before Jennifer was born.

Our social patterns have changed in other ways, too. We even eat differently now. We used to go out almost all the time but we can't do that with Jennifer. She is very picky in restaurants and won't eat a balanced meal. Now we have to eat at home, which, I suppose, is healthier for us too, but the meal planning, shopping and cooking takes a great deal of time.

*Like all the women we have interviewed, you were over thirty when you had your first child. How do you think your age has affected your experience of being a mother?*

If I were younger, I would have felt much more aggrieved and burdened by the pressures having a child involves. I've read novels in which the mother runs off and leaves the children with the father, and I think I would have had much more of an impulse to do that. Being more mature now, I can say to myself that, true, I would rather not have a child, but now that I've done it, I'm going to live with it. I simply have to compromise what I want to do with what I have to do.

*You say you would rather you didn't have a child. Do you think if you had chosen otherwise, you would regret it now?*

No. I would have felt fine. Let's say it turned out that I was sterile. I would have had no sense of loss. I never felt the need to have an extension of myself, which is the reason I think a lot of women have children. And I don't believe I would regret being childless when I got older. A lot of women think, when I am fifty-five and childless and my husband leaves me or dies, what will happen to me if I don't have a child? But I don't think like that. I don't believe in working from the assumption of disaster. Anyway, if you have a child now for the sake of the future, it will probably make the future you want impossible.

Having children doesn't protect you against loneliness. In fact, children make you more insular: the range of your friends is smaller and your relationships are shallower because so much of your energy is involved with your child. It keeps you from developing lifelong professional friends and colleagues, and from committing yourself fully to a subject you could study in your old age.

*You've made a strong case against motherhood. Is there anything you like about having a child?*

Of course. It is very touching to have a child, especially when you've just had it. I was thrilled to see that here was a real living being that I had produced, that had come out of my body. I remember getting up all the time to make sure she hadn't suffocated. And I certainly do love my child and enjoy the rewards children her age offer. They love you, they hug and kiss you, you're their mother and they depend on you to love them. I have moments of great tenderness for this creature who is so dependent and vulnerable. But to be honest—I told you this before and you were amused—I think of my dog Penny in the same way. She is a creature I want to protect, that I feel loyal to, that I would never think of doing anything to harm. And I would go immensely out of my way to do all kinds of things for her. But Jennifer's a great deal more trouble than Penny, and she takes up a great deal more of my time.

*Some women feel that having a child allows them the opportunity to re-experience some of their own childhood conflicts and to overcome them. Was this your experience?*

I think it is very dangerous to ever think of a child as an extension of yourself. If you want to relive your childhood through your offspring, you will probably force the child to act in certain ways and end up having your child resent you. I think that if you want or need to relive your childhood, you could do it much more effectively if you were writing an autobiography or autobiographical novel, or even if you were psychoanalyzed.

*Do you think that as Jennifer grows up, some of the problems you describe may diminish?*

Frankly, I don't think the ways I don't like having a child are going to change. My older friends who have children say the problems are just as bad when they get older, but there are fewer rewards. When children become more independent you miss the ways in which they were charming and affectionate with you. Instead of hugging and kissing you all the time and making you feel needed, they begin to see you partly as an enemy. But you are in fact just as responsible for their welfare, for their schooling, for getting them new clothes, and making sure they don't get pregnant or this or that. By the time they are more or less able to stand on their own two feet, they leave.

*In light of your experience, what advice would you give to other career women who are contemplating having a child?*

First of all, you must assess how much your work means to you. Women who are ambitious and truly absorbed in their work should not ruin their chances for a satisfying career just because they feel that women should have children or that they would miss out on something if they didn't.

Don't be discouraged if you're having difficulties with your career right now. Good jobs are hard to find and keep because of the economic recession, but this should not be a reason to give up your job and have a baby. Becoming a mother should never be a way of psychologically warding off a sense of failure. Some of my friends I went to college with did just that. They either had jobs which weren't that good or lost their academic jobs and were afraid they wouldn't be able to find another. They proceeded to have one or two children which they originally did not plan to have. The kids were meant to fill a gap of a certain number of years in their lives when they would otherwise have felt useless. In their eyes, the children legitimize their existence. I don't believe in that solution to the problem of identity.

One other piece of advice. I think it is extremely important to have some experience with children before you decide to have a child of your own. Most professional women have never spent much time with children; they've gone to graduate school or medical school or law school and worked very hard. When they graduate they think, Aha! I've got my degree and now it's time to have a child. Before they do that they should think through very carefully what that will mean. Maybe they should borrow a child to see what they're getting into. I really mean that. Keep a friend's child for the weekend or take one on a short vacation.

*Can you comment on any reading you have done which might help women understand the conflicts that may emerge between career and motherhood?*

I haven't followed all the sociological and anthropological literature, though I know some work on professional women and of course Rhoda and Robert Rapoport's book, *Dual Career Families Re-examined* (Harper & Row, 1976), but none of the works really discuss the ways in which one simply ought not to have children if one is really caught up in a career and feels strongly about the way one wishes to lead one's life.

I can't think of any books which really reflect the values I have except some autobiographies like Simone de Beauvoir's, and of course she was childless. Generally, books by women writers on the subject are divided into the same camps that women have always divided themselves into. On the one hand there are books about women who are utterly dedicated to their writing, intellectual women who have chosen either not to have children or, if they do, they hire full-time nursemaids while they remain far apart from the mother role. On the other hand are the books about women who are just beginning to have a minimal sense of their own selves and their capacities but are in a struggle against men whom they love but who are not taking their ambitions seriously. These books usually end on a quasi-hopeful note, with an assurance that the woman is about to embark on a life where she will combine family and career. But mind you, you never actually *see* the woman working out the conflicts.

I think there is a strong taboo in our culture, reflected in our literature, against speaking about children negatively. As a result, it is usually the husband who is pictured as the object of resentment. The children are supposedly among the things that make life palatable. Feminist literature abounds with stories of working women who are exhausted by having children and a job, yet none of them ever says they regret having a child.

*In light of the cultural taboo you speak of, why are you able to express your negative feelings about children?*

Probably because my work rather than my role as mother is the main source of my identity, I feel more freedom than most women to accept and express ambivalent and negative feelings about children. I remember shortly after Jennifer was born I had dreams in which she died, usually because of some external disaster. Even though I was horrified and would wake up very frightened, I knew the dreams were expressing some sort of wish-fulfillment. That made me feel guilty. But now I see the dreams as a reflection of my very real feeling that my child was a danger to my career and that my ambivalence about her existence was understandable and justified. I think a lot of other women have these dreams.

*That's all the questions we have. Do you have any concluding remarks?*

I would just like to reiterate my belief that women who have always been independent and derive a great deal of meaning from their work, who are good at it and will get better, and have all sorts of plans and hopes for a professional future— these women should carefully consider what a child will do to that future. There are ways that the burden of children can be minimized or reduced. But the fact is that when you have a child you must take part in bringing up that child. It takes time, but especially energy—physical energy and psychic energy—which is going to be taken away from your work and from your marriage. Marriage is something you freely choose and can un-choose, but once you have a child, you always have that child. You will certainly have it for the eighteen formative years of your career!

If I knew then what I know now, I would have decided against motherhood.

# Ellen Talbot

Ellen Talbot, thirty-nine, a Ph.D. in psychology and mother of two children, Dan, six, and Nancy, four, is currently completing a book on children's response to stress. She and her husband, John, an internist, live in the suburbs of a large East Coast city. Ellen grew up in Virginia, the youngest of four children in an upper-middle-class churchgoing family. Her father was a lawyer, and her mother was active in community organizations. Her parents encouraged Ellen to go to college and get a good education, but both were surprised when she told them she planned to go on beyond her master's degree to get a doctorate in psychology.

Ellen distinguished herself early in graduate school and four years later, Ph.D. in hand, she became an assistant professor of psychology at a large West Coast university. There she met John, who was finishing medical school. When he was offered a residency at a hospital in the East, they decided to marry and move to the East Coast. Competent, well-trained and with excellent credentials, Ellen easily found good jobs after the move. She accepted a teaching and supervising position at the hospital where John was doing his residency, and concurrently began working as a clinical psychologist at a large community mental-health center. She was soon promoted to head of the children's services division there and was next in line to be executive director of the entire center.

After her first child was born, however, Ellen resigned from the community mental-health center, and after her second child came two years later, she quit her job at the hospital as well. Although she continued to work on a research project at home, and this project later grew into a book, Ellen frankly acknowledges that she chose to exchange prominence in her career for more time to spend with her children. Aside from her lucid explanation of the factors that motivated this decision, Ellen's story is fascinating for her vivid account of the tremendous impact a difficult baby, in this case a colicky infant, can have on the life of its parents.

*Why did you decide at age thirty-two to have your first child?*

Well, it's the whole basis of your book. You begin to look at how old you are, and if you've made the decision to have children, which we had, you just don't want to wait too long. My professional training in early infant development perhaps made me a little oversensitive to the biological and genetic risks involved in waiting too long, but my decision wasn't based on biology alone. I also thought that I would have more energy for my children if I had them before I was thirty-five or thirty-six.

*Did career considerations play a part in the timing of your child?*

Not really. I was very conscious that no matter when I decided to have my children it would interfere with my career: being thirty-seven would have been no better than thirty-two. If I had waited until I was thirty-six or thirty-seven, in fact, I might have been doing something even more exciting and it would have been harder than ever to give it up.

*Did you and your husband ever consider not having children?*

Strangely enough, no, even though we had some pretty compelling reasons not to have kids. I had a nice career carved out for myself, enjoyed my work and was doing a good job. I would have been director of the whole mental-health center by now if I had stayed. We were both working full time, had plenty of money, and, my Lord, we were leading a good life —going out to restaurants all the time, to the opera, the theater, the symphony. Life would have been very hedonistic without kids. But I suppose deep down we felt: Is hedonism all we want, or do we want something more? We used to have long discussions about not having kids, but neither of us really thought seriously that we wouldn't.

*How do you account for the strength of your commitment to a family?*

I was thinking about that before you came: Why was it unthinkable for us not to have children? Part of it, I'm sure, is that both my husband and I come from good, close, loving families. If you had that kind of experience, you somehow want to replicate it, to recapture some of those good feelings with a family of your own. On top of that, I had an extraordinarily competent mother, who was tough as nails and not at all diminished by her role as housewife and mother. Consequently, I didn't anticipate losing self-respect or self-esteem when I became a mother. She made it easy for me to want kids.

There was one more reason as well which I'm slightly embarrassed to mention because it sounds like such a cliché, but I had the sense that I would not feel complete or fulfilled as a woman if I didn't have children. When I got to be age forty-five or forty-six, I knew I would regret it. I realize that back in 1965 it was still considered woman's destiny to get married and have kids, and we have since gotten beyond that kind of thinking. Yet, I wonder, how much do women want to have children because society says they should, rather than thinking, I'm a woman—I have the unique capacity to have a child and I want to fulfill that capacity. I can imagine a woman choosing not to have children and fulfilling her life in many other ways, but for me childbirth and child rearing were life experiences I didn't want to miss out on.

*How was your experience of childbirth?*

Fantastic! With both Dan and Nancy I prepared for natural childbirth. I went through the Lamaze course with my husband and it turned out to be a marvelous experience for both of us. In fact, I can't emphasize enough how much that course reduces or "binds" anxiety. People are always talking about the pain of childbirth, but Lamaze teaches that it's possible to master the pain without getting doped up with all kinds of medication.

Don't misunderstand me. It really hurt. Childbirth *is* painful. But the Lamaze breathing exercises give you something to do which distracts your attention so you can rise to the crest of each labor pain as it comes. You can also learn to push when you need to push, so that the whole birth process is much shorter. Since I wasn't medicated at all, I had all my emotional and mental faculties about me. That's probably why giving birth was such an intense experience for me. Just unbelievable. Not only the moment of giving birth, but the hours, the days that followed were an incredibly intense emotional experience for me. Childbirth can give you an emotional high that nothing in life can duplicate—unless you have another baby, and then the same thing happens all over again.

*How did the birth of your first child affect your work schedule?*

I cut back immediately. At the time I got pregnant I was really working more than full time at my two jobs. Just before Dan was born, a colleague and I were notified that our grant proposal for a research project had been funded. That was a great boon because I knew I could work on that at home. So I decided to resign as director of children's services but keep my teaching and supervising position. About a month after Dan was born I started working about eight hours a week at home on the research project and twenty hours a week at the hospital.

*At that point, did you experience any conflict between your work and your child?*

Yes, once I had Dan I was very conflicted about finding somebody to stay with him so I could go out and work even with my reduced schedule. In fact, I worried about that as soon as I got pregnant. Once you have a child, or once you even have a child growing in you, you become extraordinarily attached and protective, and you worry. At least I worried. Could I find someone who would be as good as I would be with my child, who would love him in my absence? If I hadn't been able to, I would not have gone to work.

*What child-care arrangements did you make?*

I put an ad in two newspapers asking for an older, mature, experienced woman to look after an infant twenty-five hours a week. Only two people answered my ad. I didn't hire the first woman who called because she said she had a hearing problem—she was deaf in one ear and had limited hearing in the other. So I hired the other person, who turned out to be a student. *Never* hire a student. From what other people have since told me and from my own experience, students are notoriously unreliable. They move around all the time and quit at a moment's notice. That's what happened to me.

In desperation I called the first woman back, and fortunately, she was still looking for a job. Dorothy had recently retired at age sixty-five but was still an amazingly energetic, bright, capable woman. As for the kids, she's their grandmother. She adores them and they her, but what's more, she's very stimulating to them, always taking them for walks and reading them stories. She began working for us when Dan was only a month old and she's still with us.

I can't tell you how lucky I was to find Dorothy. It's easy to find someone to take care of an infant, but much harder to find a good person to take care of a toddler or a three- or four-year-old. With a child that age you have to worry about someone being able to set limits and the whole business of cognitive stimulation. Knowing that Dorothy was available to me and that I could trust her with my kids has made my work life much less complicated and much less of a conflict.

*If you had been unable to find someone like Dorothy, would you have considered a day-care center?*

No, I didn't want to do that. I admit I have real biases against day-care centers. Since I'm a clinical child psychologist, I have very strong professional convictions about what makes for mentally healthy and intelligent children. I have consulted at a number of day-care centers and I have never liked what I saw. It may be possible to run good ones, but I just didn't want my kids in them.

That's an elitist attitude and I know it. Many people have no choice and have to use out-of-the-home day care for their infants and toddlers. And of course, I should differentiate between large centers with twenty-five kids and only three or four helpers and small neighborhood centers where a woman keeps three or four children. The first is pure chaos and can really be damaging to children, while the small neighborhood center, depending on who runs it, can actually be a good experience.

But as for me, I was convinced that it would be nicer for my children to be in their home. The older they get, the more important that becomes for them. They would much rather come home than be transported to a day-care center after school. Their toys are here, their books are here, all their drawing material is here, and they feel much more secure in their own house. If I had not found somebody like Dorothy to take care of my children at home, I'm sure that I would have been distressed enough to quit my job at the hospital and only do work I could do at home.

*Since you were satisfied with your child-care arrangements, why did you later decide to leave your position at the hospital and restrict your work to what you could do at home?*

Partly it was because Dorothy was getting older and couldn't stay with the children as many hours, but it also had to do with the nature of my job at the hospital. I was the only child specialist on the staff at the time, and there was a great deal of pressure on me to teach all the children development courses. So even though I had cut back by that time to only ten hours a week, I was teaching three seminars, and my schedule was absolutely insane. I was racing into the city twice a week, blasting my mouth off all day long at high speed, teaching, supervising, consulting, and then I would race home and be totally exhausted. Six months after my second child, Nancy, was born, I quit altogether. I had to, because I was a frazzled mess. Now, except for one day a week when I see patients privately in my office, I work exclusively in my home.

*We've repeatedly heard women say that with one child they could manage to keep up with a career, but with the second, everything came apart at the seams!*

That was true for me. Two is more difficult than one. It's not one plus one but one multiplied by a variety of factors. And although I knew that before I had the second, I would never have had just one child. I also have strong convictions about that. The life of an only child is uniquely different from the life of a child with siblings. Only children tend to be more self-centered, and while they are more mature in relating to adults, they usually have trouble relating to their peers. I see that clinically quite often. Only children are lonely children, and that's not just a cliché—especially when both parents work. So John and I were committed to having two. But I must admit, I really think that if Nancy had been our first child, we might have reconsidered and not had a second. She was so very, very difficult.

*What were your troubles with Nancy?*

She was an absolutely impossible infant. She never slept through the night, she screamed constantly, and she *never* took naps. Most babies, you understand, are the way Dan was: they sleep for two or three hours in the morning and then again two or three hours in the afternoon. During that time you can get some work done or have some time for yourself. Naturally, I expected it would be that way with Nancy. But the very first night, when I was still in the hospital, the nurses said she didn't want to sleep much, and she didn't. She screamed every night for the first nineteen months of her life, and there was nothing we could do to comfort her.

Not only that, she would spit up all the time. We had a white rug in the house and it was covered with vomit. She was the classic colicky baby, and the only thing you can do with a child like that is to medicate her, but we didn't believe in doing that. Nancy brought me in touch with the whole dynamics of child abuse. One situation in which child abuse occurs is when a kid screams and screams but there is nothing you can do to stop it or to help. You're left with an impotent rage and all you want to do is expel, extrude, get rid of the baby. I had been teaching about child abuse for a long time, but to be confronted with the feeling of wanting to throw my own child across a room was really overwhelming for me.

John was just as desperate. We took Nancy on a vacation —ha! a vacation!—to San Francisco to visit John's parents. We kept joking about putting her on the Sausalito ferry and quietly slipping away, hoping that someone on the other side would see this beautiful baby and pick her up. You see, Nancy was a perfectly gorgeous child. When she smiled, it was extraordinary. She was lucky she had that going for her because she was bad—so terrible I can't tell you.

Nancy's the kind of child you would probably have to put in a day-care center if you were unable to get help at home because the mother would have to have some relief. I would have gone bananas without Dorothy. Going to the hospital to teach those two days a week, even with my insane schedule, felt like a blessing. I was so glad to get away. Dorothy, incidentally, didn't have any more luck with her than I did, but that was one place where her hearing impairment came in handy.

It's very hard in retrospect to recapture how bad it was for us, but it was very, very serious. I started a baby book on Nancy, putting in pictures, making notes, but when I realized the notes were getting increasingly hostile, I stopped and haven't looked at it since. She was impossible. She didn't like to cuddle, she didn't like to sleep, and she wasn't happy just lying around either. You have no idea what rage a child like that can arouse. She was headed for a miserable parent-child relationship. In someone else's house I'm convinced she would have turned out to be a basket case. Thank God, she didn't.

*What factors helped you deal successfully with your anger?*

I was lucky. I had John to spell me off, and I had Dorothy. Also, I didn't take Nancy's behavior personally, and that is very, very important. If I had been an unexperienced mother who had given up a career to have a family and ended up having a child like Nancy, it would have been devastating. But since I already had one child, I knew it wasn't I who was the problem but that something inside was hurting her.

And my professional training helped. Whenever I felt destructive impulses toward Nancy I had insight into what they were about and that helped me control myself. You see, I held the intellectual conviction that it would be terribly damaging, just devastating to our relationship, if I had actually acted on my impulses and hurt her. And I also knew that once I started, it would be that much harder to stop. For all those reasons I was able not to hurt Nancy, although I have to admit I screamed at her plenty. I don't know what would have happened if that behavior had gone on and on, but it didn't.

One day everything turned around. When Nancy was two she got very sick and was in the hospital for six weeks with what turned out to be an undiagnosed hip infection. John was taking her down to the x-ray unit to have a total body scan done on her when, lo and behold, she put her head down on his shoulder and cuddled. He came home that day and said, "You won't believe what Nancy did today." Nancy had never cuddled up to us before. She was a very active, bright child, way ahead of herself developmentally, and she was always looking around at the world rather than focusing on us. But that day, for some reason, something changed. For the first time she seemed to have a primitive understanding that she needed people for support—she needed parents, and she began relating to us. Gradually our hostility to her turned around. John started having a better relationship with her almost immediately, but it took me another year to work things out.

Now we have a wonderful relationship and she's just a great kid. The same characteristics that made her difficult as a baby —that tough-as-nails constitution that enabled her to scream for hours and not fall asleep when most kids who scream like that are exhausted in five minutes—have made her a tough, resilient, extremely competent child. She's just super now.

*Earlier you discussed the difficulty you had leaving your children to go to work. Did you have conflicts leaving your work to take care of your children?*

Yes, I did feel bad giving up my position at the hospital. I liked my work a lot and I was certainly doing very well there. But that job, combined with everything else, made it impossible for me to live the kind of life I wanted to live.

Fortunately, I'm in a field which gives me a good deal of flexibility to work on my own terms. I can do research at home, or I can start a private practice and create a limited schedule suited to my needs. Now, if I had been working at a law firm, an investment firm or in any traditional male chauvinist setting where I had to make a total full-time commitment to my job—if it were all or nothing—then I would have felt much more torn, but I still would have quit when I had children. Otherwise I would have felt even more torn.

I think many working women with children are full of conflicts. Not everyone, of course. There are women who don't like parenting that much, or who had children out of a sense of obligation and are really mostly committed to their careers. For them, being away from eight to six is perfectly okay. But I didn't have kids because I had to. I personally wanted to have children, and I wanted a good relationship with them.

*Did your colleagues think less of you for quitting your job at the hospital?*

There was terrible pressure on me not to cut back. Whenever I brought up the subject they would say things like "You can't do that to us. We *need* you to teach this or that. We need you to supervise." It was a very work-oriented, guilt-inducing place and they did a tremendous job on me. But the fact is that I was working with psychologists and psychiatrists, reasonably insightful people who, when I insisted that my schedule was crazy and utterly exhausting, finally said, "You're right. We can understand your decision. We're sorry to lose you, but it makes sense." My colleagues, after all, were pretty traditional, and they believe that if you're going to raise psychologically healthy kids, you've got to put in the time. So it wasn't quite as illegitimate to cut back as it would be in other fields.

But some people, I suspect, might have thought my training and experience were going to waste because my primary commitment now was to my children. I was acutely aware of that attitude in graduate school. The faculty, most of whom were males, seemed to think they were wasting their time on the women in my class because, after all, we were eventually just going to get married and have children. They never said it to me directly, but I don't think it was merely a projection either. That irritated me then and it irritates me now. For ten years I have been racing around like mad and I have been extremely productive. Aside from my clinical work, I have published ten papers and have a book in the works. I have certainly repaid my graduate training. It's possible that I may not obtain the same status in my field as if I had gone on to take the executive-directorship at the community mental-health center or if I had continued to advance up the academic ladder, but I believe that the personal satisfaction in raising healthy kids is just as important as professional status. Unfortunately, it isn't sufficiently recognized in our culture what a difficult, complex and vitally important job it is to raise well-put-together kids. Important though my work is to me, my children are more important. As a psychologist, I have intellectual convictions about being available to them that I would have great difficulty compromising on.

*Do you disagree with women who argue that it's not the quantity of time you spend with your children but the quality that counts?*

It's true that quality is very important. It is also true that quantity without quality is not productive because you can be at home and still be a zombie to your kids. There are days when I'm under pressure to write something and, believe me, the quality the kids get ain't good. I guess I believe in a mixture of quality and quantity.

When kids are young they don't protest so much, but when they get older they begin to take offense if you're not around very much, and they tell you so. It doesn't mean that they won't survive without you—they will; it just means that sometimes they will feel a little resentful or depressed. Dan, who is seven now, has begun to resent that I don't take a more active part in his school programs. Many of his classmates' mothers help out in the early-childhood education program by teaching or leading activities. Now and then he tells me, "Well, if you didn't have to work all the time, you could come to my school and do what the other mothers do."

I don't get blasted very often, but the blasts I get let me know that I should be available a little bit more. You can delude yourself into thinking that two or so "quality" hours a day is enough for your kids, but you are the most important person in their lives, and as they get older they need more of you.

*That's interesting, because many career women plan to cut back during the first two or three years and then, once their children are in school, resume a full-time commitment to their work.*

Let me make some differentiations. The quality of what goes on in the first two or three years is absolutely critical. Everything flows from that period: emotional development; cognitive development; the extent to which the child is or is not well organized psychologically. If certain foundations are not laid then, chances are they may never be. During this period it is critical for kids to have warm, loving, concerned caretakers, whether it be their mother, their father or an outside caretaker. The problem with hiring an outside caretaker as the primary person in your child's life is that hired people tend to come and go, and during these formative years children cannot tolerate a large number of separations and losses and remain psychologically whole. That is why, when my children were infants, even though I had Dorothy, I still wanted to be the primary person in their lives.

So kids need special things the first few years to ensure that they develop healthily, but as they get older they need other kinds of equally important input. I'm not saying that all women should quit full-time jobs and stay home with their kids. In many cases that would just cause frustration and resentment and be terrible for the mother and her children. I also realize that many people work full time because they must in order to support their families. But I have seen enough children with serious or even moderate psychological problems to advise a career woman, unless she is really committed to the notion of learning something about what it takes to be a good mother, not to have a child. Kids can't raise themselves. And women who want to continue their career productivity should understand that they will have more conflicts and more work than the men in their marriages. It takes more out of a woman to do both well.

*Is that a given, or should men be asked to take more responsibility in household matters and in raising children?*

They *should* take more responsibility, but it rarely works out that way. At least that has been my experience. We have a really beautiful, egalitarian marriage. My husband pitches in tremendously: we both fix dinner, we both wash the dishes—and he's wonderful with the kids.

But on work issues, his work always takes precedence over mine. For example, when the baby-sitter calls in sick, who cancels appointments and always stays home with the kids? Me, not my husband. After that happened the last time, I asked, "How many patients did you see today?" and he said, "Well, I had one new patient and two follow-ups." I said, "Well, I canceled six patients to stay home this afternoon. That's absurd. You should have stayed home." It's curious that that should happen in our house, but some of the old traditional ways persist and I'm not sure why I don't make a bigger issue of it. Partly it's economics. John needs to become established in this community to ensure our financial future. From that perspective, it's more important for him to keep his appointments than for me.

But aside from the financial end, I think that my wanting to be available to the children is partly maternal and biological and therefore different from what John experiences. First of all, I grew 'em. I was the one who was pregnant; my sensations at birth were my sensations, not his. He was my coach and he participated in the birth, but the experience was mine. I really think that makes a difference. A lot of women would take me to task for saying that in this day and age, but I believe there *are* biological differences. Maybe it's all socially or environmentally determined, who knows, but my investment in the children is greater than John's.

*How have the children affected your relationship with John?*

Having children changes your relationship with your husband, and it changes it permanently until the kids are out of your life again. To put it simply, we just don't have much time for each other because the children have a way of usurping tremendous amounts of energy and time. Sometimes I find it extremely frustrating. We will be having a conversation and both kids interrupt, making it impossible to carry on. In addition, I don't have as much energy at the end of the day because I've been burning the candle at both ends, taking care of the kids and trying to work too. At night, once the kids are asleep, all I want to do is sink back and read.

Weekends are wild because John and I have a thousand things we love to do that we only have time for on weekends, such as playing tennis, cooking elaborate meals for ourselves, landscaping our yard, and so forth. But we also want to plan one or two nice activities with the children. Unfortunately, they don't like to do the things we like to do. We're interested in Oriental art and Oriental rugs and love going to museums and shops. When we try to take the kids along, it's usually a disaster. So we have to balance what we like to do with what they like to do. As a result, we run around like mad all day and when Sunday night rolls around we are both totally exhausted.

*What have you found to be the rewards of raising children?*

You mean what do children offer aside from making tremendous demands on your time and energy? That's hard to talk about because most of it is intangible. Creating a family simply has a good feeling about it. It satisfies some very primitive desire for closeness and love that is present in everyone, but it also satisfies the mature side of our nature, the part that wants to nourish and give love.

Children take a lot out of you, but they also bring a great deal of joy to your life. Dan will say something funny, and John and I just look at each other and smile because it's so cute. Nancy sings a lot. Sometimes I'll be driving her somewhere and listening to her sing and think to myself, She sings beautifully and that's nice. I really like that.

Both children are bright and happy, and it feels wonderful to have created children like that, not just because they reflect you—which is one reason children are so gratifying—but because they are more than you; they are their own selves as well, with their own biological givens. Regardless of the impact we have on their lives, they will develop in their own way —not independent of what we do, but in addition to what we do. That's immensely exciting to watch. Our children, I think, are turning out very well and I feel they will have good, meaningful lives. It's a wonderful feeling to think that you've helped to make that possible for another human being. That's what everyone hopes for, of course, that's the fantasy, and that's why we're exhausted so much of the time. It takes a tremendous amount of energy if your kids are going to get what they need and develop optimally, but when it happens, it's worth it.

In my field there's a whole body of literature that talks about parenthood as a developmental phase, and that's another payoff of having children. The argument goes that in bringing up children, adults are brought face to face with some of their own unresolved childhood conflicts. If they successfully negotiate these with their children, they become more mature, better integrated adults.

Let me give you an example from my own life. My parents relied heavily on spanking to discipline us when we were children. I really think they were too severe in their means of punishing us. Now, physical punishment is very hard for kids to take and it generates terrible anger. That can have dire consequences when they become parents themselves because we tend to repeat with our children what was done to us. Child abusers, for example, were often abused themselves as children. The maturing part comes if you break the pattern, intervene somewhere along the way and consciously make the choice not to repeat with your kids what was done to you. In my professional training I learned that although you need to set firm limits for your children, you do not need physical punishment to discipline them. It's much better to use purely verbal means. So neither John or I *ever* hit our kids.

My mother was sure that our children were going to be outrageously disorderly and out of control. She thinks all psychologists' kids are crazy. But now she can't get over how well behaved my children are. They get into mischief and they're fun-loving, but basically they are very well-behaved children.

I think I've really turned something around in my psyche by controlling my impulse to express anger physically, and in the process I've learned a lot about my family and myself. I had to think a great deal about my response to anger when Nancy was a baby because if I ever had the impulse to hit, it would have been vented on her that first year, and the result would have been disastrous.

So parenthood is clearly a maturational process. If you take it seriously and do it well, you become responsible not only for the lives of your children but for the way you interact with them. I think that can enrich many other interactions in your life as well. From my standpoint as a psychologist, that's a very good by-product of having kids. You get a lot of ghosts out of your closet.

*What career goals have you set for the future?*

Well, our grant runs out in a few months, and even though my partner and I are flirting with the idea of applying for another one, I want nothing so much as a period of six months in which I can do practically next to nothing. You see, I have been working nonstop throughout my marriage, including after the children were born.

Now I'm working mostly at home on the book, but it takes much more energy to work at home than it does anywhere else. I'll be intensely involved in analyzing some data and trying to integrate them into a section of the book, and just as my thoughts are beginning to take shape, the phone will ring, somebody's at the door or one of the children is crying and I have to see what's going on. I'll take care of the interruption and then have to get myself involved in my work all over again. It takes vastly more energy if you have to shift back and forth like that all the time. And even though I'm officially supposed to be working fifteen hours a week on the project, we have a publishing deadline on our heels, so in practice it comes out to much more. As a result, I am always exhausted. That's the consequences of trying to maintain a high level of mothering and a high level of writing and research at the same time.

I love leisure time but the way my life is organized now, I rarely have time left over for myself. All my friends at the tennis club have long lunches with wine after we play tennis and I'm greatly envious of them. I have to race home, pick up the kids at nursery school and get down to work. My friends are envious of me, I know, because I have a career and they think I'm doing important things. So we envy each other. But ever since my marriage and particularly since I've had the children, I know something is missing from my life, and recently I have become aware of what that is: I am no longer doing all the things that used to enrich it. I used to sing a lot and play musical instruments, but not anymore.

So, I promised myself that when I finish this book I'm going to do something bizarre, like learn to play the oboe or join a chorus. And I'd love to play more tennis. I also want some time occasionally to stay at home and read—nothing serious, just junk novels and stuff. Basically, part of me is a lazy person who loves to do nothing.

So in the future I never intend to take on a full-time work commitment that will demand the tremendous amount of time and psychic energy that my previous jobs have demanded. I have different priorities for my life now. My most important priority is to have more time to do things with my children. When Nancy asks to go swimming, I want to be able to take her swimming! I'd also like to work in Dan's class every Thursday from one to three, or whatever. I miss not being able to do those kinds of things with my kids. Those activities aren't absolutely necessary to my children's well-being, but they would make life nicer for them.

Once again, it has to do with what I want for my children. I not only want them to be psychologically well integrated and well functioning, but I want to have a really good relationship with them. I can tell that whenever I've been under pressure and not as available as I'd like to be, the kids, especially Dan, begin to pout and become difficult. As soon as I jack up the input just a little, they bounce back again.

But in the main, I think it's just fun to do things with my children. I don't want to wake up one day with my kids grown up and say to myself, "Gee, I could have done some really neat things with my kids, but I've missed the opportunity. I wonder why?"

# Nancy Bryan

Nancy Bryan, thirty-five years old, is an advertising executive in Chicago and the mother of three-year-old Marcia. Her husband, Phillip, is the general sales manager for a major food company. They live in the northern suburbs of

Chicago, about an hour by train from Chicago.

Nancy and a younger brother were raised in a suburb of Boston. Her father was a sales executive and her mother was a traditional housewife who enjoyed staying home to care for her family. Nancy attributes her strong interest in work to the influence of her father: "I was his firstborn and he treated me like a son. He wanted me to develop my talents, be independent and have a career."

After majoring in business in college, Nancy devoted her twenties to establishing herself in the advertising world. Talented and productive, she had little trouble finding good jobs in New York, where she lived for five years until she married Phillip and moved to Chicago. There she quickly ascended the career ladder of a large advertising agency until she was lured away by a rival firm. She was pregnant at the time.

Although Nancy worked for eight years in a predominantly masculine profession, she felt that she never suffered discrimination in terms of equal pay or equal power. It was only during her pregnancy with her daughter and later when she had her child that she discovered that the rules of work in the business world were not set up to accommodate mothers.

*You had just reached a new career plateau with high pay and foreign travel. What was your reaction when you discovered you were pregnant?*

I was delighted! While I hadn't been trying to get pregnant, I wasn't trying to avoid it, since I wasn't using contraceptives. I figured if I became pregnant, that was okay, and if I didn't, that was okay. My husband was delighted too. We had been married for five years and we had just gotten to the point where we were ready to have a child. Up until then we felt we still needed time to get to know each other better, and even at thirty I knew my work life wasn't really settled.

*Did your concern about the biological clock affect your timing?*

Yes, I think it did. I understood that when a woman gets to be around thirty-five, more problems can arise if she becomes pregnant. My doctor reassured me that if I was in good health and wanted to delay having a baby, that would be fine. The only problem, he said, is that after thirty-five it becomes a little more difficult to conceive. If for some reason I didn't become pregnant easily and had to use the fertility-drug treatment, that could take a couple of years. So I didn't think it would be wise to defer much longer.

*Why did you and your husband want to have children?*

I don't really know. We never discussed that question and neither of us consciously thought about it individually either. We just assumed that one day we would have children, and the only point of deliberation was when the best time would be to begin our family. Now that Marcia is almost three, I know what it means to have a child in my life. But at the time I had absolutely no idea. It was just something you did, that's all.

*Did you feel any social pressure to have a child?*

Not from my friends. Most of them were in similar situations to my own. They married a bit later than the norm, deferred having children till their thirties, and then they were too busy making their own decisions to worry about me. I did get family pressure, however. Not from my husband's family—they were great—but from my own. From about the end of my first year of marriage it was: "Well, Nancy, don't you think you ought to have a baby?" To put that in perspective, where I came from in Boston, most of my high school friends married right after college and got pregnant right away. I was something of an oddball. I moved to New York after I was graduated from college and didn't marry until I was twenty-six. My parents, and especially my mother, were always comparing me to their friends' daughters. So there was pressure, but I just ignored it.

*How was the experience of pregnancy for you?*

I really liked being pregnant. I felt a little nauseated the first couple of weeks, but I had no morning sickness or other physical problems. I ate well—had a marvelous appetite throughout—and went out and bought all sorts of terrific maternity clothing.

I continued to work throughout my pregnancy. In my eighth month I attended business conferences in London and France and felt perfectly fine. In fact, I had a ball! Once in a French restaurant when I was having a business lunch, the maître d' brought me a complimentary glass of wine and said, *"Pour le bébé."* When I returned to the States on Air France, the stewardess put me in first class so I would be more comfortable. Toward the very end of my pregnancy I gained too much weight and swelled a bit because I was overdue. But for the most part I was in great shape physically and psychologically.

Interestingly, my problems came not from my pregnancy, but from the way the men in my company regarded it.

*How did your male colleagues react to your pregnancy?*

My company was very conservative, and I was the first professional woman to continue working through my pregnancy. I must say their reaction was awful. Most of the men were in their sixties, but even the younger staff members, those in their mid-thirties or forties, had outdated notions of what pregnancy means to a woman and how she should act. They seemed to feel that pregnancy is some sort of illness and that pregnant women should be at home. Partly I think they were just uncomfortable having a pregnant woman around, and partly I think they were offended that I would opt to work during pregnancy rather than stay home and make my unborn child the primary focus of my attention. The most devastating aspect of their response was that they wrote me off as a professional peer. All their wives, if they ever worked at all, quit, never to return once they had their babies. Naturally, they all assumed that I would quit too.

As soon as I started to show, one of the younger men asked how long I had known I was pregnant. When I told him I had known two weeks after I missed my first period, he said, "Don't you think you should have told somebody? We have to make plans." I said, "Look. It's none of your business. I'm not planning on changing anything." One of my associates confided to me that the president of the company said to him, "Well, Nancy *says* that she's coming back to work, but we know that she's not going to. She doesn't realize what it takes to raise a child, and once that kid comes along, she'll never return to work."

*How did those remarks make you feel at the time?*

Terrible! I had been there four years conducting myself as a serious and productive professional, and suddenly they were questioning my commitment to my job. I knew that I would remain committed to my work and return to the agency soon after I had the baby, but I had to put up with these men who were second-guessing what I was going to do. Also, their remarks about the strain I must be under being pregnant and commuting to Chicago and doing full-time work set off conflicts in me for the first time. I began to wonder if maybe I should be at home. I think it affected me so much because I was getting pressure from my parents as well. They kept asking, "When are you going to stop working and get prepared for this baby?" Frankly, I couldn't understand what I was going to do for a couple of months to get prepared, but I was constantly going back and forth about whether I should quit my job, take a leave of absence or just keep on working.

The only positive support I had was from Barbara, my

administrative assistant, who is a very sharp woman with a teen-age daughter. One morning when I was beside myself trying to figure out what to do, she said, "You know you really don't have to make a decision now. You're maintaining your pace and legally they can't fire you. If you don't want to stop working, there is no reason you should quit your job." That made me see that I didn't have to make a decision at that point. I could just keep on working until the baby was born and then see what I wanted to do. That was a tremendous relief.

*We understand that late in your pregnancy a rival company offered you a job. How did that come about?*

When I was about five months pregnant I was approached by the president of another company who said he was interested in hiring me. He wasn't the least bit concerned with my being pregnant. In fact, he officially offered me a job at the beginning of my seventh month, and said I could start then or after the baby was born. Since I felt that in good faith I couldn't start a new job at the beginning of my seventh month, I told him I would give my answer a few weeks after the baby was born. As it turned out, I had a difficult delivery and my recuperation period was a little longer than I had anticipated. But my new boss didn't seem to mind at all. He even sent me flowers when I was in the hospital. He was trying to woo me over, of course, but it was a nice touch. I still don't know to this day if I turned sour on my old agency and decided to leave because of the way they treated me when I was pregnant, or if I was just ready for a change. In any case, I told the new firm I would start work right away, as soon as I cleared up my desk at the other place. But I was so overwhelmed when I got home with the baby that I didn't actually start work until three months later.

*Tell us about your experiences with a newborn.*

Oh Lord, we were so unprepared! I had been planning on breast-feeding. I imagined that you just hooked your baby into your breast and it would automatically stop crying. I was so confident that I didn't even have a single bottle in the house. No one bothered to tell me that some women can have a lot of trouble breast-feeding. Often the milk doesn't come in quickly. So there I was with a screaming baby and no idea what to do.

The books I had read said that when a baby was little it would feed for about an hour and sleep for four hours. That sounded pretty good to me, but let me tell you, *my* kid didn't read those books. She was up all the time. She never slept. It was totally overwhelming, and for a while I thought I'd go bananas. Until you've had one, you have no idea how much a baby can disrupt your whole existence. If someone had told me what it would be like that first year, we would never have believed them. Here you have this small thing that is completely, utterly, totally dependent on you. You can't plan a schedule because things come up unexpectedly, and you never know when and if the baby is going to go to sleep. It's horrible. You can't eat dinner, you can't do this, you can't do that. Your whole life is wrapped up around servicing this child.

These are the things nobody prepares you for, including all those charming "how to" books about pregnancy, childbirth and taking care of a baby. These are the things you can never know until you experience them for yourself.

*Was it difficult starting your new job?*

It was at first, but I started out slowly, going in once a week, twice a week, to get my feet wet and meet the staff. When Marcia was five months I went to the London office to meet the folks there and really got into the swing of things. At that point I was working for one of the agency's subsidiaries. Then a position opened up in the parent company—it was a promotion, actually. The condition was that I would work four days a week and ultimately go full time. They didn't care where I worked those four days. It could be at home or in the office, as long as I produced.

*Could you work at home with an infant in the house?*

Not always. Sometimes I would spend all morning with Marcia, and when twelve-thirty came around I would put her to bed for a nap so that I could work for two hours straight. But of course, she would decide she was not going to take a nap at all that day and the work I'd planned would never get done. Still, the problems weren't insurmountable because I was lucky to find Annette, an excellent baby nurse to take care of Marcia. She had been the head nurse of a maternity ward at one of the local hospitals and came very highly recommended. A few days after I got home from the hospital she came to help me and she's been with us ever since. A godsend!

*Do you have any other help?*

Well, in addition to Annette, I have several other people who work for me for short periods. It's a three-ring circus around here and I juggle everybody and everything. Sally, a teen-ager, comes three days a week to clean for me. I do no housework myself. I don't have the time, and also I'm a lousy housekeeper. Sally usually comes in the afternoon or evening and gives Annette a break from the baby. The baby loves to follow her around the house to "help" her or watch what she's doing. We also have a dog, so I have the young girl next door, who adores dogs, come by in the evening to walk her.

*How much does your support cost and what kind of income do you need to afford such help?*

Last year I grossed about $23,000 working a combination of full and part time. My husband makes about $50,000. We pay our nurse $25 a day, which is really quite low, since the going rate for a well-trained child caretaker around here is $4.50 to $5 per hour. The other help runs about $1.50 to $2 an hour. I figure it comes to roughly $110–$120 a week. But after I deduct taxes and child care, I net something like $25 a week. You see, we're in a tax bracket where the government takes a huge chunk. We take every deduction in the world, but we're in that middle-income bracket where you get screwed. For example, I can only deduct so much for child care, whereas someone in a lower bracket can deduct a lot more. My husband and my accountant say that they're glad that I enjoy what I'm doing because I sure ain't making much money out of it.

*With abundant household help and a flexible work schedule, it sounds as if you have found a workable solution for combining your career with your new role as mother.*

I did, but it didn't last. Everything was fine until my boss changed and I was no longer responsible to the man who had originally hired me, the person with whom I had worked out my flexible arrangement. I wound up working for a very bright woman who was a few years older than I, very career-oriented, and married but with no children. While officially I could work at home and come in when I wanted to, in practice the demands she made were very different. There were meetings, for example, that I never used to be expected to attend, but she insisted I be there—and these meetings usually took place at eight-thirty in the morning or after dinner at night. It got so that on many days I was working ten to twelve hours, on top of my two hours for the commute. I would have to leave the house in the morning before the baby woke up, and by the time I got home she was already asleep.

*Why would your new boss make such demands?*

There's no mystery to that. She lost no time in telling me: "If you are in a high-powered job and really committed to your career, it, not your family, should come first." She herself had chosen not to have children because for her, career is number one. If that's how she wants to live her life, it's fine with me. The trouble came when she started imposing some of her values and expectations on me.

*Could you have accomplished all your work on a more flexible schedule?*

Of course I could. On the days when I came into the office I worked until seven, eight or even nine at night to finish whatever I was doing so that when I got on the train to go home I could feel comfortable about not coming to the office the next day. I would also work on Saturdays and Sundays. But for this woman, it didn't matter how much overtime you put in; she thought you should be in the office every day from nine to five minimum.

*Your story suggests that professional women who are also mothers will have to struggle not only with "old guard" men but with "new guard" women as well.*

Oh yes, we're going to see more of this. More women than ever before are working, and it's not the way it was twenty years ago, when it was assumed that if you got married, you had kids. Clashes are bound to occur because women who do not have children just can't understand the feelings of women who do.

Let me give you an example of what I'm talking about. One day when Helene (my boss) and I were talking about the requirements of my job and specifically my inability to get to a meeting because I had to take my kid to the doctor, she said to me, "Nancy, if you have competent help, it shouldn't matter if your child is sick. Your nurse can very easily take that child to the doctor." I answered, "True, very true. It's just as easy for my nurse to take my daughter to a doctor. But I'm still the child's mother. Maybe she doesn't want the nurse when she's sick. She wants her mother." It's hard for somebody who doesn't have children to sympathize with that feeling and be willing to let the rules bend a little.

*We would hope that women in power would try to make it easier, not harder, for other working women as well as men to combine work and family roles. How would your boss respond if you told her that?*

She would probably say, "Unfortunately, the way the rules are written today, men control the power structure. If women want to be accepted as true competitors in this world, they have to play by male standards. If men are going to be available to their clients around the clock, then women will have to be available as well. No excuses." She herself is a real hard-nosed competitor, and she stands up very well against the men in the office.

*Can women with children be—in your boss's words—"true competitors" in the business world?*

This is where the waters get murky. Women want to be treated as equals at work, but if they have opted to have children, they do have heavy responsibilities at home.

One day at work I got a phone call at ten in the morning from Marcia's school telling me that she had come down with the measles, and they asked me to come to school right away and pick her up. They had been calling my nurse but there had been no answer. So what do you do? You go to school and pick up your kid. The nurse had been shopping for me and missed the phone call by five minutes. Meanwhile, I'd given up a half-day of work.

Women who opt to have kids must make compromises and trade-offs, and that can be maddening, like being stuck at home during a snowstorm listening to "Big Bird Sings" while your major office competitor handles your presentation to your client because she lives closer and has no children and doesn't have to worry about a caretaker being afraid to drive in bad weather.

*If you had even more supports, perhaps a live-in nurse, would that make the conflict between motherhood and career less of a strain for you?*

No, it wouldn't. And that brings up another problem. I have been incredibly fortunate in the kind of child care I was able to arrange. I found a marvelous woman who gives my child a great deal of love, and Marcia adores her. But while she is an excellent caretaker, she can't give the baby the stimulation I think is important. She can read to her, perhaps, but she's not going to pick her up in the middle of the afternoon on a nice day and take her down to the zoo and explain to her about all the different animals. I guess that when you grow up the way I did with the idea that education is the most important thing in the world, you want your kid to have the very best. You might suggest a more educated caretaker. But what woman who is that educated is going to be a caretaker? Would you want to stay home and take care of kids all day? I wouldn't. If you want your child to have the kind of stimulation you think is important, then you have to be the one to give it.

This is not so critical when the child is an infant. Then it mostly need lots of love and care. When Marcia was about a year old it really struck me that she was in the take-off period. She was just starting to talk and make all sorts of interesting connections. We were absolutely amazed to see how sharp and bright she was, but I guess everybody tells you what a bright little kid they have. In any case, I began to feel that if I didn't personally take the time to help conceptualize things for her or give her the direction she needed then she might miss out on something vital. That's too great a price for her or me to pay for my work.

*Did you look into day-care centers? Some of them stress cognitive development.*

No, I did not. It's very rural where we live and there aren't any kind of day-care centers around. But even if there were, they probably wouldn't appeal to me. I feel that at her age, Marcia still needs the constant one-to-one attention that she couldn't get in a group situation. Even with as few as five kids in a room, she wouldn't get that extra hug or the love I feel she needs. A day-care center might be fine for the intellectual stimulation, but I have my doubts about it on a five-day, full-time basis. On a part-time basis it might appeal to me, but there aren't any around.

*To sum up your predicament, then, you increasingly felt that you needed more time to spend with your child, while your boss was pushing you to make a greater time commitment to your job. Did she give in or did you?*

Neither. I'm no longer working in Helene's department, and she is no longer my superior. I've been moved to a different department and a different position and it's worked out much better for everyone concerned. Now I work on an average of three days a week on alternate days. On working days I usually leave the house around six-thirty in the morning and don't return home until eight or eight-thirty. The next day I can focus my full attention on Marcia. It's not a frustrated or resentful attention, but a very positive one.

*Does your part-time position set you back on the career ladder?*

From a short-term standpoint it has substantially set back my career goals. But since I want more input into my child's development at this point, I'm willing to defer my career goals for a few years. Once Marcia starts school, I can go back to my original goal.

Now, it's true to some extent that I am taking a risk in my

present job. But fortunately I'm in a career where you don't really have to stay in one job. In fact, if you want to advance, it's better to job-hop a bit. So if I find myself in a dead end here, I'll move someplace else.

*Sounds like an old story—the woman doing all the accommodating and taking the career risks. Shouldn't men compromise their careers for their family as well?*

I think they *should* have to make compromises, and eventually they will. It's inevitable. The longer women work and get a taste of the intrinsic enjoyment, the heightened sense of self-esteem, and the economic rewards of working, they are not going to want to give it up and be tied to a house and children. I have a good friend who gave up her job to stay home with her baby and she is going crazy being stuck in the house all day. It may be a challenge to guide your child's development, but not on a twenty-four-hour-a-day basis. Educated women are not going to want to stay home and minister to their children. The men will have to take a much greater part in both the household and child-care responsibilities.

Too often men who don't want to take care of the kids use the excuse that they are not as qualified as a mother. Now, that's ridiculous. Let me tell you, I have absolutely no qualifications to take care of a child whatsoever. And Phillip does just as well as I do. We both just play it by ear. There have been times when I've just thrown up my hands and said, "I've had it." Phillip has just stepped in and taken over, and he manages beautifully.

*Since you and your husband both have careers, did you succeed in altering the traditional sex-role responsibilities?*

We've had many, many discussions over the division of labor in this house, and recently there have been some modifications. But this brings up another important problem. I happen to have a very supportive husband, who is open to the idea of cooperating with me in the care of our child; he gets up in the middle of the night when Marcia is sick and helps with feeding her and so forth. But when it comes to the planning and the preparation, everything still falls on me. For example, my husband does a great deal of the shopping. Terrific! But I am the one who has to draw up the list and tell him what to get because he can't put two and two together to figure out that if there's no milk in the refrigerator, we need milk. Milk has to be on the shopping list. I've heard from many other women that one of their biggest problems is that no matter how supportive their husbands are and how cooperative when it comes to the planning and thinking, the female has to help the male out to help her. And that takes time and energy.

*What effect has the baby had on your relationship with your husband?*

It's been an uphill struggle! I think you'll find this is typical. When it was just the two of us I had the freedom to pick up the phone anytime and suggest dinner out or a movie or just taking the afternoon off and screwing around. When a child comes into your life, you can't do that anymore. You have a little being to take care of and you have to be thinking ahead all the time. The baby becomes primary in your life because she needs you much more than your spouse does. My husband resents it, and he's not alone.

It's difficult for a husband *not* to feel displaced after a child is born because a child takes so much looking after. And I don't care if you have a full-time housekeeper or not, you're the one who does most of the planning and thinking about the child. You take your kid for shots, you watch for hives and it's you who have to tell your housekeeper how to change the menus. So it's not that you love your husband any less, it's simply a question of limited energy. When Marcia was an infant I had no free time at all to devote to myself or my spouse, and I think that is true for most women who work and have kids and a husband.

Now that Marcia is a little bit older and not so incredibly dependent, it's become easier on both of us. The baby still prefers me as a mother, and I think that would hold true across the board, but Phillip and I are getting better at sharing responsibilities. During the week we take turns being with Marcia in the morning. Phillip will leave the house late one morning and I'll leave late the next, and we try to split duties fifty-fifty on weekends. As a result, I don't feel as resentful as I used to when everything was falling on me, and Phillip doesn't feel so left out anymore.

But that didn't happen overnight. It took a maturing of our relationship to get to the point where we could talk freely about the resentments that were building up on both sides. It's so easy for the woman to think all the gripes are on her side because she's the one who's doing everything, but a husband who feels he's being shut out has plenty of grounds for complaint too. It's up to both partners to air out these concerns rather than let them build up until the two of you end up screaming and yelling at each other.

*You waited until you were in your thirties to have a child. What advantages and disadvantages have you found in being an older mother?*

One disadvantage is that I get more tired. Little kids run around and have boundless energy. I just don't have the same energy I had five years ago. Another disadvantage is that I sometimes get impatient to jump back into my job full time. I feel I could accomplish more, move up faster. When you're in your twenties, things don't seem so urgent; you feel you have more time.

On the other hand, and this may sound contradictory, I've mellowed since I was in my early or even middle twenties. I tend not to get so upset about not advancing more quickly.

I've also obtained a high enough level of professional competence to know some job will always be waiting for me. That makes me freer to take some time off for free-lance mothering.

*Do you plan to have a second child?*

I have very mixed feelings about that. I have two friends, both super career-oriented women who worked all the way through their first pregnancies and went back to work straight from the hospital. When they had a *second* child, everything went to hell.

One was a real estate broker with a four-year-old who then had twins. She couldn't manage both and quit working. The other, a graphic designer, had her second child when the first was about twenty months old. During the day she spends all her time with the first child—who has since become much more demanding and babyish—and then she's up half the night with the newborn. Her husband helps her out, of course, but he is working full time, and let's face it, he needs his sleep.

A second child is probably even more difficult if your first child is older—say, two or three. The older child needs outside activities and exposure to other children, while the infant needs constant feeding and mother love. You have to work at two different ends. Personally, I don't know if I can take another child, especially another infant.

*Do any of the feminist critiques of motherhood correspond with your experience?*

I'm not all that familiar with the literature, but I disagree with anyone who dumps on motherhood in general, saying that if you aren't out working you are worthless, or that raising children is not as satisfying as working and everybody should go out and get a job. Some women really enjoy staying home with their kids and they shouldn't be made to feel guilty about not working. It is a question of options. However, women who are forced to stay home for one reason or another, who want to get out and work but can't, they ought to be encouraged to find jobs.

*What are the greatest rewards and pleasures you've gained from having this child?*

That's hard to say. Different kids mean different things to different people. Some women I know simply adore having children clinging to them and being dependent on them for every need. I respond more to different things. For instance, I think it's an absolute gas when I walk up the sidewalk at night when I come back from work and I hear this little voice yelling "Mommeeeeeee!" and I see this little girl come running out of the house to give me a kiss. I also love to sit with Marcia and watch her go through her alphabet book. She already knows almost all of the letters and half of the numbers. Well, that gives me a great deal of pleasure. Marcia is a marvelous child because she happens to be a very happy person. She's bright, she's sharp and she's fun. Let's just say that she's a part of our lives and a delight to have around.

And, oh yes, there's one more pleasure you get in having a child which I've just recently become aware of. It has to do with the pleasure of being a family. That didn't happen right away. When Marcia was an infant we didn't have much sense of being a family unit. There was just us and this kid that we would carry around with us everywhere. But as soon as Marcia got to be older, she became a little person we could communicate with and take on outings, and the whole picture has changed. Now there's a wonderful interaction between Phillip, myself and Marcia. Last week we took Marcia on her first train ride. She just loved it and we all had a blast. Next month we're going off on a vacation together and I think that will be great fun too. So becoming a family is a major payoff. In fact, it's the best reason I can think of for having a child.

*What are your moments of greatest frustration?*

The worst part was when Marcia was an infant. There I'd be at three in the morning with this screaming child on my hands with no idea what to do. Let me tell you, at those times I had second thoughts about what I had gotten myself into. And there are times now when she can be pretty difficult. I'll take her to a shoe store and she'll absolutely refuse to take her shoes off—things like that. And she's capable of some pretty obnoxious temper tantrums. The other hard times are when Annette is on vacation or sick. I can get very resentful because I have to stay at home with Marcia when it's important for me to be at the office.

*Do you have any thoughts on women who are opting to be childless?*

I can understand choosing not to have a child—especially once a woman gets used to running her own life and having a wonderful close relationship with her husband. When another human being comes into your life, naturally your love and attention are going to be split. If you don't want to give up that special relationship, or have some serious doubts about giving up some of your freedom—and you *will* have to do that—it's reasonable not to have a child. Also, if your career really comes first and you are one hundred percent dedicated to your job and want nothing more than to succeed in it, then I don't think that you should have kids. Most women look at motherhood very unrealistically. You just can't imagine the time, the responsibility, the commitment to another human being that motherhood involves. Maybe if you did, you wouldn't get into it! If deep down you don't want a child or even if you have serious doubts about it, don't have one.

*What advice can you offer career women who definitely want a child?*

The key to combining a child and a career is flexibility. If you are rigid in your demands, if you must have only a full-time job or only one type of job or one type of child care, even if you insist on such-and-such a relationship with your spouse, it's not going to work.

Now, I know it's not so easy to get flexibility in your job. The kind of work I do, which involves copywriting and preparing ads, allows for it. If I'm writing a creative program for a client, it doesn't matter where I write as long as I get it in on time and it's done properly. But if a woman has a secretarial job and is needed at her desk to type or answer the phone for someone five days a week, she obviously has no latitude at all.

The other reason I have some flexibility is that I know I have something special to offer my company. I'm very creative. Whole campaigns are run on my ideas. If you are one in twenty doing the same thing, it's obviously much harder to negotiate special terms. But once you feel you are indispensable, you can take your request to your superior and say you really like working there and you know you make a good contribution and then state the trade-offs you're willing to make. If women were a little more ballsy, they'd find they could get more. I don't know how true this is for educational or other fields, but once a business has made an investment in you as an individual, they don't want to lose you. You're a capital investment, so to speak.

*That's all the questions we have. Do you have any final comments?*

You've covered all the major areas: the child-care issue is important, the relationship with the spouse is important, and flexibility in your work is important. The way things are set up today, you can't have everything. You have to juggle the time you spend with the baby, the time you spend with your husband, the time you spend on the job. What you give up is time to spend with yourself. If I find half an hour a week to read, that's a lot.

But you have to remember: the first year is the worst; gradually it gets better. Once the child moves into a different stage of development, communicates better with you and develops its own set of friends, you in turn will move into a different phase of your life. So cope as best you can during that first difficult period of motherhood. That will pass and you can look forward to a much easier, more rewarding time.

# Anne Gibson

Anne Gibson, her husband, Steven, and her two sons, Jeffery, age eight, and Paul, age two, live in a university community in New England. At age thirty-eight, Anne is a tenured professor of political science specializing in comparative political systems and a prominent member of her profession.

Unlike the other women we have included in this section of the book, Anne did not take for granted that she would have children. She always knew she'd have a career, but she didn't believe she would necessarily become a mother. When she started going out with Steven she told him that she did not want to have children. Nevertheless, when Anne was thirty-two, they had their first son, and their second followed five years later.

As committed feminists, in practice as well as in theory, Anne and Steven arranged their lives so they could each take an equal part in raising their children and have equal time to pursue their careers. Anne also managed to negotiate a flexible working schedule at her university, and this, along with sharing child care with Steven, greatly lessened her conflicts. But not all their problems were solved by any means. Throughout the interview Anne reflects on how difficult our society makes it to combine children with career, and offers a vision of how circumstances might change in the future to make it easier for men and women who work to be responsible, committed parents as well.

*Why did you once think you didn't want to have children?*

Well, my mother was a full-time homemaker who, for reasons to do with her childhood, could not bring herself to enjoy raising children without feeling drained by it. She quite explicitly pushed me away from identifying with her role, and she did this, as she saw it, for my sake. She used to say, in effect, "Anne, don't be like me. Don't live my life." Mother enjoyed her marriage, but not her children. My brother and I had the feeling we were a burden to her. Whenever I asked for nurturing, she'd look as if I were eating her up. Naturally, I expected a child would have the same effect on me, and I'm sure that has something to do with why I didn't want children. She had wanted a career and had to give it up "for us." I understand how she must have felt. I don't know if she would necessarily have been happier if she hadn't had children, but the experience of motherhood was not positive for her, and I didn't think it would be for me, either.

My father loved his job, was well thought of in his profession, and I came to want a career like his, one that involved travel and responsibility. On the most basic level, it seems to me now, I identified with my mother, and I'm sure that's why my experience of sexuality, childbirth and breast-feeding have been gratifying. What I was attracted to was the male *role*. My father got great satisfaction from doing interesting work, and for a long time I thought that would be enough for me. I couldn't see any reason to include children in my life, too.

*What happened to make you change your mind about motherhood?*

I credit Steven with most of that. Living with him made my feelings change gradually. In a quiet way he communicated a confidence that I could be a mother without the risk of feeling unhappy and depressed and burdened down. That didn't happen right away. I'd say the process of change took about ten years. Others come by this feeling naturally—I had to develop it in adulthood. When we were first married, despite all my outward signs of being an independent and autonomous woman, I was in reality quite dependent. Steven seemed to gain satisfaction in giving me sustenance. And it was important for me to see that nurturing could satisfy rather than hurt the nurturer. Steven was unlike my mother in this crucial way, and I felt re-mothered by him, gradually in the course of living and working together. He is an utterly warm, loving, steady, trustworthy, reliable person, the son of a mother whose identity was entirely that of "mother." Steven re-mothered me, and in the process allowed me to grow into a far more nurturing kind of person myself.

After we were married for a few years, the idea of nurturing a baby, and raising a child, slowly began to appeal to me. Steven wanted that experience too. It was understood that if we had kids, he would share equally in taking care of them. I guess the most important thing that changed my mind about wanting children was how I felt about Steven. I loved him very, very deeply, and wanted to create a child with him, a joint product of our relationship. As I say this, it sounds silly —too much how one is supposed to feel. At the time we didn't talk about our feelings in just those terms, but in retrospect, that is, in fact, how I—we felt.

Steven was ready to go ahead almost any time, but I felt the need to wait until I got my Ph.D. and had a job as an assistant professor so I could feel safe enough to have a baby and not worry about my career. I was afraid that if I didn't get a regular full-time job first, I would go the way of most women in academia and be shunted off into a research post or part-time lectureship. It took me until I was thirty to get everything together. When Steven and I were finally ready to try to conceive a child I felt terrific. That was a very giddy and exhilarating time. Everything had worked out well and I felt I was doing exactly what I wanted to do with my life.

*What was it like being pregnant and teaching at the university?*

Well, being the only pregnant woman teaching on campus, I initially felt very awkward and anomalous and that must have shown. I was in a women's group and I recall several people questioning my attitude about being pregnant. They told me I should feel good about it and I said, "Oh yes. You're right. I do feel good about it," but, in fact, I felt very deviant. Finally I handled those feelings by turning my pregnancy into a virtue. I thought to myself, Well, if I'm going to be in this fix, why not do it up right, just be the pregnant professor and let everyone pat my belly. I became a one-woman crusader for combining pregnancy and work. I was there as proof to the world: "It can be done, it can be done." I kind of whistled that one out. My second pregnancy, five years later, was no big deal.

*You were thirty-six when you conceived your second child. Were you worried about your age?*

I might have been, but thank heaven for amniocentesis! I was just at the lower end of the age range for which that's recommended, and at first I wasn't planning to have it because I was afraid the procedure was too risky. But then I chatted with a neighbor who works with retarded children and she told me how heartbreaking it is for the parents when they learn that their child will never grow up psychologically and may never even be able to count to ten. That made me decide to look into amniocentesis a little more carefully and I discovered that the risks weren't nearly as bad as I had thought. My chances of having a mongoloid child at my age would be about one in one hundred, while the chances of having a miscarriage because of an accident during the procedure were only one in five hundred. At least those were the statistics for the medical center where I was planning to go. Steven and I were reassured and we decided I should do it.

I'm very glad I did. The procedure itself is very quick and almost painless. It took about five minutes and the only thing that hurt was when they put in the Novocaine. For a lot of women the one-month waiting period for the results can be pretty tense, but I somehow managed to just shut it out of my mind. When the results came in they were normal and we were asked if we wanted to know the child's sex. Steven and I were divided on that. I wanted to know and he didn't. But I couldn't resist asking, and that's how we found out we were going to have another boy.

Amniocentesis is a revolutionary development for women who want to postpone having children until relatively late in life, because nature just isn't on our side with that one. I think that every woman worries that maybe something is wrong with her baby, but for older women that becomes a realistic fear. Just knowing that your baby will not have Down's syndrome or one of a number of genetic abnormalities is an enormous relief. And I'm convinced that freedom from that fear allows you to become attached to this little unborn person you're carrying sooner and more deeply than you would if you were always thinking that maybe something's wrong. Amniocentesis doesn't dispel all your worries, of course, but at least you know you're not taking much more of a risk than a twenty-year-old mother-to-be.

*What were your experiences with childbirth?*

Both were good births without complications. Labor with Jeffery was easy and fast. I had a more difficult time with my second baby, Paul. But Steven had arranged for a close friend to take Jeffery so he could stay right there in the hospital with me the whole time. At night they brought in a spare cot and during the day he would lie down on a window sill. We joked that he was doing a couvade.

The most vivid memory I have of childbirth is how I felt just after I delivered my first baby. I remember feeling extremely confused about where I was and who I was, and for a moment I experienced a tremendous fear that somehow I had become my mother. I even looked down at my arms fully expecting to see my mother's chronic skin rash. It was an unbelievable relief when I saw I didn't have it.

Since then I've heard other women say that they've had a similar experience in childbirth and that giving birth often provokes a crisis of identification with one's mother. When that happened to me it was particularly terrifying, I think, because I had spent years and years trying to dissociate myself from my mother, and for a brief moment there we were—one and the same.

But as soon as that moment passed I began to feel deliriously happy because it was clear that I was still me, with a full-time teaching job, and a husband who loved me and supported my work, and who wanted to share equally in bringing up our children. Ultimately that brief period of identification with my mother was very liberating because it helped me realize clearly once and for all that I wasn't my mother and didn't have to lead her life. That gave me a marvelous sense of freedom and possibility.

*How did your agreement with Steven to share child care equally work out in practice?*

People often ask me about that and they usually expect me to describe a long battle of the sexes in which I struggled tooth and nail for my liberation. It wasn't that way with us at all. Steven had agreed to share child care with me because he is as committed a feminist as I am and believes we should have equal time to do our work. Besides, he genuinely *wanted* the experience of sharing equally. The underlying agreement had been firmly established a long time ago; we just needed to work out some of the practicalities.

We didn't make all kinds of rigid rules where every task was split down the middle and we were both supposed to do exactly fifty percent of each, or insist on six and a half hours and two minutes a day for Steven to be with the children, and six and a half hours and two minutes for me. What did matter was that in the long run we each got an even crack at our work. That was our guiding principle: equal time free for our work. When I was breast-feeding each baby I had to be with them more than Steven, of course. I used to take them with me to school and nurse them in my office. But during that period Steven did all of the housework and all the shopping to even out the time. He was a little put out because he felt he was getting the short end of the stick, doing the boring part while I got to be with the babies and was having all the fun. But after about eight months, when I wasn't breast-feeding anymore, we worked it out so we had equal time with the children and equal time for household chores.

*Do you find that you and Steven are equally skilled in child care and child rearing?*

Are you asking if Steven can "mother" as well as I? Absolutely. As far as the physical tasks are concerned, he is every bit as competent as I am. The most important part of child rearing, I think, is psychological, and in that realm we tend to complement each other.

I am familiar with the argument that women are biologically better primary caretakers because the bond they develop with their offspring through pregnancy and childbearing is deeper and more empathetic than the bond the father has with the child. I find that argument quite simply wrong. It's true, of course, that Steven and I had a different biological relationship to our children. I did carry them in my womb, I gave birth, I breast-fed, and those are biological facts. But does that mean, on some deep-down residual level, that I have a more profound relationship with the children than Steven has? I have to honestly answer no to that. Steven has been involved with our kids from day one, and he is equally attuned to their needs, sometimes more so than I am. What's important is not the biological bond itself, but the meaning people attach to it. Now, it's interesting that often when one of the children wakes up at night I can always hear it very keenly, whereas Steven can't. Possibly there is something biological about that. But whenever that happens, and it's Steven's turn to get up that night, I just poke him with my foot under the covers and he wakes up and sees to the child. Big deal. That's just about as far as biology determines the arrangement. Five minutes later I'm asleep.

It's so easy to think that what we see around us every day is "natural" or biologically "given." In fact, the social and cultural rules by which we live our lives are far more important in determining our behavior. In American culture it isn't considered manly to take care of children, and as a result men often affect an *un*natural stiffness and incompetence around babies. But all you have to do is get away from the Anglo-Saxon tradition, and it's amazing to see how "maternal" men can be—in Mexico or China, for example.

Even in our neighborhood, where most of the men lead very traditional lives and are away from home all day and come home late from work, we see evidence, especially in the two fathers across the street, of tremendous psychological involvement with their children. They gravitate to talking about their children, and if you watch them, you can see that they are deeply into what their kids are doing. Burt, a neighbor of ours, can be involved in a conversation with me, but if his two-year-old goes for a cup on the coffee table, he's there in a flash to keep that cup from falling over. I think if society gave our men half a chance and rewarded them for their "maternal" feelings, they could easily strengthen their bonds and commitment to children.

The amount of commitment Steven is willing to give to his children is unusual in our society, I know. His family circumstances made him question his values long ago, and it was important to him personally that he be close to and involved with his kids. He has been, and I know this has meant a great deal to him. Just recently he had his twenty-year college reunion and was supposed to write a short summary of his recent activities. Now, most of the men wrote things like "The wife Sally and I are renovating our Victorian," or maybe they wouldn't mention Sally at all but would say that they still loved wine and blondes—all that defensive adolescent stuff. Steven's paragraph was so different and so moving, to me. After describing his work, he wrote about how he enjoyed taking care of our children and wouldn't trade that experience for anything in the world.

*What do you think has been the effect of shared child care on the children?*

I think the effect has been very positive. As I said, Steven and I tend to complement each other's personalities in a way that seems to be beneficial for the children. For instance, Steven tends to be more cautious than I am in what he lets the children do, while I'm more likely to value exploration over caution. We've had some arguments over that, but basically I'm very glad Steven is cautious, and the combination of both our attitudes gives the kids a nice balance. To give you another example, Steven disciplines the kids a little differently than I do. He's very patient with them, but at the same time very firm. He can always get them to do whatever he wants, but in a very nice way. I'm not as patient, and I'm working on that, but I think sometimes my style of discipline has its advantages, too. So the main effect of sharing is that the children are exposed equally to both our personalities, and optimally they get the most desirable parts of each of us.

They get full exposure to both our faults, too, of course, but because we share I think the effect of our faults on them tends to be minimized. Having a backup person eliminates much of the stress of child rearing. Those "breathers" let you recuperate so the children are likely to get one of us at our best and avoid one of us at our worst.

*How have the children affected your relationship with Steven?*

Well, we worried beforehand that children would take something away from our relationship. We baby each other a lot and we were afraid that once we had real babies some of that might go away. But it didn't. To a large extent that's because we're able to afford baby-sitters. If you can buy time away from the kids to be with each other, you can pretty much establish the same relationship with your husband that you had before. At least that's how it's worked out for us.

I know many women say that once they have children their relationship with the husband starts to unravel. I suspect that's due in part to the husband's resentment at being displaced as number one by the baby. But a lot of that syndrome disappears when you actually share child care equally. Your husband doesn't feel displaced. He's in there with both hands and feet. He doesn't have time to feel displaced. Ironically, in our house it began to work the other way a little bit. After I had Paul I began to feel that Steven had appropriated Jeffery, and *I* was beginning to feel left out. We had sort of teamed up: Paul and I were a pair, and Jeffery and Steven were a pair. We realized that wasn't good and began to switch partners more. I'd take Jeffery, and Steven would take Paul—or the four of us would do things together.

*What has been the impact of the children on your career?*

Well, I must say it was quite different from what I had expected. I thought I could easily continue my career pretty much as I had before and be a good mother at the same time. No problem. My model was Margaret Mead's description of an Arapesh mother. "Casual competence" would be an apt term for these women. Mead described how they would go about their duties casually and competently, scaling fish or thatching huts, while at the same time taking care of six children, feeding them all, seeing to their needs. I didn't see why I couldn't be like them, casually, competently getting it done, whistling all the way.

But that's not the way it happens. Once you have children, your priorities change and you change. I now have two little human lives that I am partially responsible for, and when one of my children becomes ill or requires my special input, that casual-competence model goes out the window. When I have to make a choice between my children and my work, I choose my children. I'm not saying that the children have made me any less committed to my work in the sense that I love it any less. And in terms of writing, I have managed to be as productive as anyone in my department. As long as everything is going smoothly and the children seem happy and content, it's business as usual and I work in high gear. But if Paul is sick or Jeffery is cranky and not doing well in school, I step back from my work and take the time to deal with whatever the problem is. My children come first. No question about it.

Actually, with my first child, Jeffery, I could follow the old Arapesh-mother model. I was on a grant and not teaching most of that first year after he was born, and Steven, who had switched careers, was in law school then and studying at home. We would put eight-month-old Jeffery's chair between us on the desk, and he would go to sleep to the hum of my typewriter. Even if one of us was talking on the telephone, we'd be looking at Jeffery and he would feel very centered on and content. The synthesis of work and child rearing couldn't have been more ideal.

The problems came when I went back to the university and started teaching full time. Even with Steven sharing fifty percent, I was having trouble doing anything more than teaching my classes and being a mother to Jeffery. I had almost no time to continue my research and finish the book

I was writing. I really began to feel the pinch then because that book was vital to my getting tenure at the university and keeping my job. I suppose I could have managed to get more writing done if I had been willing to be a zombie in the classroom and hold office hours for fifteen minutes a week, but I love teaching and did not want to short-change my students. The solution as I saw it was for me to cut down on my course load and teach half time. With fewer courses to prepare, I could give the students I had more attention and also have more time to write.

Unfortunately, at my university there was no such thing as a regular part-time position. Temporary people like instructors or teaching assistants could work part time, but not permanent faculty. Actually, half the men in my department did teach part time, but they spent the other fifty percent of their time in a research institute, and that was okay. But it was not okay if you wanted to share fifty-fifty with your family. That was against the rules.

To me that seemed terribly unfair. It meant that any woman or *man* who had child-care responsibilities and needed extra time for writing would automatically be at a disadvantage where it counted most for their career. Since women generally do most of the child care, they're the ones who usually suffer the consequences. I saw half-time regular positions as an essential option to gain if we were to stop the university's discrimination against faculty women. So a group of women and I fought for that and we won.

*How did you get the university to change the rules?*

We presented the reasons why regular part-time faculty positions were desirable to the other members of the faculty-wide women's caucus, and they agreed we should take up the cause. We got organized, passed around petitions and generally made a lot of noise. First, I got a letter from a top administrator at the university flatly saying no, what we wanted couldn't possibly be done. Later I talked to him on the phone and he said, "Well, you have a good case, Professor Gibson. I think we can make an exception for you." I answered, "No, I don't want to be an exception. Why shouldn't this kind of job flexibility be available for every man and woman working on this campus?" Then he said, "Well, for *women* it's understandable. Maybe we could make that option available for women." I said that wasn't acceptable either, and I pointed out that it would be unconstitutional to change the rules just for women. That was the end of the conversation.

Then, not long afterward, my petition for a part-time professorship was granted and that option is now written into the affirmative-action plan at the university. It's a university rule now. That doesn't mean that the administration is advertising it; they're trying to keep it as hush-hush as possible. But the word has gotten out, and several people I know are taking advantage of the part-time option.

*Did Steven encounter problems where he worked because of his responsibility for the children?*

You bet. Especially when he was just getting started in a law firm. He ran smack into the sexism that is usually reserved for women who have children. The only woman working there was childless, and he was the only man in the office with any child-care responsibilities. They frequently scheduled meetings to begin at four-thirty and running right through the time when he was supposed to pick up Jeffery from his after-school day care. When he asked if meetings couldn't be held a little earlier, everyone really laid into him, especially, I'm sad to say, the woman. She was very unremitting, saying that he had decided to have a child and that now it was his problem. She was saying, in essence, "This is a work place, and family responsibilities just don't count here." We were pretty taken aback because Steven works for a public-interest law firm and people there consider themselves relatively enlightened and progressive.

Yet Steven's office, like the university where I teach, like almost every other work place in this country, is set up to accommodate the childless person. Too many women naïvely think that once they get a good job in a traditionally male institution, they've got it made and their battle with sexism is over. But just let them decide they want to have children and they'll realize the battle has just begun. The rules governing the way these places operate, whether they're informal or built into the organizational structure, totally filter out of their system anything having to do with family or children. They're child-free, airtight. Rules are made to suit the traditional male who has a wife to take care of the children. In Steven's case, that wife was me and the pressure he was getting from his law firm made things very hard for both of us, especially when we had our second child. That was a terribly difficult period.

*What complications and difficulties did your second child bring?*

Well, I think it began with my pregnancy. When I was pregnant with Jeffery I felt very calm and good and he came out a placid, easygoing child. But during my second pregnancy I was not in a very good state of mind, even though we wanted a second child very much and had planned the pregnancy for just that time. Steven had gotten deeply involved in several politically important legal cases and that took him away from the house a lot. I really didn't resent that he wasn't there more to help me with Jeffery because he had taken over most of the child care the previous year when I was struggling to get tenure at the university. He took charge completely so I could go on a study tour of China for one month with a group of social scientists. But it was a hard period for me and psychologically I was pretty agitated most of the time. Paul came out irritable and colicky, and I honestly think that was a reflection of the way I was carrying him. You don't just carry a baby in the womb; it's in the psyche too.

To compound matters, Paul was a month premature and at first had to be fed every two hours. I lost so much sleep I couldn't see straight. On top of all that, Paul's birth hit Jeffery very hard. Having been an only child for five years, he had a lot of trouble adjusting to his new brother. So that was one of those periods when I had to let my work take second place so I could stay on top of things in my family. Fortunately, the university allows more flexibility than most institutions so I could manage that, but Steven, as I told you, was in a much more rigid situation. We ended up hiring someone to come in several hours a day to give us some help with Paul. Eventually the baby straightened himself out, ate normally and slept through the night. Once I got back into some sort of routine, we started looking into child-care arrangements for Paul outside of our home, and into after-school programs for Jeffery, who had just entered first grade.

*What are your views on day care?*

I personally do not buy the myth that you have to be with your child all the time or you're not a good mother. Dr. Spock sold our mothers' generation of women the belief that children are like "empty vessels" and everything they do or become is due to their parents' influence. That made many women think they had to stay home all day watching over their children's development or feel very guilty if they didn't. A lot of people now think that made for overinvolved mothers and some pretty neurotic kids. In any case, a woman who works because she wants to or has to cannot be that kind of mother. She has to have help in taking care of her children, and day care, as long as it's high quality, is fine.

*What do you think makes for quality day care?*

Well, I'm certainly not talking about large institutionalized day-care centers where there are a few harried adults to take care of hordes of disgruntled, disaffected children, and the kids have to line up to go to the bathroom. That can obviously be a damaging environment, especially to very young children. But if you can find a place with a stimulating, enriching environment, where the ratio of children to adults is low— say, one caretaker to three or four children—so that each child can get plenty of personal attention—and the adults are warm and loving people and like children, the children should do very well. It's also important that the caretakers remain constant so the children can get to know them and feel secure. If all those factors are present—and I'm afraid they're not in most day-care settings in this country—there is every reason to believe that children do just as well in day care as they would if they were home all day with their mothers. Depending on the home and depending on the mother, they might, in fact, be a good deal better off in day care.

*How did you go about finding a good day-care setting for your children?*

For Paul, who was about a year and a half, Steven and I spent two weeks going through about twenty-five private day-care homes. We interviewed all the women who ran the places— unfortunately, there weren't any men—and judged them by a kind of seat-of-the-pants reaction. If the woman seemed nice and talkative, and warm with the children, we would put her down on our "possible" list. Finally we came across Patsy. She had only two other full-time children and one child part time. We were terribly impressed with her and still are. The atmosphere of her home is wonderful. Whenever you go in there you hear lots of laughter, but it's never frantic—just good vibes. And she's always taking the children to the park or to a museum, and sometimes she even has puppeteers come to her house. She uses a toy library, so the scene is always inviting and slightly different each week. On top of all that, she charges only one dollar an hour. We told her that's ridiculous, she should get three times that much, but she won't raise the fee.

We gradually increased the time we left Paul with her. First it was just one hour a day, then two hours, and so on up to eight hours, and it's working out beautifully. That may seem like a very long time for a small child to be away from home, but Paul has managed to arrange his sleeping habits around his absences from us. He wakes up at six every morning and then takes a three-hour nap at Patsy's. At night he doesn't go to bed until nine or nine-thirty. When I come home from work, he's right there saying, "Hi, Mommy!" As it turns out, we're with him literally half his waking day.

For Jeffery, unfortunately, we haven't been able to find a good after-school day-care program. There is a program at his school which runs from three in the afternoon to six in the evening, but it's very mediocre. They have just one playground teacher to supervise about thirty kids, and the children just float around the playground rather aimlessly. Jeffery was in it for a while, but we've taken him out of the program and we're glad we did. He liked it fine, but he wasn't getting enough stimulation there, and his school work was beginning to suffer. Now we take turns being with him after school, and he's really shot ahead under the new regime. His schoolwork has greatly improved, and he's starting to enjoy reading. But it's not easy for either of us to arrange to be home by three every afternoon. It's just a shame that this country isn't better at developing quality day care for working parents.

*Do you have a vision of a child-care system that would better meet working parents' needs?*

As a matter of fact, I do. First of all, I think the family and children should go public. They should be integrated with work into the daily fabric of life. Instead of parents depositing their young ones in day-care centers in the suburbs while they go off to work in the cities, there should be well-equipped, fully staffed child-care centers in every place of work. Take, for example, a law firm like Steven's. I can envision a garden on the first floor, and adjacent to that a modified cooperative child-care center. It wouldn't be for just the women on the staff. Every lawyer's child would be entitled to attend. By the collective decision of the members of the firm, one or two well-trained, experienced child-care people would be hired to take major responsibility for running the place, but everyone who had children—possibly those who did not—would sign up and take turns assisting the full-time staff. Naturally, this law firm would allow the parents of small children to work on a flexible, modified schedule so most of the children would not necessarily have to be in the center all day. On the other hand, since lawyers are sometimes likely to work at night and on weekends, a reduced staff would have to be there after hours to meet those needs.

Sweden, for example, offers this arrangement, and it isn't unheard of in this country. I heard just the other day that the nurses in a hospital nearby were organizing a campaign to have a child-care center built on as a separate wing of their hospital. And a stodgy manufacturing firm in Boston is experimenting now with a child-care center for its women employees right in the basement of the office building. I think we could have such things in work places of almost every kind. That would be better for the kids, and better for the parents, too, I think. They miss something by being cut off from their kids all day.

*What have your children added to your life?*

My female students often ask me that question. They see me highly geared into my professional life and wonder, Isn't that enough? Why have kids, too? I can understand their questions, and I tell them it is certainly possible for childless women to lead happy and fulfilling lives. But I also try to explain to them just what the rewards for me have been. That isn't easy to do, because having children has become such an "of course" kind of thing for me that I hardly know how to articulate the gratifications. They're certainly there, or why else would we be thinking of having a third child?

I could start by saying that there is something uniquely wonderful about having a close relationship with little beings who are part of you but at the same time very much their own selves. My boys don't look a thing like me and their temperaments so far don't resemble mine. But there's an important bond between us, nevertheless. I know they're mine, that I influence them and that I will remain a part of whoever, whatever they become in life. Without the children I wouldn't have the same deep sense of continuity or the same involvement in the future.

Now, to be perfectly honest, not only have children added to my life, they have also taken away. Frankly, I covet more time to do my work, and I can't travel as much as I'd like to or as much as my work sometimes demands. In that sense the children detracted from my work, but they've also brought unexpected rewards. Being a mother has opened me up, deepened me as a human being, made me more sensitive to a wider range of human emotions, and that has positively improved my thinking as a social scientist. So for every hour the children may have subtracted from my reading, writing and travel, they have given me back much more by changing me as a person and deepening my insight.

I find it hard to compare the pleasure and satisfaction my work brings me with the pleasure and satisfaction my children bring. The rewards I get from these two realms of my life—my work and my family—are not interchangeable. One does not substitute for the other. I would expect a man who was in touch with himself would feel exactly the same way.

*You began your family in your thirties. For you, what have been the advantages and disadvantages of being an older mother?*

Oh gosh, I can only think of the advantages. Steven and I feel the kids have given us a new lease on life, an extension of our youth. Even though they consume enormous time and energy, we feel "younged up" in their presence. It's great! I am very healthy, so I haven't felt at a disadvantage physically. Being in good shape is the key to that, I think.

There are distinct pleasures of late motherhood, but I want to emphasize as well that I really didn't have much of a choice, because I wanted to have a career. In academia there is a great deal of pressure to be very productive the first seven years after you get your Ph.D. In that time you're supposed to publish a lot and really make a contribution. At the end of that time your career is reviewed, and then it's either "up" or "out." You get tenure—permanent job security—or you lose your job the next year.

I waited until I was thirty-two to have Jeffery and thirty-seven to have Paul because I knew I had to get my career established before I could deal with the pressure of adding children to my life. As it happened, it worked out just fine for me. But I would hate to give a blanket endorsement of late motherhood for that reason. In some sense it's merely an accommodation to the traditional male way of setting up a career which requires us to make the big push in our twenties. That suits the traditional male just fine because he doesn't have to worry about having babies or taking care of children. He has a wife to do that for him. But if the wife wants children and a career, too, that's too bad for her; she has to defer.

There's no intrinsic reason why careers quite simply have to be set up so rigidly. The reason is historical—careers were designed for men. They could easily be restructured to accommodate women who don't want to wait until their thirties to have children, or men who don't want to miss out completely on their children's early years. Some changes are already being made in the medical profession to make that possible. A few medical centers allow part-time residencies so that doctors in training don't have to work twenty-four hours a day anymore.

That gives young men and women doctors the emotional and physical energy to start a family earlier if they like and play a real part in bringing up their children. When the children get older and don't need their parents as much, that's when they can begin practicing medicine full time, and that makes sense.

But the way most professions are set up today, the rules are oriented totally toward the life cycle and social role of men. If a woman wants a career and children, too, she'll have to defer almost as a necessity, even if it's not her real choice.

*What advice do you have for women who want to combine career and children?*

My first piece of advice would be to recognize that your ability to be a good mother depends in large part on the support system you develop, and I don't just mean baby-sitters or household help. Every person has dependency needs, and I know that the ability to care for those who are dependent on you is related to how well you're able to get your own needs met. Talk all this over thoroughly with your man and negotiate your commitment and his. Then, as soon as you get pregnant, start looking for several good baby-sitters who will be available to you when you need them. That's critical. You might even consider making up with your mother-in-law and having her move in next door.

My second piece of advice is that you analyze your work situation and consider what might be changed to help you manage a career and a family. Push for paid maternity leave of the kind they have in most enlightened countries. In Sweden the husband or the wife can take nine months off with pay and up to three years' leave of absence without pay, with no risk of losing their job. Why shouldn't we have the same? Push for flexibility in your working hours, for optional part-time work or whatever you feel is necessary. But don't wait until you're pregnant to try to get the rules changed. Start planning ahead. It's very difficult to make any major changes on your own, so try to organize the men and women in your place of work, starting with those who have a stake in the changes. First, get together with other women who have children or are thinking of having them. Then find the men who are fathers and concerned about their father role. You might even talk to the wives of the men working with you; they'll probably encourage their husbands to support the policies you want. Have an evening in your home for everyone and talk about what needs to be done. If women and men workers fight together, more can be accomplished than you think.

*Do you have any final reflections?*

I've talked a lot these past few hours about the particular problems I've encountered combining children with a demanding career and the personal solutions I've found to make that possible. There's nothing wrong with personal solutions —we all have to survive. But we also have to recognize that unless we fight for something more than just ourselves, nothing is going to change for women as a group. It took the power and the push of the women's movement just to shove a relatively few women into elite positions in institutions, organizations and professions. I worry now that some women will say, "I've made it and to hell with everyone else." That's a shame because most of these women are where they are because of the women's movement or because other women individually have cleared their way. So women who have gained power and status should especially try to make it easier for other women to get jobs, keep jobs and have their children too. It's a moral obligation. No question about it.

# EXAMINING
# THE ISSUES

Will pregnancy and motherhood affect the way my professional competence is perceived and evaluated?

How much child care should I relegate to others?

How will having both a career and a child affect the relationship with my mate?

Can I predict how much conflict and stress I might have if I combine children with my career?

In our mothers' generation, most women who worked out of choice rather than necessity interrupted their careers when they got pregnant and while they were raising their children. Typically, the female-dominated professions—such as nursing and teaching—allowed for this career pattern. But fewer women today choose to interrupt their career for any length of time, and those who move into traditional male work roles have fewer options to do so. Thus, the question arises of how pregnancy and motherhood might affect the way in which a woman's professional competence is perceived and evaluated.

Another issue for career women today is child care. Every woman has her own ideas about how available a mother should be to her children. Usually these are based on a model of her own upbringing (or a reaction to it) and on what she has read or heard about the prevailing theories of child development. Many of the undecided women we interviewed wanted to hear what career mothers had to say about what it takes to be a good mother and how much child care one should relegate to others. Another question they frequently raised had to do with the effect a child might have on their relationship with their mate. Everyone knows that children alter the relationship between parents. But what particular issues might arise if a woman is involved in a career? Not surprisingly, the question most frequently asked by those trying to make up their minds was whether or not there is any way to *predict* in advance how much conflict and stress they might have if they have a child.

Heldmann, Talbot, Bryan and Gibson were selected for this chapter because of the different positions they hold on the issues of combining children and career, and the broad range of experience which their accounts provide. The problems they encountered when they added children to their lives are similar to those most other career women will confront; the differences will likely be in terms of *degree* rather than *kind*. Drawing primarily on these four interviews, we can provide some answers to questions raised by undecided women who were concerned about the consequences of combining children and career.

*Will pregnancy and motherhood affect the way my professional competence is perceived and evaluated?*

In most professions a high level of commitment to work is one of the most important values of behavior, and those who want to advance in their career must demonstrate this quality. Just getting the work done is not enough. Commitment is a more intangible quality, which has to do with communicating to others that work is the highest priority in one's life. Because of conventional sex roles, commitment in professional men is usually taken for granted, but often questioned in professional women. If they are married, women are assumed to give primary allegiance to their family. Most women are fully aware of these cultural stereotypes and often feel they must work harder than men in order to prove themselves. But sometimes their efforts do not yield rewards. Women with children frequently find themselves in this double bind: as professionals they are expected by their colleagues to give their all to their work, but as wives and mothers they are expected to give priority to their families. The problem may first arise when a woman becomes pregnant; the experience of Nancy Bryan was not unique.

Bryan was the first professional woman in her conservative company to choose to continue working right up until the time she had her baby. And this was something her male colleagues found difficult to accept. Not only did they view pregnancy as some sort of illness that should keep a woman at home, but Bryan suspected that she offended the men by *not wanting* to leave work so that she could devote all of her attention to her unborn child. Despite her reassurances to the contrary, the men were certain that after she had a baby she would not come back. By her account, they wrote her off as a professional peer. After four years of serious work, her commitment to her job was suddenly in question.

A television producer in New York told us that when she became pregnant she talked to her station manager, who was quite willing to accommodate her request for some flexibility in her work schedule. But during her fourth month of pregnancy new management took over the station, and she felt especially vulnerable to her new boss's evaluation of her work. If she didn't keep up with the demands of the new regime, which required that everyone be available "twenty-three hours a day, regardless of family or other obligations," she believed that her commitment would be suspect. Unfortunately, she developed complications of pregnancy, but she attempted, nevertheless, to maintain the expected work pace. Under continued pressure from her job, she took a business trip to California against her doctor's advice, and soon after lost the baby. Looking back, the producer speculates that "had I been out of commission for a broken leg, I think that would have been okay. My problem was not something my boss either liked or indulged."

One physician commented that when she got pregnant during her residency, she felt that some of her male peers and instructors expected her to drop out, but she completed her training on schedule and set up a practice of her own. Frequently she worked in the evenings and spent time at the hospital on weekends as well. Now she gets messages from her male colleagues which imply that quite inappropriately she is neglecting her responsibilities as a wife and mother in favor of professional commitment: "Every so often I hear remarks about how hard it must be on my husband when I get up and leave in the middle of the night. During my training they doubted my commitment to my work, and now they imply that I have too much."

Though this dilemma exists for many career women, our interviews showed that the problem is certainly not universal. When Bryan joined a rival firm, her new boss apparently had no qualms about hiring a pregnant woman. Gibson was self-conscious during her pregnancy when she was one of the very few female professors on campus and the only one expecting a baby, but she did not report that anyone questioned her professional competence or commitment. One of Marlene Heldmann's male colleagues, who she says divides women into two classes—women who work and mothers who stay at home—let her know that he was surprised that such a work-oriented woman had become a mother. But everyone else at the university was very impressed that she could handle both roles. When Talbot restricted her professional work to activities she could do at home, she was sure that some colleagues felt her training and experience were wasted. But she handled the issue of commitment by redefining it in her own terms. In her opinion, professional commitment need not be demonstrated only by following the expected career path in accordance with the established rules of the game.

*How much child care should I relegate to others?*

All of the women we interviewed had been liberated from the notion that prevailed during our mothers' generation, i.e., that nearly everything children do or become was due to the influence of their mothers, who were expected to be around the home all day to provide their offspring near-constant attention. In fact, we met a couple of women who held the opposite view: that children's personalities and their potentialities are basically set from birth, and their maturation is essentially a process of "unfolding." In accordance with this idea, these women felt that as long as a child's basic needs were met, the particular child-care arrangements made mattered surprisingly little, and so did the amount of time children actually spent with their mother.

The four women interviewed for this chapter varied considerably in their ideas about child care and how available a mother should be. But the most striking contrast in views was between Ellen Talbot and Anne Gibson. According to Talbot, the more available a mother is to her children, the happier, more secure and better psychologically integrated they will be; her presence is especially crucial during the first three years of the child's life. Talbot has strong reservations about day-care centers and believes that children are much better off when cared for in their own home. Gibson questions the belief that a child's well-being will be impaired if the mother is not generally available. She is comfortable placing her eighteen-month-old son in a family day-care home for eight hours a day, and feels that most children develop just as well and will be just as happy in day care which meets quality standards than if they were home all day with their mothers.

Many of the undecided women we interviewed and a number of the mothers expressed a lot of confusion about how much a child really needs to be with its mother and the effects of various modes of child care on development. When these women turn to the experts for the answers, they don't get much help. Currently there is a great deal of controversy about how much a child needs its mother for optimal psychological development. Some theorists hold that a small child benefits from having its mother as primary caretaker because a mother is more likely to be especially devoted to her own child and will take particular care to provide the necessary stimulation for her child's emotional and intellectual growth. As primary caretaker, moreover, the mother can offer the child the consistency of care which some experts believe is essential for a child's emotional security and its ability to form strong attachments later in life.

The majority of recent studies of children in day care, however, suggests that women who work full time are doing no harm whatsoever to their children as long as their day-care arrangements meet quality standards. These include a relatively high ratio of adults to children (one adult for every three or four children), warm, loving, consistent caretakers and a stimulating environment. The fewer the children in the group, the better it is for the child. Dr. Jerome Kagan of Harvard found in his university-run day-care center in Boston that infants and toddlers developed emotionally and cognitively in the same way as carefully matched control groups of children raised by their mothers. Even when the children were separated from their mothers all day, five days a week, their bonds of attachment to their mothers were as strong as those of children raised at home. Research also suggests that children of mothers who choose to work outside the home are better off—other things being equal—than children whose mothers stay home but are discontented with their role as full-time mothers and housekeepers.

*How will having both a career and a child affect the relationship with my mate?*

Quite a few undecided women expressed concern that if they added a child to their already busy lives, they would place a great strain on the relationship with their mate. They told us stories about their friends with careers who found that things began to unravel on the home front after the birth of their child. Even when the child grew older and more independent, its needs, along with the demands of the job, usurped so much of the women's time and energy that the relationship with their mate continued to suffer. The undecided women wondered if this would necessarily be the case with them.

Heldmann insisted that a child drives a wedge between its parents. Certainly this was true for her. She and Peter did not get closer after Jennifer was born. In fact, it was quite the opposite. Both worked full time and could rarely find time to be together. Vacations were not the same with a child along, and because they felt they should be spending leisure time in activities their daughter would enjoy, the couple had little opportunity to pursue their favorite pastimes—reading, relaxing and going to museums. Talbot, too, felt that children change a woman's relationship to her husband. In her case, limited time and energy were the cause: "To put it simply, we just don't have time for each other anymore." It has been an uphill struggle for Nancy Bryan and her husband since her daughter was born, and she thinks this is typical for most couples. In her opinion, it is difficult for a husband not to feel displaced by the baby and resentful that he is no longer the primary other person in his wife's life. Even working part time when Marcia was an infant, Bryan had no free time to devote to herself or her spouse, and she is sure that this holds true for most working women with children.

Anne Gibson's experience was in sharp contrast to those of the other women. She and her husband worried beforehand that children would take something away from their relationship with each other. But that did not happen. She attributes their continued closeness to two factors—time away (together) from children, and sharing child care. The Gibsons were able to afford baby-sitters, and in their opinion if you can buy time away from the kids to be with each other, you can pretty much establish the same relationship as you had before. Gibson also had heard many women say that children negatively affected the relationship with the husband because the men resented being replaced as number one. Her solution to this problem is to share child-rearing tasks because a man who is "in there with both hands and feet" doesn't have time to feel displaced.

Deane Bunce, a health-care organizer and administrator, found that she and her husband grew closer after their baby was born. She mentioned the same two factors as Gibson as the reasons why the quality of their marital relationship actually improved. Taking time away together from their child was essential for "rediscovering passion" and working out any tensions and strains that were developing in their busy lives. Since they could not afford sitters, they worked out cooperative day care with their friends, caring for the others' children overnight and occasionally on weekends. Both she and her husband arranged to work part time so they could each help take care of their son. Because they were both equally involved in child care, they grew closer by sharing an interest in this essential and time-consuming activity.

All the women we talked to agreed that their husbands should share in household and child-rearing tasks. The extent to which they actually did, however, varied considerably. Since many of the women we interviewed worked full time and lived in urban areas where the ideas of women's liberation had supposedly permeated the culture, we expected to find a greater incidence of shared child care than we did. The husbands of two of the four women included in this chapter did share equally, but this was not representative of our larger sample. Over and over again in our interviews we heard echoes of the complaint of Bryan and her friends: no matter how cooperative and supportive their husbands were, they were mothers' helpers rather than equal partners in the child-rearing enterprise. In addition to doing most of the direct child care, the woman is also the primary "psychological" parent responsible for most of the planning, worrying and decision making regarding children and household matters. This extra burden takes both time and energy away from work and adds to a woman's general level of stress.

Recently there have been a number of studies in which middle-class men and women in dual-career families have been interviewed about the allocation of tasks and responsibilities in the home. Researchers report similar findings: while more and more men and women have come to express the rhetoric of equal sharing, the division of labor as actually practiced has been slow to change, even in families where professional women work full time. To understand why the rhetoric was not translated more often into action, we asked the women we interviewed about it. Many said that their mate resisted the idea or accepted the idea but resisted the action. Sometimes, though, it appeared that the extent to which a husband shared had mostly to do with his wife's explicit or implicit assumptions about whether men *should* or *could* take on traditional female tasks.

Ellen Talbot does not make a big issue of her husband's work taking precedence over her own, because she feels that his job is more important than hers for the family's financial future, and so it is more appropriate that his work come first. She also believes that her investment in the children is greater partly for "biological" reasons, and thus she does not expect him to be quite as involved in the children as she is. Nancy Bryan also feels that mothers are somehow "privileged" caretakers of their children. At age three Marcia still prefers to be taken care of by her mother, and Bryan thinks this would hold true for all children of that age. Deane Bunce called our attention to the fact that some women are overly possessive about their babies and push their husbands away from caring for them by assuming a "super mother" competence, even if they don't feel very secure themselves. She considers this a form of female *macho* which programs men to feel foolish and inept around babies and children, and frightens them away even if they really want to take an equal part. This tendency should be guarded against by every career woman who has children. But among the women we interviewed, most felt that when sharing child care was an issue, their husband's *macho* was a bigger problem than their own.

*Can I predict how much conflict and stress I might have if I combine children with my career?*

Like Talbot, Bryan, Gibson and Heldmann, nearly every woman we interviewed agreed that deferring childbearing into their thirties lessened the pressures of combining children and career. Still, each found that children interfered with her work and that the conflicting demands of the two roles created strains and tensions. The character and intensity of the conflicts varied substantially, however, and we were interested in discovering what accounted for the range. In considering the stories in this chapter, along with all those we heard from the many other women we spoke to, four factors appeared most important in determining the level of conflict experienced and the ease or difficulty the women had in coping with the strain: (1) the demands of the job, (2) attitudes toward work, (3) beliefs about and availability of child care, (4) the experience of motherhood. An undecided career woman might well find it useful to evaluate where she stands on each factor when trying to predict what her experiences might be if she adds a child to her life.

## DEMANDS OF THE JOB

The demands of a woman's job and career are usually the most important determinants of the conflicts she will experience combining children and work. Obviously, jobs vary greatly in the amount of time and energy they require and the flexibility they offer in arranging the hours and place where the work can be done. If a woman has a job where she can come in late or leave early or take time off in the middle of the day to tend to a child's special needs or deal with a family crisis, she will certainly be able to reduce the stress of meeting the demands of her two roles. In general, professional women have much more autonomy and flexibility than other working women. But this is not always the case. Professional and managerial positions frequently involve a great deal of responsibility, long hours, travel and almost round-the-clock availability.

Options for maternity or extended leaves, split or shared positions, and part-time work are other aspects to be considered in assessing the demands of the job. In male-dominated professions it may be especially difficult for a woman to cut back and work part time (even if she can afford to do so) without forfeiting her chances for advancement or jeopardizing her career. Sometimes it is argued that the job requires full-time involvement for satisfactory performance. This may be true in some cases, but often the more important factor is the cherished prevailing idea of single-minded devotion to work expected of professionals. As a lawyer, Gail Gordon (see the Introduction) could have found part-time work, but not as a high-powered corporate lawyer. But Talbot was in a field that offered a number of interesting options for professional work which were less demanding and time-consuming than the administrative and clinical positions she had held before her children were born. As a highly trained and experienced psychologist, she could teach part time, start her own private practice as a therapist, or do research and writing in her home. At one point Nancy Bryan was able to arrange a part-time position that allowed her to alternate days of work with days she could be with her child. She was able to negotiate this special status partly because she didn't have to be in a particular location to do her work and partly because she had made herself "indispensable" to her firm and used this leverage to bargain for special terms—a strategy suggested by many career women we interviewed. Gibson, instead of negotiating a special status, fought to change the rules of the institution so that the option of part-time tenured positions would be available to her and other women and men.

Different pressures are created by different careers, depending on how they are structured. Gibson described the typical features of the academic career. In the first seven years at a given institution one must publish a lot and make a contribution to the field. At the end of that time it's either "up" or "out." On the basis of one's evaluated work, the individual is either given security of employment or terminated. Many women who have academic careers or other careers set up along similar lines feel they are under a special kind of time pressure. If they were to divide their commitments between work and family before they pass that all-important hurdle, they fear they might lose too much, not have a chance to recoup their loss, and thus be set back permanently in their career. Other kinds of careers allow for a more flexible pattern of time in and time out. In Nancy Bryan's field it is better to "job hop" a little in order to advance. This gives her some advantage, and was the reason she took the risk at her current job of demanding special part-time status. She could easily switch jobs if she didn't get the terms she wanted; also, she felt she could later make up for her reduced productivity and continue up the career ladder.

A lot of women are surprised to discover that mobility in their career requires a lot more than getting the work done and doing it well. It is usually important to be involved in informal and formal networks of professional colleagues, which often means a great investment of time. This can be a "hidden" demand in a job, and one particularly difficult for women with children to meet. One banker told us that "with a lot of day care and a husband who shares I have managed to work full time since my daughters were born. But I don't have time left over to do the kinds of things you're expected to do if you want to get ahead—like having a drink with colleagues after work, entertaining a lot, or going out of town to meetings."

In addition to the demands of the job which are externally imposed, there is a subjective element as well. Heldmann believes that to do her scholarly work well she requires unbroken stretches of time. Despite the flexible hours, she is convinced that combining children and career is especially difficult for professors because of the pressure to publish: "You're never off, and you're always behind." However, other academic women we spoke to, also under pressure to publish, found that the limitations of time imposed by a child actually helped them be more efficient and productive. One single mother discovered that she could accomplish more in her writing in four hours than she could when she had all day. When trying to predict the degree of conflict a woman will experience between family and career, one's tolerance to pressure, efficiency in work, and circumstances needed to do work well must also be taken into account. A job with demands that seem overwhelming to one person might be handled more easily by another.

## ATTITUDES TOWARD WORK

The career women we interviewed varied greatly in terms of commitment to work, ambition, and the pleasures and satisfactions they gained from their job. We found, as one might expect, that highly work-oriented women who placed a great emphasis on advancing in their career were more likely than the others to experience intense conflict when the demands of motherhood clashed with the demands of their job. Many women modified their attitudes toward work after they had children, and often this modification lessened their conflicts. During her twenties, work was everything to Anne Gibson, but after she had children she came to value a whole range of experiences she had not known of before. Though her career as a productive scholar continues quite well, she says that because work is no longer "everything," she is not resentful of the times she has to step back to see to the special needs of her children. Nancy Bryan commented that she has "mellowed" since her twenties, and when she had to cut back to part time for the sake of her child, she was willing to accept a temporary setback in her career. And Ellen Talbot felt little conflict pulling back from her prestigious and high-powered job, because her priorities in life substantially changed when she had children.

When a woman who has been deeply involved in her work and career does not modify her attitudes after she bears a child, the conflict can be intense. Marlene Heldmann is a case in point. Before she had Jennifer her major interests were books, ideas and teaching. After the baby arrived, her interests did not change in the least. As a result, even though she had taken a leave from the university that year and had great flexibility in the way she could organize her work, she felt intense frustration and resentment when her child upset her usual mode of working and "consumed" her time.

Can a woman predict whether or not she will modify her attitude toward work once she has a child? Our interviews suggest not always. We spoke to an engineer who had not expected a child to alter her relationship to her work; it did, in a subtle but important way. "I expected that having a child would take up time and energy," she said, "but not change fundamentally my relationship to work. But since I've had a child, I've changed. Now I don't have to 'do' all the time. I can just 'be.' Putting my little girl down a slide seems a worthwhile and pleasurable experience. I'm still as dedicated to my work as before, but I no longer feel the same kind of urgency or intense drive."

Another woman, an architect who worked in an all-male firm for ten years, told us that she had worried before she had her son, when she was thirty-six, that motherhood would cause her to change her priorities radically. "After being in a world of men for so many years, I feared that once I entered the world of women and experienced motherhood I would be flooded with feelings so warm and satisfying that I might never want to go back to the competitive world. I thought perhaps my commitment to my work and my ambition would leave, never again to return. But that didn't happen. Three months after having the baby I was ready and eager to go back to work full time."

Though there may be some surprises in the outcome, an undecided woman should reflect on how she might feel if the demands of motherhood took away from her work, and her peers advanced in their careers and passed her by. All the women we spoke to were uniform in their view that unless a woman could imagine modifying her ambition and achievement, at least for a short period of time after she had a child, she could anticipate a good deal of conflict and stress.

## CHILD CARE

We consistently found that the degree to which a woman felt she must be available to her child, her attitude toward day care, and her willingness to relegate child care to others (including her mate) strongly affected the ease or difficulty she had in combining children and career. Whether or not child care was a source of conflict depended less on a woman's beliefs about what was appropriate than on the options and resources she had available to implement her preferences. Talbot wanted to spend a lot of time at home with her children and still engage in professional work. She was fortunate to have the financial resources and to find a highly qualified person to come in and care for her children at home. Many women, however, fared less well. They had difficulty finding and sometimes affording the kind of day care they wanted. Even when availability and cost were not factors, they frequently had problems adjusting their work schedule so that it would dovetail with the hours of their caretaker or day-care center. Bryan, Gibson and Heldmann could afford

high-quality child care, yet all of them found the issue somewhat problematic. Bryan placed a high premium on the development of her child's cognitive skills but was unable to find
anyone she felt would be qualified for this task. Though she
considered her baby nurse an excellent caretaker, she did not
think this woman could offer Marcia sufficient intellectual
stimulation. In Bryan's opinion, only a well-educated caretaker could do this as well as she, and she doubted that such
a person would be willing to stay at home all day with someone else's child.

Anne Gibson and her husband spent weeks interviewing
women who ran private day-care homes to find a place for
their toddler. Finally they discovered Patsy, who they think
is superb. But they ran into trouble making arrangements for
their older boy. They could not find a good after-school program for him, so they had to interrupt their work day in order
to pick up the child from school and stay home with him in
the afternoon. Marlene Heldmann tried a wide range of day-
care homes for her child and was satisfied only with the
cooperative center where the food, the activities and everything else were a matter of joint policy for the parents. But
the co-op didn't work out because parents had to help out one
day a week, and that proved to be too great a strain for
Heldmann. She had to settle for a conventional day-care
home that costs more and offers less. For many professional
women like Gail Gordon, the corporate lawyer, even the
highest quality day-care centers would be insufficient to meet
their needs. Gail and her husband frequently work late in the
evenings and on weekends and also travel a lot for their jobs.
Only a live-in housekeeper could fully meet those needs, and
like many women, even those in dual-career families, she felt
that the cost would be out of their range.

Whether lack of availability of quality child care, cost or
an inflexible work schedule is the reason (and sometimes it is
all three), feelings of acute stress and conflict are generated
in mothers who believe their children are not getting the

proper care—be that insufficient attention from them or from qualified substitute caretakers.

## THE EXPERIENCE OF MOTHERHOOD

The way in which a career woman experiences motherhood has a lot to do with both the type and intensity of her conflicts. The more a woman enjoys being a mother and the greater the degree to which the pleasures and rewards offset the inevitable frustrations of hard work involved in raising children, the less likely she is to feel resentment toward the duties and obligations of motherhood. For example, Gibson experienced the close relationship she has with her two sons as "uniquely wonderful" and feels that her deep sense of continuity and involvement in the future exists because of that bond. Being a mother has also brought her the unexpected rewards of improving her thinking as a social scientist and of making her more sensitive to a wide range of emotions. Because she feels that for every hour the children have subtracted from her reading, writing and travel they have given her back much more by changing her as a person and deepening her insights, she experiences less conflict between family and work. Nancy Bryan felt differently about motherhood at different stages of her child's development. During Marcia's infancy she had second thoughts about what she had gotten herself into, but as the child grew older she discovered a great pleasure in being in a family unit. Bryan cut back to part-time work because she believes that her daughter needs her personal input for her maximum cognitive development. A mother who did not take as much pleasure as she in watching her child grow and develop might well have been resentful of being set back temporarily on the career ladder.

Unlike the other women we interviewed, Heldmann did not find motherhood enjoyable. In contrast to Bryan, who very much enjoys going through the alphabet with her daughter, Heldmann finds that kind of activity nerve-racking. Talbot expects that her relationship with her children will become better and better as they grow older, but Heldmann anticipates that things will get worse, since she feels that as children grow up, they begin to see their parents as enemies. Both Gibson and Talbot stated that they gained valuable insight into themselves and broadened and matured as adults as a result of their contacts with their children. This was not true for Heldmann, and in any case she was convinced that it would be easier to gain insight and maturity by "being psychoanalyzed or by writing an autobiography" than by being a mother. Although there were some aspects of motherhood that Heldmann liked, the pleasures were not sufficient to offset the strains and tensions she felt when her child interfered with her work.

The women who enjoy motherhood most may not feel resentment of their children's demands, but they may experience conflicts of different sorts. For example, women may want to spend more time with their children than their job or career will allow. Certainly this was true for Talbot, who was in conflict before she quit her job at the hospital not only because she believed that mothers *should* be with their children, but also because she very much *wanted* to be with them. This was true for many other women we spoke to as well.

Even if a woman enjoys being a mother, the difficulties of combining children with a career can be seriously intensified if she has a child with a troublesome temperament. Why some infants are born placid, happy, good sleepers, easy to feed and easy to calm, and others are colicky, irritable, difficult to soothe and to satisfy, nobody knows for sure. Some people believe a child's temperament has to do with the emotional state of the mother during pregnancy, but there is no research that proves this conclusively. While behavior is certainly affected by the interaction of the child with its parents, some aspects of behavior are inborn: children come into the world with different constitutions, different temperaments, different energy levels, different thresholds of frustration, and different degrees of emotional resilience. The experiences of Talbot and Gibson illustrate the way the "nature" of a child can ease or create difficulties for a woman combining children and career. They each had "easy" first babies, which allowed them to work at home while their infants slept. Both, however, had difficult second children who totally disrupted their lives for a period of time, during which they had to pull back substantially from their work.

In general, we found in our interviews that women like Heldmann who felt no strong desire for a child but had a baby simply because they "never expected not to do it" were the least likely to enjoy motherhood. Those who were most definite about wanting children were the most likely to have positive subsequent experiences. But just as one cannot always predict in advance how one's attitude toward work might change after having a child, it is equally difficult to know beforehand how much one will like being a mother.

### INTERACTION OF THE FOUR FACTORS

Demands of the job, attitudes toward work, beliefs about and availability of child care, and the experience of motherhood determine a woman's ease or difficulty in combining children and career. In the first three factors, *flexibility* is the key to reducing conflict. The fourth factor cannot be discussed in such terms, but the experience of motherhood does play an important role in determining how much flexibility a woman may need in the other areas. For example, if a woman really enjoys being a mother, she may *want* a less demanding schedule. If she has a child with special needs, she may *require* one. Though each factor is important in and of itself, what actually determines one's overall level of conflict and stress is how the four interact and combine. By examining how the women in this chapter fared on each factor, we can gain insight into why Marlene Heldmann finds combining a career and child so frustrating and why the other three women have been able to reduce their conflicts to their satisfaction.

Heldmann's problems derive primarily from her having a very demanding career and a strong commitment to her work which she did not modify once she had a child. Her willingness to relegate the care of her child to others did not solve her problem, because she feels that the amount of day care she needs is too much for the emotional health of her child. That puts her in the painful double bind of fearing that she will have to sacrifice her child or her career, or both. Since she does not enjoy motherhood, her resentment is further compounded by her feeling that her daughter is a threat to her career. On top of everything else, her daughter has always been a very poor sleeper, and as a result, Heldmann does not get sufficient sleep and is thus deprived of the energy she needs to do her work. Nancy Bryan's experience suggests that if there is inflexibility on some of the factors, flexibility on others can compensate. When Bryan's beliefs about child care clashed with her superior's belief about what it takes to be a good advertising executive, she resolved her conflicts by modifying the demands of her job.

Ellen Talbot holds a strong conviction that a mother should be generally available to her children, and on this point she is unwilling to bend. But her profession allowed her to continue to do interesting work on her own terms without compromising her commitment to be with her children. She gave up prestige and status when she left her position at the hospital, but this was a source of little conflict. Her second child was very difficult, but the flexibility in her job and her attitude toward work allowed her to make the career adjustment needed to ease her strain. Anne Gibson was in conflict when her responsibilities as a mother threatened her chances for success in her career, but she resolved her dilemma by securing a part-time tenured position. She utilizes a lot of high-quality day care, and her husband shares in all aspects of mothering. Relegating child care to this extent allows her time to teach, write and publish without feeling that she is sacrificing the emotional well-being of her children.

The women we've interviewed offer a number of suggestions for the kinds of adjustments and accommodations women can make in order to ease the strain of combining their family and professional roles. But the problems encountered by most women who are committed to both their career and to their children cannot be resolved adequately at the individual level. Their "private troubles" are also public issues that require collective solutions at the societal level. Counseling women to better juggle and balance the demands of family and job is important. But we must also change social attitudes and social institutions: work needs to be reorganized, for both men and women, sex roles redefined, and more high-quality child care should be made available.

The United States lags far behind all other industrialized Western nations in the quality and quantity of public and private day care available to its citizens. Developing a system of high-quality child care should be a national priority. Even career women who can find and afford housekeepers or sitters or private day-care homes would benefit if we had programs in this country to upgrade the training, status and pay of child caretakers and public funds to subsidize experts in early-childhood development and education who could consult with the staffs of day-care centers and day-care homes.

Finally, though women have been flocking into the labor force, men have not been heading back to work in the home. Thus as women take on demanding careers in addition to their responsibilities in the home, the danger emerges that the "Mystique of the Feminine," so oppressive to our mother's generation, will be replaced by the "Mystique of the Liberated." This new mystique embodies the notion that any woman should be able to manage both a career and a family; if anything goes amiss in either sphere, she has only herself to blame. The few exceptional women who are able to do it all with competence and ease become the yardstick by which others measure their own success or failure. In order to shatter the liberated—superwoman—mystique we must direct the spotlight toward the social system in which we live and understand that the social supports which could make it possible for most women to combine children and career without great conflict and strain simply do not exist at present in this country.

Though it is useful to continue to ask what a working mother can do for herself, we must also pose the question: What can *society* do for all women?

# GOING IT ALONE
# AS A SINGLE MOTHER

## Janice Ritter

Of all the women interviewed for this book, no one expressed
a wish for a child more intensely than Janice Ritter, a professional artist and now the mother of three-year-old Maria. If
Janice had met and married a man who wanted to become
a father, her desire for motherhood would not have been
problematic. But as Janice realizes in retrospect, Eliot, the
man she was married to for eight years, fit the pattern of all
the other men in her life—he was creative, successful, stimulating and encouraging to her in her work, but totally uninter-
ested in having a family. When her marriage ended, Janice
was thirty-two and she found herself in the same dilemma as
many other women who want to have children but are alone
and up against the clock. Afraid that her time to have a baby
was quickly running out, she began to consider an option
which was previously unthinkable—becoming a single
mother. Despite tremendous insecurity, uncertainty and little
positive support from family or friends, she deliberately got
pregnant and proceeded to have a child on her own.

Janice did not find single motherhood a breeze. She had
money worries, job worries and child-care worries. And she
soon found out that it wasn't easy trying to be a good artist
and raise a small child at the same time. Nevertheless, the dire
predictions of many of her friends did not come true. In the

interview Janice tells how she managed to cope under difficult circumstances, and how the birth and rearing of Maria helped her consolidate her identity as an independent woman and contributed to her success as an artist.

*During your marriage, did you and your husband consider having children?*

During the first few years we were married the subject of children rarely came up. Our life style was unconventional to say the least, and there was really no way children could have fitted in. We lived in a poor industrial section of town in an old dilapidated brick building. Eliot had bought the place and converted it into a combination home and studio for us. It was quite a trip, just like a James Bond movie where you walk into this run-down, tacky tenement house and suddenly find yourself in an exotic, elegant living space. It was gorgeous, with twenty-foot ceilings, skylights, beautiful redwood walls and plants all over the place. There was plenty of room to live in and it was an inspiring place to work, but that neighborhood was no place for kids. There were no parks nearby, the closest schools were probably pretty bad, and the idea of a private school didn't appeal to me politically. So, clearly, if we were going to have kids, we would have to move.

Whenever I brought up the subject of children and how terrible our neighborhood would be for them, Eliot would tease me by saying that I could move to the suburbs and he'd stay where we were. I felt a little threatened by that, but I was willing to put off having kids for a while. We were totally taken up with our projects, worked almost all the time and were very compatible under those circumstances. Life seemed good enough as it was.

*When did the issue of children become important for you?*

When I was about twenty-seven or twenty-eight, I began to think more and more about having a baby. Around that time Eliot entered and won a competition to design a city-hall plaza, and for three years that became the intense focus of both our lives. It wasn't that my work stopped being important for me. I continued to be productive, selling a lot and having shows in art galleries and museums. But I began to recognize that work for me was not an all-encompassing passion the way it was for Eliot. I needed something else in life. I wanted to be a mother.

Eliot's lack of interest in having a child was making me feel unloved. By the time the plaza was finished—and it was a great critical success—I was pretty sure that he did not want to have children—ever. I remember his saying at one point, "If you ever feel that the issue of having a child is so important that you would want to leave me if I were unwilling, let me know and I'll make a decision." But I never wanted it to come to that because I was sure he would decide he didn't want kids and that would be the end of our marriage. I was terrified to draw the line. I kept hoping that eventually he would change his mind about children and that would make everything okay.

*Did the issue of children play a part in the breakup of your marriage?*

Yes, it did, but in a roundabout way. Maybe a year or so before we actually separated, I had some unexplained bleeding. My doctor decided to do a D & C, a fairly routine operation, but it really set something off in me. When I went to the hospital it seemed as if I were going to have an abortion, even though I knew I was not pregnant. The nurses didn't know who was having a D & C for abortion and who was having it for other reasons. After the operation I started crying hysterically, and one of the nurses said, "Oh, that's all right. Next time you'll have the baby."

That really made me feel terrible because I was afraid that something was seriously wrong with me and I would *never* be able to have a baby. All my confidence that I could get pregnant if I wanted to was gone, and I felt it was all Eliot's fault. I had waited too long to have children because of him, and now it was too late. I was very, very angry. We began to argue a lot about children, and that put a terrible strain on our relationship. I even moved in with my sister for a month. When I came back, we talked and talked about how much I wanted to have a baby and I began to think things might work out. I didn't know that Eliot had met another woman. When the end came it was exactly like in Ingmar Bergman's *Scenes from a Marriage.* One day Eliot came home and said, "I'm leaving for Paris tomorrow." And that was that.

*How do you explain the intensity of your desire to have a child?*

That's a hard question. I always took for granted that I would have children. It was part of the way I saw my life: you grow up, go to college, get married and then have kids. During my marriage when we were living a very carefree existence and few of our friends had children, I tried to put my heart into thinking I could live my life without them, but I just couldn't. Deep down I knew that unless I had at least one child, I was going to be a permanently disappointed individual.

I'm not sure where that feeling comes from. My mother was not the stereotypic housewife totally involved with her kids. She was a pediatrician. She did stay home maybe the first couple years after my sister and I were born, but during most of our lives she worked full time in a clinic and had housekeepers to take care of us. I think a more important influence on my desire to have children was Susan, my younger sister. We are just a year apart and very much alike and share many interests. In fact, we've both become artists. When Susan got married I remember thinking that I didn't mind that she got married first but that I would be jealous if she had a child before me. She did, of course, and now she has three. That was really hard for me to take.

My only consolation was that I was the more successful

artist. She stopped painting when she had her kids, and I was way ahead of her in terms of my reputation and the number of shows I had had. But then, when her kids were still pretty young, she started painting again. She was really amazing. She got up at four in the morning to go over to a friend's studio so she could have a few hours to work before her kids got up. I was terribly impressed with that and couldn't help thinking that she deserved more credit than I did. Susan was doing her work in spite of, on top of, having kids, and somehow for a woman that's the way I thought it should be done. No matter how great everyone thought my work was at the time, I couldn't give myself as much credit for it because I wasn't doing the whole routine.

You have to remember how it was, even as late as the mid-sixties. Women didn't get much feedback on their "great" accomplishments. I thought it would be much nicer to say, "I've opened at this and that museum, I'm working on this and that project, and, yeah, I have kids, too. I'm a good mom," or whatever.

As I think back on it now, another part of my wanting children was that I was afraid I might fail as an artist, or just turn out to be a mediocre artist. Having a child, then, was also a way of hedging my bets because it would provide me with an excuse.

*If you had been more confident in your talents as an artist, would you have been less likely to have a child?*

The rewards of being a fine artist can be wonderful, but they can also be very fleeting and I didn't want to bank my whole existence on that kind of satisfaction. After I complete a painting that I think is great, I do feel super. But then I begin to worry, wondering if I'll ever be able to do that again. I want something in my life that will have more lasting value. Also, I sometimes feel that it is indecent to spend so much time on something like painting, which I think of as a totally selfish preoccupation. I thought that nurturing a child would be a way of finding a better balance in my life. I also wanted to have someone share in my accomplishments so that what I was doing was not just for me but for both of us. So for all those reasons I felt being an artist just wasn't enough. I also wanted to have a child.

*When did you first consider becoming a single mother?*

About a year and a half after my divorce. I was thirty-three and getting a bit panicky that my time to have children was running out. I went to my doctor to have a gynecological checkup and told him how concerned I was about having a baby. He said that I was perfectly healthy and that up to thirty-five or thirty-six there was absolutely no problem. He couldn't understand what I was worrying about. He talked as if three years were a lifetime, but it's not much time if you have to meet someone you love, who loves you, and who also happens to want to be a father. Even if you establish an absolutely fabulous relationship, it doesn't necessarily mean that the first thing you're going to want to do is add a child to it. I broke down and cried because I couldn't see how I was ever going to get it together in time.

Then my sister told me about a friend of hers from San Francisco who had become a single mother. She was a psychiatrist who had been married and then divorced, and had since gotten into a very casual relationship with a man much younger than herself. She told him she really wanted a child and promised him that he would have no responsibility; she wouldn't even tell him if she became pregnant. He had no objection and she had a baby.

Most people I knew condemned what she did but I was just thrilled when I heard about that. It was the first time it had ever occurred to me that a woman could do that. Up until then I was so blinded by convention that I could only imagine having children in a partnership where two people who loved each other both had to want it. The idea of doing it alone, as an independent person, was suddenly very attractive to me. I thought it was the strongest thing a woman could do.

My sister's friend lived in a commune, which made it relatively easy for her to have a baby. A group of professional men and women had rented a whole floor of a huge apartment with four or five bedrooms and a big living room and kitchen they all shared. There were several other children in the house and someone was always available to look after them. Also, she had a job that paid her enough for her to work only part time and still make a decent living. My circumstances weren't nearly as good, but from her I got the germ of the notion that a woman didn't necessarily have to see a child as a gift from someone else, something you have to wait for, pray for and worry that you might never have. You could give a baby to yourself. Just make the decision and go ahead and do it.

*Did you ever consider adopting a child instead of bearing one of your own?*

No, probably because my vanity was tied up with having my own baby. I just loved looking at my sister's children and seeing how much they looked like her. I wanted the experience of having a child and having it be mine. If I had been married and for some reason couldn't conceive, I might have tried to adopt. But as long as it was biologically possible to have my own, adoption didn't seem to be a reasonable substitute. In any case, it would have been virtually impossible for me to adopt as a single mother. I have married friends who have tried to adopt for years and couldn't. You have to make all kinds of statements about your personal beliefs, your ability to support a child, your compatibility with other people, your role in the community, and so forth. Those are things that no one asks if you're going to have a baby on your own, and I didn't want to go through all that mishmash for nothing.

*What responses did you get from people who learned of your intention to have a child?*

I talked about it a lot with friends and mostly I got negative responses. When I told my friend Betsy, who's also an artist, she said I have everything that she wants—time, space and freedom—and that I was crazy. What she said worried me because she had a husband to support her and still had so many problems. I would have a baby to take care of and the total responsibility of earning a living, too. When would I have time to paint? On the other hand, there were differences between us. I had already established my professional reputation and thought, Well, I can take a few years off from painting if I have to without risking too much. People won't forget me and I'll get back to it in two years or so.

Just about everybody I told was suspicious of my motives. A lot of people thought I was just being selfish. They were right in a way. I wanted to have a child for myself. But then, isn't that why other people want children—for themselves? I felt sure that once I had the child I wouldn't be selfish. Anybody who wanted a child as much as I did would have no trouble putting that child first.

Fortunately, not everyone was negative. A few of my friends said to go ahead, and I was very grateful for their support. In any case, no matter what anybody had said, I was going to go ahead and do it.

*Did your family support your decision to become a single mother?*

Quite the opposite. My mother was appalled when I told her I wanted to have a baby by myself. She thought I was being self-indulgent and urged me to consider the problems a child might have coming into the world under such circumstances. As if I hadn't! My father seemed more concerned about how a baby would affect my future relationships with men. He said if he had met a woman who had a child in this way, the child would constantly remind him of the woman's other relationship, and he would feel jealous and not want to get involved with such a woman. That bothered me a bit, but then I thought, Well, it's different now. We live in a world where so few marriages last and so many children are part of relationships that existed previously. His concern is really outdated.

My sister and her husband weren't much help either. Susan had a friend who got divorced very soon after having a baby and ended up being virtually a single mother. Apparently the relationship between the mother and the little boy was terrible. They were much too close and the woman had no distance from the child and couldn't control him at all. Susan thought maybe that was inevitable if you were raising a child on your own. There was nothing I could say to counter that argument. I didn't know if it would be different with me, but I sincerely believed it would.

My brother-in-law kept telling me that I didn't know what I was getting into, that I was just being romantic and had better come down to earth. But I thought I had a pretty realistic idea of what I was getting into. I knew I wouldn't love washing diapers and getting up in the middle of the night all the time. But I had a strong faith that even though it would be hard and I would be angry and upset at times, it would still feel worth it to me.

*Having decided to bear a child, how did you intend to get pregnant?*

I wasn't sure what to do. I remember telling one man that the next time I got into a relationship I was simply going to announce that I wanted to have a baby, and that would be that. He was horrified and said that almost any man I'd meet at this stage in life would probably have had all the kids he wanted to have, and by making a kid part of the deal, I would probably never have another relationship.

Another man I knew, a neighbor, found out that I wanted to have a baby by myself and he begged me to go out for coffee with him because he *had* to tell me about this terrible thing that had happened to him. He had been going with a woman for a long time and was close to marrying her, but then decided not to. She wanted a child badly and decided to get pregnant anyway. She let him know afterward. He was *furious*. He told her she had to get an abortion, and when she refused, he abandoned her on the spot and has never seen her again. He thought that what she did was a terrible violation of his right to decide whether or not he wanted to be a father. Since then he's joined some men's liberation rap groups and has had a vasectomy. I understand his feelings but I think they are extreme.

Still, that story had some effect on me and I toyed with the possibility of sleeping with four or five different men and never knowing who the father was. If nobody wanted to accept that kind of responsibility, why make it clearly anyone's responsibility? But basically, that strategy didn't appeal to me. I *did* want to know who the father was and that's why I didn't consider artificial insemination either.

*How did you finally choose a father for the baby?*

I began dating Tony, a man I had known as a friend when I was still married. He was also an architect and was married then, too. When Tony got his divorce we began seeing each other.

I knew from the beginning that Tony was not an appropriate person for a long-term relationship. He was too much like Eliot. Though he was in some ways warmer, he was equally selfish and equally self-involved. He was very attractive, and he was an important connection for me to the art world. Maybe the greatest appeal was his fertility. He had five children from three previous marriages. He didn't live with any of them and that told me a lot about him. But his kids were absolutely darling and he was very nice to them when he was with them. His youngest daughter became the exact prototype of the kind of child I wanted to have. Pretty soon, when we were making love, I started to take chances.

*Did you let your lover know you were trying to get pregnant?*

Sort of. At one point, when he became aware that I wasn't using my diaphragm, he said he didn't want any more kids and when I said he wouldn't have any responsibility he still said nothing doing, that he would feel responsible if I had a child.

After that the subject was officially closed, but I felt we had both clearly made our stands. And even though Tony was aware of what I wanted to do, he continued to make love even when he knew it was risky. So I took that as a sign that on some level it was okay with him. At the same time I had no illusions about him. If I did get pregnant, I knew I would be very much on my own. To make that absolutely clear, I didn't even tell him when I found out I was going to have a baby. We weren't seeing each other as much by then and he left for Europe without knowing, about a month after I got the news.

*What was your reaction when you found out you were pregnant?*

I was really startled. I mean, I knew that was what I had wanted to happen, but when it did, I felt this incredible terror. A large part of it was my being so totally alone, with no one to support me, and not really knowing if I would be able to make a good enough living. Then I started to be afraid I would never be able to paint again. Everyone had told me it was impossible to do good work with small children but I had always pooh-poohed that. Now that I was pregnant I began to fear that maybe they were right. What had I done to myself?

Part of my misery was that I was very sick during the first three months of pregnancy. I had all these grand notions that I would be able to do everything and be everything, and now I discovered that I had been totally unrealistic. I was soooooo sleepy all the time. I was teaching at night and would sleep all day and drag myself out of bed to get to my classes. I could barely climb the hill to where my classes were being held. So that was a very hard period for me. Friends were counseling me to at least consider getting an abortion, but despite all my misery I knew I wasn't going to do that. Later in the pregnancy I got my energy back and felt great.

*Did you ever tell your former lover that you were carrying his child?*

He found out for himself when he came by to see me shortly after he got back from Europe. He asked me what I was going to do and I repeated what I had told him before. I wanted this baby and he had no responsibility for it. He didn't react as if something terrible had been done to him or that he had been dreadfully deceived. Deep down, I think, he may have been angry at me but it didn't show on the surface.

By mutual agreement we decided not to renew our relationship, but he did ask me to tell him when the baby was born so he could come to the hospital to visit. I would have loved it if he had offered to come to my Lamaze classes, too. But he didn't, so I went to them by myself.

*Was it difficult being a single mother in your childbirth preparation class?*

I had been in a lot of conflict about whether or not to go to the Lamaze classes because all the films I had seen were built around the beautiful relationship that develops between a man and a woman when they experience the birth process together, and I thought, I just can't go through with it. It's really going to make me feel deprived. But then I realized that was just ridiculous. If I didn't have natural childbirth and let myself be knocked out by anaesthetics I would deprive myself of something even more important—the whole experience of giving birth—simply because I couldn't face what I had presumably already come to terms with—that I was having this baby by myself. Being the only single person in the class was a bit of a problem, but the teacher acted as my coach and arranged for a woman who was training to be a Lamaze instructor to be with me during the delivery. The labor was kind of long and difficult, but I was well prepared and glad that I was conscious when Maria was born.

*The first few months of having a baby can be difficult for any woman. Did you have any special problems as a single mother?*

When I left the hospital my mother came to stay with me for three weeks. By that time my whole family had become very supportive. Mother was a tremendous help, and immediately after she left, my closest friend came down from Boston. Then a month after that, my sister came. So the first three months weren't too bad. My first crisis came right after my sister left and Maria and I were alone for the first time. I was under terrible pressure to get a grant application in and I had a dreadful time getting it done. Usually I work at night so I don't have a million calls and interruptions to break my concentration. But Maria was never a good sleeper and I never could count on her giving me that night time to work.

That's when I felt it would be nice to have a husband to spell me so I wouldn't feel so completely overwhelmed. But I think that a woman who had been married and then divorced would find it even more difficult than I did to handle a child alone. That was *not* the bargain she made with life, because she had planned to have a child with another individual who was supposed to help take care of it. So even though it was hard on me, I never expected anything different, and I accepted what followed from that. How you manage has a lot to do with your expectations. Don't get me wrong; it was a very stressful time, but it wasn't awful. I never felt, Oh my God, what have I gotten myself into?

*Does Maria's father give you any support at all?*

He hasn't paid anything toward her support, but he was willing to sign a contract acknowledging that he is her father. That was something I really wanted him to do because I wanted to protect my daughter from being legally a "bastard." I couldn't be sure that wouldn't cause her trouble later in life. I had read in a book called *Sex, Living Together and the Law,* by Carmen Massy and Ralph Warner, that you can have a legitimate child even if you're not married to the father just as long as the father acknowledges that the child is his and does certain things under the law, like helping with financial support and visiting regularly. Tony wasn't willing to do all that, but he agreed to sign a statement saying that he would. Another thing Tony has done is to include Maria in his Blue Cross medical coverage plan. That's no skin off his back, of course. He has so many children on that already that it doesn't cost him a cent extra to add one more. That's all he's done for us. I didn't expect anything more.

*Do you think Maria will miss anything important because she doesn't have a father?*

I do think a father can be important to a child, even though I'm not sure what my father contributed to my life. I know he loved us in his own way, but he was always off somewhere on business or locked up in his workshop, and we didn't see him very much at all. I have special fantasies about father-daughter relationships, even though they aren't based on my own experience. I can imagine a father being real huggy and thinking his daughter is beautiful and spending a lot of time with her, and so on. But I didn't have a father like that and I know you can get along without one.

*Does Maria ever ask who her father is?*

That's an interesting subject. It first came up when she was about two, and we were visiting my parents in Arizona. They had come to pick us up at the airport, and when we got into the car, I said, "Hi, Mom," and Maria asked, "Is that your mommy?" I said, "Yes, and that's my daddy." She said, "No, no, no. That's *my* daddy." My father answered, "No, I'm your granddaddy." But she called him Daddy anyway, and whenever people would ask her about her father she told them about my father.

*Do you ever plan to tell her who her father is?*

Actually I did tell her just recently, because I thought she was becoming old enough to understand things better, and I was feeling a little deceptive letting her call my father Daddy. We had recently begun to see a little more of Tony, so she knew him. I told him she was interested in the subject of "daddy" and said I'd like to tell her he was her father. He said that would be okay with him.

Then, the next time she was talking about my father as "Daddy" I told her about Tony. At first she wouldn't accept that he was her father and insisted that my father was her daddy, but when Tony came to visit a few days later, Maria greeted him with "Hi, Daddy!" and he was really pleased.

Shortly after that happened, I accepted a good full-time job for next year in Washington, D.C., and we're moving away at the end of the summer. When I told Tony we were leaving, he said he would like to see more of Maria, and since then he has really increased his input. Last weekend he gave a birthday party for her and bought some really fabulous presents. I know what's happening, of course. Since he knows we're leaving, he doesn't feel so threatened by us and can be more generous. Still, it's been wonderful for Maria to get all that attention from him. Once we move away, Maria will have somebody she can think of as her father and have some very nice memories of him when we look at his picture in the scrapbook. And also she'll get to see him whenever we go back to New York. She'll be very much like a child from a divorce where the parents are on good terms but don't see each other very much. Taking everything into consideration, I think things have worked out very well with Maria's father.

*How have you managed financially?*

Well, it's a miracle, but I've been doing pretty well. I'm rarely overdrawn, but when that happens I have to rush around and borrow some money or draw on what I call my security fund. That's the money I got in my divorce settlement, about $6,000.

My known income, which is about $4,800 a year from my part-time job at the art center, would qualify me for some welfare programs but I've never applied for anything like that. To tell you the truth, my situation fluctuates so much that I'd always be going on and off welfare and that would be more trouble than it's worth. All sorts of extra things turn up for me. Someone will leave unexpectedly at the center and I'll get extra classes to teach, or suddenly everybody wants to buy my work and I make some money in sales. I don't know how I do it, but I usually find a way to double my income by the end of the year and I've never felt terribly strapped for money.

*What kind of child-care arrangements have you made?*

Many people have offered to trade off days of baby-sitting with me—I stay with their kids one day, the next day they stay with mine. But frankly, it's easier for me to make all my own arrangements than to try to coordinate with other people's schedules and be indebted to them. So I'm more inclined to find somebody I can pay. I don't have all that much money, but I really need time more than I need money.

When Maria was just four weeks old I started teaching one night a week at the art center and had to find a baby-sitter. A local child-care referral service helped me find baby-sitters for that one night a week. It was a harrowing experience because no one was willing to be committed for every single Wednesday evening for ten weeks. So inevitably there were Wednesday-night crises when the baby-sitter wouldn't come and I would be frantic to find a last-minute replacement. And that's been a pattern ever since I had Maria.

I don't have anything like family out here, with the possible exception of my ten-year-old neighbor. That may be the answer to a single mother's problems. Have a dedicated ten-year-old who loves babies live next door. I didn't even have to pay her because she just loved Maria and wanted to be with us all the time. She was too young for long-evening baby-sitting, but during the summer she was a godsend during the day.

It's really extraordinary how things have come along at critical moments to bail me out. One winter I was holding down two jobs at once—one at the art center and another at a museum. That was the hardest period of my life. I wanted to earn enough money so I could have the summer completely free to do my own work. Miraculously, a friend materialized who was trying to decide whether she wanted to have children, and she volunteered to take care of Maria from nine to five for fifteen weeks! It was quite a strain for her, but she carried it through and it was a tremendous relief for me. But I don't always have such good luck. When I can't find friends or baby-sitters to help me with Maria, I have to put her in family day-care centers.

*Does your demanding work schedule require that you use day care more often than you would like?*

People tell me all the time that I'm not with my daughter enough. They say that six hours in day care or eight hours in day care is too much for an infant, or for a two-year-old, or whatever age she happens to be. I've gotten a lot of negative feedback on that. But I look at it this way: if she seemed miserable all the time or as if she were suffering in some way, then I might agree that I was doing something wrong. But that just isn't the case. She's a very sociable, easygoing little person. Everyone tells me how independent she is and that she's a pretty neat little kid. Maria has loved the people I've left her with, and frankly, I think they give her more than I am able to give her. I'm very tired and crabby when I've been teaching and painting all day, and I don't have the energy to sit down and play games or read to her when I come home.

I think another big reason why I don't feel guilty about leaving her is that I really have no choice—I *have* to leave her with other people because I have to work to support us. It's the women who don't *have* to work who feel guilty about leaving their children, and they try to get me to feel bad too.

The same thing goes for how you feel about the kind of place you put your child during the day. Last summer I got into a tremendous fix and didn't have the time to find the perfect child-care situation for Maria. I had been evicted from my apartment because the landlord didn't want babies and I had to find a new place for us to live. On top of that, I was putting together an important show. I put Maria in a day-care center near my house, even though I didn't like the place all that much. They refused to let mothers come in and help the child get settled in the morning. They insisted that you drop off your kid at the door, and if your child cried, they said they could handle it. In the end it worked out fine. When I came back to pick up Maria in the afternoon she was always cheerful and seemed to like the teachers and the other children.

*What has been the effect of having a child on your creative work?*

Well, in terms of the time I've had to spend on my painting, the effect of a child has been negative. If I had continued doing the same kind of work I was doing before Maria was born, there wouldn't have been a problem. I could keep grinding it out at a pretty good pace. But I couldn't do that and remain a good artist. I feel that good artists are never static. Their work shows a never-ending progression and unfolding of new ideas. Now you can have a million and one new ideas every day, but it takes time to work them out, and since Maria was born, time is something I don't have enough of.

So that's the loss involved in having a child if you're trying to be an artist at the same time. But there are some important gains as well. There are things that go along with having children that can be wonderfully inspiring to an artist if you keep your eyes open. The whole women's movement in art has been supporting that idea, that images of children and images of the home—subject matter that men have rejected for years as kitschy or put down as mere "women's art"—are as important in their own right as any other choice of content. Maria's toys, even images in her books, have found their ways into my work and she is the best subject for my painting that I've ever had. I've always thought of an artist as someone who has images inside his head just burning to get out, but I never experienced that feeling until I had her. So it's a trade-off. Maria gives me tons of inspiration, but she takes away time for me to work out my ideas. As she gets older I'll have bigger and bigger blocks of time to myself, so I don't think lack of time will be a lifelong problem.

*How has being a single mother affected your relationship with men?*

Everyone told me it would affect them adversely. But even before I had Maria, I didn't believe that was true. I felt that a baby would make it more likely that I would eventually establish a good relationship with a man. Here was my reasoning: I felt under such tremendous pressure to have a child that I simply wasn't able to relate to men properly. When I met someone, I wasn't thinking, Do I like this person? Would I enjoy going out with him? All I could think about was, Is this man a candidate to be the father of my baby? Would I want to spend the rest of my life with him? I figured that once I had a child, there wouldn't be that particular pressure anymore and my relationship would naturally be easier.

I'm sure I'm right about that, but I really haven't put it to the test. I just haven't met anybody that I've really been that interested in, and to tell the truth, with my work and my teaching I just don't have very much energy for men these days. To have another relationship just means having to arrange for more baby-sitting.

I miss having a relationship in some ways, but I don't feel the same desperation to have a man around as I did in the old days, to prove to myself I was lovable. Now that I have Maria, I feel much better about myself and I don't need that kind of external validation anymore. Sure it would be nice to have a relationship with a man too, but I don't feel a sense of urgency.

*Other women contemplating single motherhood might wonder how you can nurture your daughter if there is no one there to give you emotional support.*

The emotional support you can get from a child is not the same as from an adult, of course, but it's not totally lacking either. Maybe the first two years it's all give, give, give to a little person who doesn't give anything back, but that changes. Maria's getting to the point where, if I'm upset about something, she'll say, "Oh Mommy, don't worry. It will be all right." So I'm beginning to get some feedback.

*Some people worry that the pressures and strain of single parenthood might lead women to take out their frustrations on their children. Does this ever concern you?*

Not so much anymore, but sometimes when Maria was real tiny it did. I remember the bad state I got into one night when I had a tremendous amount of work that just had to get done, and it looked as if she was never going to stop crying and go to sleep. Even though it was eleven o'clock at night, I picked up my daughter and went to the neighbor's next door and asked them to watch her for a while till I could calm down. I was at the point of shaking her, I was so angry. At times like that I would think, Thank God I'm not seventeen and feeling trapped or that I'm not a little less mature—whatever it is that saves you from actually taking it out physically on your kid.

Sometimes, if she's pestering me, I yell at her and become some sort of screaming shrew and I'm always sorry afterward. Those are the times when it would be good to have some relief, someone to take over when you're too tired out from trying to do too many things at once. But I doubt that's a pressure for single parents only. It seems to me that a married woman who doesn't work and is stuck inside the house with the kids all day would be under greater stress than I am and just as likely to take it out on her kids.

*Do you have any advice for women contemplating single motherhood?*

Well, I can't come out and say, "Go ahead, do it, everything will work out fine," because Maria's only three and the score isn't in yet. I have friends who seemed to give their children wonderful homes, but when the kids got to be teen-agers or young adults they just went off the deep end. At this point I get a lot of nice feedback from other people that Maria is not the kind of child most people think a single mother will produce: she's not terribly dependent, overly demanding, insecure, whatever. I know I don't handle anger very well, and I worry that Maria may end up yelling at other people too much because she'll think it's okay to just explode when you get mad. But basically she seems to be doing fine, and I feel she's going to be a strong little person. She has to be, to put up with me. She knows she's loved—there's no question about that, and I think that's what children need the most.

*Are there ever times when you regret your choice?*

When I think of how depressed I was during those years when I was afraid I would never have a child, I'm confident that I made the right decision. What I do find myself wishing sometimes is that my life had been different, that I hadn't had to do it on my own, that I would have had another person there who wanted to have a child with me. I envy women who are married to men who are good fathers. It's their project together and that must make raising a child even more satisfying.

Still, I don't regret having a child alone. What I worry about more is what I would do if something happened to her. It's not that I'm so dependent on my daughter. People recognize that I am very selfish about my time and don't spend it all on her. It's just that I know she's there and we have each other to love and to hug and to hold, and that she's a receiver of hugs and kisses and a giver of hugs and kisses. That's an answer to something that a person needs in life. I wouldn't know how to do without her, that's for sure.

# Margaret Donahue

Margaret Donahue, thirty-six, and the mother of four-month-old Billy, predicts that the conflicts she experienced in deciding to become a mother as a gay woman will not be uncommon for other lesbians who find themselves "up against the clock": "While lesbians in their twenties may claim they are never going to have kids, they don't realize that just around the bend, when they hit thirty, they may well change their minds. If they do, they'll find themselves in the same dilemma I was in."

Margaret was born in the Midwest, the eldest daughter in a family of five children. Her father was a corporate executive and her mother was an active church and community volunteer worker. Both parents were well educated and encouraged their daughter to go to college and prepare for a professional career. Margaret majored in political science in college and went on to receive her doctorate in 1969, a time when it was becoming increasingly difficult for new Ph.D.s to get work. When her job applications were rejected, she came to a rude awakening. "All my life I was raised to think that I would go to college and then to graduate school so I could have a career and make a contribution to the world. My contribution would be to improve society through social and political change. I expected to be paid for my work, make a decent living and have a meaningful life. Unfortunately, the shrinking demand for Ph.D.s and my admittedly radical values made me unmarketable in the established academic world. Maybe in China or Cuba they pay you to make revolutions, but not in the United States."

Rather than compromise her values to make herself more palatable to academia, she moved to San Francisco, supported herself by taking a part-time job in a factory, and began active work in the women's movement. It was during this time in her life that Margaret came out as a lesbian. "I met all these women who were really strong, learning new skills, and who didn't seem to be held back by anything. They were lesbians and I thought they were great. I also felt that my relationship with the man I had come to San Francisco with was not working out. I knew that if we didn't make it, I was not going to start struggling all over again with another man. I thought it over for several months and then settled the issue when I came out as a lesbian with a friend who was active with me in the women's movement."

But there was still an unsettled issue in Margaret's life that had concerned her for many years: Should she have a child? At age thirty-five, and by her own assessment ap-

proaching the biological deadline, she felt she could postpone the decision no longer, even though her life circumstances were far from ideal. Her part-time job gave her little financial security, and in addition to the stigma she
could expect as a gay mother in conventional society, she
anticipated lack of support from some members of the gay
community who were opposed to lesbians having children.
Finally there was a practical problem to solve: How would
she get pregnant?

*When did you first consider becoming a single mother?*

Not until I moved to the West Coast. Before that, I would
never have dreamed of becoming a single mother. Where I
came from they were called "unwed mothers" and I thought
of them as poor uneducated women to be pitied. But when
I moved to San Francisco it seemed as if every other woman
I met was raising children by herself. Some had previously
been married, but many had not. At first it was just straight
women, but as my friendship circles changed, I met lesbian
mothers as well. After a while I forgot that wasn't the way it
always was; it seemed quite natural.

My first lover in San Francisco had a son, and when I
moved in with them I experienced a strong desire to have a
child of my own. But then it was mostly on the fantasy level.
I was hoping that maybe a little girl, a two-year-old who for
some reason needed a mother, would just walk into my life.
Instant Motherhood! Then I actually met a woman with two
children who needed some time off and asked me to take care
of her kids. Faced with the real possibility of children, I
thought, Oh God, I'm not ready. So that fantasy went out the
door.

The real turning point for me was four years later. I had
an experience that put me in touch with my desire for a child
in a deeply physical way. I was doing body therapy and my
therapist asked me, "Is there a big insight you want to get out

of this? A revelation?" I said yes, there was, but I had no idea what it would be. We were working at the time on my stomach and she encouraged me to let my stomach muscles relax totally. That night I got into the bathtub and really let my stomach hang out. Then it hit me hard. I said to myself, I really want to be pregnant and I've *always* wanted to be. That's a real part of me that I've been denying myself. I wanted a baby so much at that point that I knew I was going to go through with it.

*Why did you want to have a child?*

Maybe it was my socialization as a female, maybe it was my own personal psychology, but I've always wanted to have children. I felt very close to my mother and strongly identified with her. Since she had children, I always assumed I would have children too. Isn't that the way it usually works? I can remember that as a little girl I had fantasies where I could literally see my children in my mind, two boys and three girls. I never really saw a husband in the picture, which is sort of interesting to think about.

Also, I've always enjoyed kids tremendously, so that's got to be another part of it. I loved to baby-sit when I was young, and even did it when I was a graduate student. In graduate school a really traumatic thing happened to me. I got pregnant and had to have an abortion. That was illegal back then and I was scared to death. I didn't have any conscious conflict about the abortion because there was no way I could have taken care of a child. Having a kid would have closed off all my options, and I felt it would be the end of my life. But unconsciously the abortion must have set off a real crisis because afterward I became depressed. I talked to a therapist and got in touch with how much I really wanted kids. We worked it out that I didn't have to have five kids like my mother—one or two would still be "having children"—and there was no hurry. I still had lots of time in the future. That settled the issue for the moment, but it kept coming up again and again at various times in my life.

*What did you expect a child would add to your life?*

I'm not really sure what I expected. I know I thought children would add a new dimension to my existence, that they would make my life somehow more meaningful. That was becoming increasingly important to me because the work I got paid to do was totally alienating. The work I do on the side—my political work and especially my writing—gave my life meaning, but there were clear limits to the satisfactions even my writing gave me. It just didn't substitute for the rewards you get when you bring up a child. I guess I believe that when you nurture a child and raise a child you are forced to make deeper commitments in life. You have to put out more, take greater risks, and you're not as safe. It may be scary, but your life has more meaning.

When I was younger I believed that this "meaning" I keep talking about—which, for me, is simply the sense of doing something that is good not just for yourself but for others as well—would come through my work. But I found out the hard way that in this society it's hard to earn a living from work that has any meaning to it, so I felt a child might provide some of that for me. I'm not saying that having a child is the only way or even the best way to put meaning into your life, but that's the way it felt for me.

*How did you translate your desire for a child into action?*

As a person I'm a cautious, rational type. My typical process is to think things through before I go ahead. I said to myself, Every few years you go through this thing about having a baby. Now it's time for you to work it out once and for all, or let go of it and do something else. So I began right away to assess my resources. My first question was, "Do I have enough money to support a child on a day-to-day basis?" I had taken on an extra day of work to save up some money, but when the baby came I knew I would be cutting back. I finally settled the money issue by accepting that I was never going to be totally financially secure, and that was okay. My friends in similar situations have managed; I would somehow manage too.

My next question was, "Will I have help from my friends in raising my child?" I didn't have a lover at that time. I didn't have anyone who was very close to me and would promise to help me through the ups and downs of being pregnant and being a mother. So I had to know what other support I could count on. In some ways the lesbian community provides a very good place to bring up kids. Many of us live communally and therefore we avoid the terrible isolation so many straight women experience who are stuck alone in their houses in the suburbs. On the other hand, not all lesbians like children or want to take part in raising them.

*Many straight women do not want to raise children either. Do you think there are special reasons that account for this sentiment among lesbians?*

When I think about the gay women I know personally, several important reasons come to mind. First there is a myth in the air that says if you don't have children you can escape oppression as a woman; you can beat the system, sneak by without getting caught, and maybe you're going to win. I know where that comes from. Many women grew up and saw their mothers suffer a lot of oppression as *mothers,* as opposed to oppression as women. Naturally, they want to escape that.

Secondly, there are some lesbians who don't like to be around children very much because they're scared or nervous or feel inadequate around them. Others, I think, have internalized the straight world's belief that lesbianism is a disease. Unconsciously they say to themselves that this is the way they are and they have to accept it, but it would be wrong to take the risk of passing it on to children. I even had some remnants of that attitude. When I was trying to get pregnant but didn't right away, I would say to myself, I'm too old, I don't have enough money, and I'm a lesbian. Maybe I'm not supposed to have a child. I was shocked to hear myself saying that, and thought, Where is that guilt from? I didn't dream it could come from inside me, but it did.

*What kind of support did you feel you could count on from your friends?*

Well, when I began asking around, people told me they were interested in putting in limited time with my child. Based on how other lesbian mothers I knew lead their lives, I had a picture in my mind of what it would be like: I would get together a support system of a number of women who would have energy for my child, but that would periodically fall apart and I would have to get it back together again with other women. In between I would be solely responsible for the child. I decided that, well, I wish it could be better, but that's okay. I can still go ahead. There was one more particularly difficult problem. I had always assumed that I would have a girl, but of course, that's not guaranteed. I had to honestly answer the question I asked myself: "Am I prepared to raise a boy?"

*What did you expect would be the problems in raising a boy?*

My friends had already told me that they would have more energy for a girl than a boy, and I understood what they were saying. I am not a separatist, but when I came out as a lesbian, I did want to be away from men for a while because I didn't like the person I became around men. I felt I needed the space to unlearn bad habits and to discover new things about myself. Over the last few years I've met men who were struggling with their sexism and developing their consciousness and I've felt warmly toward them, but I wasn't sure I had the energy to raise a nonsexist boy in a sexist society like ours. I just didn't want to have to deal with those issues. I had a brother who sensitized me to sexism but good. He was seventeen months younger and we were classic sibling rivals. He was a super-*macho* little kid and did *macho* things to me that I still resent. If I had a boy I figured I'd have to deal with that all over again.

Still, I tried to talk myself out of being biased in favor of a girl because it would make it easier trying to get pregnant if I didn't have a preference, but to be honest with you, I couldn't do it. Finally I decided it was okay to want a girl just as long as I felt I *could* raise a boy. My closest friends were all raising boy children and I could see that they were just children, human beings, not *men.* Then I started hearing about ways you can increase the chances of having one sex over another. An article on that even appeared in *Look* magazine a few years ago. At that point I decided I would do everything I could to have a girl, but if I did have a boy, that would be acceptable. I could handle it. In fact, I even got to the point where I could see an advantage of having a boy. I'd find it easier to separate from a male child, be able to let go when I should.

*As a gay woman, how did you plan to get pregnant?*

At first I thought I would just find someone to sleep with and get pregnant, but when I thought it over, I decided against doing that because I didn't want to take the risk of a future custody fight. I'm sure you know that the courts try to take children away from lesbian mothers. Of course I knew I could get anonymity by sleeping with several different men and not telling them what I was doing, but frankly, I thought that would be too much disagreeable work.

Then I connected up with a woman who was trying to get pregnant by artificial insemination. At first those words really bothered me. Whenever I heard the words "artificial insemination" a horrible image of cramped fetuses growing in test tubes would spring into my mind. But now my attitude has changed. As I see it, all it involves is a different way of transporting the sperm from the man to the woman, and it gives a woman much more control over conception.

My friend knew of a doctor who had a system of donors, but she didn't want to go to him because he was kind of piggy and she didn't want to risk having some obnoxious thing said to her. Artificial insemination is a real simple technique, but the implications for your life are immense and you are very vulnerable when you're doing it. So my friend found a women's health clinic that ordered the sperm from the doctor. All she had to do was pick up the sperm at the clinic, take it home and put it in her vagina with a syringe. She started trying in July, and by August she was pregnant.

*Did the same clinic assist you in getting pregnant?*

I considered going to that clinic, but then I decided I would rather get a sperm donor through my own political friendship network. Todd, a gay man I knew from a teaching project, offered to help me find a gay male who would be my donor. He also volunteered to be the go-between and bring the sperm from the donor to me. We set up a simple system: on days when I was ovulating, Todd would deliver the sperm in a jar to my house or to someone else's house and I would pick it up later. I never met the donor because I wanted the whole process to be anonymous. It seemed a lot better that way. I wouldn't know who he was, he wouldn't know who I was, and there would never be a custody battle.

*What information did you have about the donor?*

Well, I know what I requested. I asked for someone with a healthy background, no genetic or inherited diseases, and no allergies. I wanted medium height and dark curly hair, but eye color and nose type didn't matter. Then I figured that while

I was at it, I might as well throw in straight teeth. I had a lot of teeth problems as a kid and I knew I wouldn't have the money to pay for braces. I was also hoping for a mellow, cuddly baby, so I tried to think of what characteristics in the father would increase the chances for that. It made sense to me that if someone slept well at night, that might be some indication of serenity, so I asked for a real good sleeper. It wasn't scientific, but it couldn't hurt.

It occurred to me early on that there were distinct advantages to getting pregnant my way. I was in the rare position of choosing some of the characteristics I wanted in my child. Now, I should make clear that I'm not talking about all that eugenics-movement crap where they're trying to breed a superhuman race. In fact, I intentionally did not ask for someone smart or with a high IQ. I wasn't trying for some sort of superchild. I just wanted a healthy, normal, cuddly baby.

I did ask the donor to be white because I wasn't sure I would be able to provide the child with another culture, and I felt that would be my responsibility. If my friendship circle had been different, I might have made a different decision on that one.

*How did you artificially inseminate yourself?*

I had thought about using a syringe like my friend, but then I heard about a group of lesbian women on the East Coast who were inseminating themselves using a turkey baster. That's right, the kind you keep in your kitchen. I know that sounds a little strange, but I thought it was a wonderful idea. A turkey baster fits so much better into women's culture than a syringe, which is really more a part of the male control culture. So I used a turkey baster and there was nothing to it.

The technique is really very simple. It's just a matter of getting the sperm and inserting it into your vagina. Contrary to what most people think, you don't have to be extra careful about light or air or heat or anything. In fact, it almost seemed too easy. The first time I got inseminated I went for a walk afterward and realized that I was in a strange state, thinking, My God, I could get pregnant fooling around like this. I had spent fifteen years of my heterosexual life worrying about getting pregnant, and all of a sudden I was giving my body totally new messages. It was kind of mind-boggling.

*How long did it take you to conceive?*

I tried six times over an eight-month period, and the sixth time was the charm. That's no more than it takes on the average for a woman to get pregnant the traditional way, and I had promised myself that I would try at least that many times before I questioned my method. But it was hard waiting, harder than I let myself realize. Each time I got my period was a terrible letdown—all that planning and emotional and psychic energy gone to waste. It wasn't until I was five months pregnant that I realized how difficult the waiting period had been for me.

*What was your reaction when you discovered you were pregnant?*

At first I was very, very happy, just overjoyed that things had finally worked and that I was really going to have a baby. But as soon as the initial euphoria wore off, I felt panicky. All the doubts I had ever had came back and hit me full force. What had I done? Was I sacrificing my life? Would I have enough money? Would anyone really help me out? Somehow I managed to convince myself that I had everything together, but then three weeks later I would go through the same thing all over again. It was such a big change that no matter how much I had thought it through beforehand, I was never sure I had made the right decision. So I did worry a lot but I enjoyed my pregnancy too.

When I look back I realize that my fears were intensified because I was *choosing* to have this baby and believed at the time that I would have no right to complain if things didn't work out. Some people said as much to me, like "Well, it was your choice to have a baby," in a tone that implied that since I wasn't a kid and therefore should have known what it would be like to be a single mother, I had forfeited my right to feel oppressed or unhappy.

Sometimes I still feel that way emotionally, but intellectually I don't buy that argument at all. It's a real "blame the victim" trip and I think a lot of women get caught in that nowadays. They may really want to have a child but may not be in a good place to have one—they may be alone, or they don't have enough money, and they can't get a decent job. If they do go ahead and have a baby and then get into trouble, they feel they can't complain—they asked for it.

When you think about it, that's really absurd. Women have a right to have children, if that's what they want. They also have a right to a decent job that pays a decent wage. And there should be federally funded day care so a woman doesn't have to pay half her salary for someone to stay with her children. It's plenty hard for a woman alone to have a child and make ends meet, believe me. But if she doesn't make it, the failure is not hers, it's society's. She is caught up in the system and doesn't have decent options.

I feel a responsibility to fight for changes in this society that will make it easier for poor people or single women to raise children, but I'm not responsible for the way the world comes to me.

*You were thirty-six when you became pregnant. Did you worry about your age?*

Thirty-six didn't feel very old to me and I was quite healthy. On the other hand, I was defensive about a lot of things at that time, including my age. I had visions of going to see some establishment male doctor for prenatal care and saying, "Look, I'm thirty-six years old, I'm single, I'm a lesbian, and I don't have a lot of money. I know you think I'm overweight and too old to have a baby, but I'm not going to take any crap from you."

I also went through a very heavy thing about whether or not to have an amniocentesis done, and that relates to my age. I went to the University of California Medical School to read up on the process and talked to several people there about whether or not I should have the test. I decided finally that it wasn't worth the risk for me. According to statistics, only one percent of the women age thirty-five who take the test find out about some chromosomal defect, whereas a half percent of women have spontaneous abortions two or three days afterward. I would have been interested to know about the sex of the baby in advance but not enough to risk the pregnancy, and I certainly would not have had an abortion if it turned out to be a boy.

*What was your experience of childbirth?*

I think it was as good as it could possibly be in this culture. I did all my prenatal care with midwives and had the labor at home with about ten of my friends there to help. They were holding my hands, rubbing my feet and rubbing my back; whatever I wanted, they would do, and there were enough people around so that I knew I could ask for anything without asking too much. The midwives were very experienced; they knew just what to tell me to do, but more important, they knew how to say it to me. The labor was beautiful. It went on and on, but I was on top of it all the way and it felt very good.

But then when I got to the point of pushing, I pushed and pushed, and nothing happened. As soon as we realized that the head was not getting through the pelvic bone and the baby was in trouble, we all got into the car—it was a station wagon, so I could lie down—and rushed to a nearby hospital where the midwives had connections. As it turned out, I had an emergency Caesarean.

When I was coming to, after the operation, I heard one nurse saying, "I didn't think they allowed home births for first children," and another nurse said, "Well, she waited half her life to try to have a kid." That hurt, but on the other hand, they were also being very nice to me, and I was so euphoric that it didn't matter what anyone said. The baby had swallowed some meconium as he was being born, which is acidic and can infect the lungs, so they had to give him oxygen and antibiotics. I'm still anti the whole medical establishment, but I was very grateful then for the intense support a hospital can give. The baby was huge—nine pounds, three ounces.

*How did you feel when you found out it was a boy?*

Very, very disappointed. I was so sure it was going to be a girl. But when they put the baby on my shoulder and he was so alive, and I could feel his muscles moving and the blood pumping through his veins, it seemed like a miracle and I lost my feeling of disappointment. I knew I would have to grapple with the issue of how to raise a male in this society, but that was okay.

*How did your parents react to your having a baby?*

First let me say that my parents have known for some time that I'm a lesbian, and they accept that. They come and visit me and whomever I'm living with at the time. Our differences aren't around my being gay but around my lifestyle, and especially how I live my life around money. They don't like it that I've had all this good education but don't have a good job and earn good money. In the past few years they've even softened about that, and they're feeling more kindly toward me now.

So when I had Billy they were delighted, really thrilled. My mother was a little upset when she first heard I had conceived through artificial insemination, but when she found out I had asked for good teeth, she began to see it in another light. She was the one who had to take us to the dentist when we were kids, and had to deal with our hurting mouths because those wires were killing us. My dad is always joking about the list I made of donor characteristics: "Well, did you ask for a good tennis player?"

*How supportive were your friends after the baby was born?*

When I came home from the hospital, they were terrific. A friend from out of town came to stay with me for a week. Other friends did the shopping and brought me in food. Once two women came over and I gave them seven loads of wash to do and they did them. More recently, people just volunteer to baby-sit, although, since I'm nursing, I don't make much use of that. The support I find most valuable is when somebody comes to visit and she picks up the baby and walks around with him for ten minutes while I make my bed and have breakfast. Just that much is immensely helpful. It makes all the difference between feeling crazy and tied down and really enjoying your baby.

*How are you managing financially?*

Right now I'm living on pregnancy disability and AFDC [Aid to Families with Dependent Children], but soon I expect to be working part-time two days a week. Then I'll be living on $600 a month take-home pay. As Billy gets older, expenses will go up, I suspect, and I'll have to work even more. In the past I have made the choice to work less and earn less money in exchange for having more time and energy to devote to my own interests. But now, with a child to support, I won't be able to do that as much.

*What kind of child-care arrangements do you plan to make?*

I would love to find a day-care center, but for infants there is hardly anything in this city. The waiting lists are endless, and unless you have the right contacts or special skills in going through bureaucracies, you just can't get your kid in. When I go back to work I'll be working two long days a week and I'm looking for friends who will stay with Billy from eight in the morning till two in the afternoon. Then Vickie, a teen-ager who lives with us in the house, said she'd take him from two until I get home at six. If I can't find people to help me in the morning and early afternoon, I'll have to see what else is possible. Maybe I'll have to find day care in a private home, but that would cost a bundle.

*Besides more accessible day care, what other resources would make it easier for you to be a single mother?*

At the top of the list would be better housing. I would like to see reasonably priced small units where I could live with my child, but at the same time be close to other women like me. That way we would have a communal life with shared spaces where the children could play together, but if someone decided to go off on her own, the arrangement would be flexible enough so that we wouldn't have to find a whole new house or a whole new group of people to live with.

As long as I'm indulging in fantasy, I'll throw in one more. I would like to get paid for the labor that I put into raising a person who is going to be a worker when he grows up. It's not easy putting in so much work to raise a child and then not get paid for your labor, especially when you live in a society that measures your worth according to how much money you make. I feel I'm doing valuable work for society and I shouldn't have to go on welfare in order to survive.

*So far, what have you found to be the advantages and disadvantages of being a single mother?*

The main disadvantage is financial. I'd like someone to help share the economic burden of raising a child. On the other hand, it's an advantage to know that you can support yourself and your child by yourself and that you don't have to be dependent on anyone, especially a man. Most men today are so emotionally underdeveloped that women end up having to meet their childish demands on top of their children's demands. Raising a child without a man simplifies your life.

*What do you plan to tell your son about his father?*

I'll tell him that his father was a politically conscious gay man who shared my values and that he can be very proud of him. I also plan to be open and direct about the way I got pregnant, but of course I will tell him in different ways at different ages. I'll say that I was a lesbian and wanted to have a child in a way that would best protect me from losing him. Since I feel positive about what I did, I think I can teach him to feel the same way. The only reason I would be less than honest with him would be if I were under pressure from the state and might lose him if he knew how he was conceived. I have friends who can't tell their children they are lesbians because they fear the kids will tell their fathers and then they might lose them in a custody case. That's a very heavy situation, for kids basically know what's going on but they become confused because no one can tell them the truth.

*Do you think there are any disadvantages to your son's not having a father?*

Not really. My whole family was raised without a father. He may have been there physically, but not emotionally. My mother was the one who really brought us up. I hope Billy will see some positive male models, men who are leading their lives in a nonsexist, nonracist, nonclassist way. He'll see plenty of women doing it, but he'll need to see *men* as well because he's not female.

On the other hand, I really don't see why a positive father model is any different from a positive mother model. Billy will have the advantage of growing up free from a narrow conception of sex-role stereotypes. He'll see women doing everything one has to do to be an adult. In fact, he probably won't even understand what male-female role stereotypes are. He'll get some of that *macho* stuff from kids at school, I guess, but he'll also be around other children raised without traditional sex-role models. I have many friends who are trying to get pregnant, so I know there will be other babies around like him.

*Would it make a difference to you if he grows up straight or gay?*

It doesn't matter to me whether he's gay or straight. I'm primarily concerned that he grow up to be a decent human being with the right values about life. I hope he will be less competitive and less power-trippy in his sexual relationships and in his relationships in general than most men—gay or straight—are in our culture. I hope he will be able to be gentle and tender and cherish his partner, whatever his partner's sex happens to be.

*What moments with your baby bring you the greatest happiness?*

Well, I remember when I first saw Billy, the day he was born. He seemed like an incredible gift. I didn't know who had given him to me, but I had been given to. Now he's a little person and I feel he really digs me, and that's an incredibly good feeling. Just holding him in my arms is overwhelmingly wonderful. And I can't tell you how much it means to me when he smiles. Before he started to smile, we related to each other on an instinctual level. He needed me and I responded with animal-like protectiveness and caring. But when he smiles, he becomes a social being who gives to me and I give to him. His changes make me change.

I really am very proud that I had a baby and that I have thus far nourished a healthy human being. It's hard to come out and say it because it immediately makes me start to feel vulnerable. After all, how do I know how he will turn out? But right now, having a child to raise feels like a very important and satisfying thing to do.

*Does motherhood bring you frustrating moments as well?*

Sometimes when I'm breast-feeding, Billy wants to suck and suck, even after he's finished eating and I have no more milk to give him. I get to a point where I can't stand to let him do that anymore and unless there are other people in the house who can take him, I just put him to bed and let him cry. He doesn't cry long and then he goes to sleep, but I worry about that in myself—that I can run out and be unable to give one iota more. At those times I think, Oh God, I've been taking care of this kid for only three or four *months*—I have friends who have been at it for fourteen *years.* How am I going to keep on doing this?

At those times I get in touch with a little regret and wonder whether, if it weren't for my sex-role socialization, maybe I wouldn't have felt I had to have a child and I could have put all my energy into my political work or my writing, and really have done something great. I don't feel that way often, but when I do, I think to myself, Well, you made a choice and part of that choice was taking the risk that you might regret it someday. Most of the time, of course, I don't regret it and I'm thankful I had the guts to make the decision to have Billy.

*What advice do you have for women contemplating single motherhood?*

I don't think anyone can tell another person whether she should have a child or not, but one piece of advice that was very helpful to me came from a single mother, someone I didn't even know very well, and I'd like to give that advice to someone else: If you can see your way clear, go ahead. As long as you are prepared to be flexible about your support system and accept that it will ebb and flow, you can do it.

If you're looking for more encouragement and support, I would advise joining a group of other women who are thinking about becoming single mothers. I did that and it was very helpful to me. I saw that wanting a baby by myself was not just some weird fantasy of mine, but that many other women wanted the same thing. I also met women who felt they could afford to have a baby, even though they didn't have $10,000 in the bank and a tenured position somewhere. At the first meeting I attended, a woman brought in her baby who was conceived by artificial insemination and we all sat there wide-eyed in wonder. We were all thinking of doing the same thing ourselves, but to see a real live baby conceived this way—with ten little fingers and ten little toes—helped us get over our misgivings and disbelief. That was a real inspiration.

*Are you thinking about having a second child?*

To my amazement, that's a big issue for me. Since I've had Billy, I do think about having another baby.

Now, this is where the theme of your book—up against the clock—really hits home for me. Deciding to have a first child at thirty-five didn't seem like such a big deal. But if I want to have a second, or even a third child, I'm really crowding the clock. I've read that it's common for women whose babies are two, three, four months old to feel they could go on having babies forever, but I don't have forever anymore. If I really intend to have more children, I must get started deciding immediately, start up my decision-making process all over again.

# Carol Ruth Silver

Civil rights lawyer, law professor, trustee of the First Women's Savings and Loan Association, and member of the San Francisco City and County Board of Supervisors, Carol Ruth Silver is also the single mother of two boys, Steven, seven, and Jefferson, eighteen months. She was born in Massachusetts, the daughter of liberal democrats who instilled in their daughter a sensitivity to the world's problems and a desire for a career in which she could do something about them. By age thirteen Carol knew precisely what she wanted to be when she grew up: a civil rights lawyer.

Unlike many committed career women who become so absorbed in their work that the issue of having children does not arise, or at least not until they find themselves seriously up against the clock, Carol always knew she wanted a family. The conventional path would have been to get married and settle down, but that was not for her; she was not about to give up her work and doubted if she could find someone who would fit into her career plans. Convinced that she would not find the right man to marry, at least within her time limit, which she thought was close to running out, she decided to go it alone.

After she stopped taking birth-control pills but still couldn't become pregnant, she consulted a gynecologist, who told her she would not be able to conceive. This condition Carol attributes to the pill, which she had been taking nonstop for many years. Disappointed but no less certain that she wanted a child, she decided she would try to adopt. Four years later she became the adoptive mother of Steven (Ah-Hwei), a three-year-old Taiwanese orphan. To her astonishment, two years after that, Carol discovered she was pregnant. An issue she thought she had settled when she adopted Steven once more loomed large. At age thirty-seven, more involved in her career than ever before, she decided for the second time in her life to become a single mother.

*What was your reaction when you discovered you were pregnant?*

I was thrilled, absolutely thrilled. Ever since the doctor told me I couldn't conceive, I always had a lingering feeling not so much of inadequacy, but of something being wrong with me. When it happened, all I could think of was, Wow! My body finally got it together. I might have had some subconscious flickers of doubt about what I would do. After all, I was thirty-seven years old with a five-year-old son and already planning my campaign to run for a seat on the Board of Supervisors. But consciously, I had only one thought: I was going to have a baby.

*What was the reaction of the baby's father when you told him you were pregnant?*

First of all he was surprised, since I had bitterly complained to him about being unable to conceive. That response was followed by some resentment. He had a child by his first marriage and wasn't planning on having more children. He went through the "you can't do this to me, I can't afford another child" bit, but finally he accepted the inevitable. He knew I was going to have the baby and I was going to do it on my own terms. I told him he could stick around and rant and rave or he could leave. He chose to stick around and rant and rave. Eventually he relaxed and enjoyed the whole thing.

*Did the possibility of marriage arise?*

No. He was recently divorced and utterly down on marriage as an institution. I tend to agree with him. Marriage involves a number of promises of long-term commitment; otherwise it's just a legal contract. It may be that I have been a divorce lawyer too long and have seen too many pathologies in the thousands of divorce cases I have handled and therefore cannot recognize a nonpathological relationship when I see one.

But I have never met anyone that I was sure I would stay with for a long time, or he with me. Without that kind of devotion I see little utility in getting involved in the legal and other hassles that a marriage entails.

*Were you concerned about the stigma attached to being an unwed mother?*

Not really. But when I adopted Steven I was highly amused by the flurry of media interest in what I was doing. Reporters in particular were careful to distinguish between a single mother who adopts a child and a single mother who has a child out of wedlock. Adoption was a wonderful, marvelous, exciting, laudatory act, whereas being an unwed mother was considered a social tragedy. I can't see any difference myself. Everyone knows that the sexual revolution has come—if not come and gone. These days it is socially unacceptable to announce that you are celibate.

Since I was by then a highly visible political person, of course I had to be concerned about public reaction. As soon as I learned I was pregnant, I sent off an announcement to Herb Caen, the local gossip columnist for the San Francisco *Chronicle,* who dutifully ran it in his column. I made it public to guard against a whispering campaign. You can't whisper about something that everybody knows.

*Did you experience any social pressure not to have the child?*

None at all. I don't believe anyone could have felt that it wasn't responsible for me to bring another child into my life. I was well known throughout the city of San Francisco as being a single mother rearing an absolutely delightful, charming and beautiful little boy who was the envy of many other mothers. Had Steven not turned out well, had he been autistic or developmentally retarded with any hint that his condition was environmentally caused, people would have had good reason to disapprove, and I would have thought twice about it myself. As it was, I got nothing but positive feedback. I was given masses of secondhand baby clothes and equipment, including three baby carriages.

*San Francisco is a very liberal city. What if you were to move elsewhere?*

I do have some concern that in another area and in another place Jefferson may have people attempt to stigmatize him. But stigmatization is an internal thing. You can't be put down for being Jewish, or Catholic, or pink, or tall or fat, or what not, unless you internally accept that what you are is something bad. I think that Jefferson will have the internal strength to know there is nothing wrong with what he is. If someone were to say, "Neah, neah, neah, neah, neah, you're a bastard," he would feel that they were jealous of him for the advantages he has had, or that they were just crazy.

*You were thirty-seven when you got pregnant. Were you concerned that there might be problems because of your age?*

The first thing I did was ask a gynecologist what the dangers were. Then I took a bunch of tests, including an amniocentesis and the Tay-Sachs test. Since everything seemed normal, I went ahead.

*Did your pregnancy have any effect on your work?*

No, in fact most of my clients and colleagues didn't even realize I was pregnant. The very last week before the baby was born I was working on a thorny legal problem that I just couldn't seem to figure out. The baby was due on Friday and I was supposed to have the problem solved by Wednesday. I was frantically calling people and researching like crazy, but it wouldn't solve, it wouldn't solve. Friday came and I said, "Goddamit, this baby is going to get here before I figure this thing out. That can't happen." I worked all through the weekend, and on Monday, at eleven in the morning, I went to the courthouse to file the papers that took care of the problem. As I was walking out, the first labor pains began. It was mind over nature; my career had dominated my physical state.

*What was your experience of childbirth?*

It was dreadful. It hurt enormously. I had gone to Lamaze classes with my sister, and everyone led me to believe that if I learned to push and pull and breathe correctly, it wasn't going to be so bad. But after four or five hours of labor I began to think, Why did I do this? It's not worth it. Nothing is worth this. It was the only time I had real doubts about what I was doing, but by that time it was too late.

I was in heavy labor with my sister coaching me, and the baby's father, too. Having both of them there was a big help. I recommend that anyone going through the birth process get as many people as possible to participate. Labor never stops and if your coach has to leave for a minute even just to go to the bathroom, you're still there. If you have several people, they can spell each other.

*Do you expect that the baby's father will play any role in his life?*

I think it is clear to him that I will never make any legal claims on him for child support, nor will he ever attempt to claim custody of the child. However, if something were to happen to me, I know he would feel enough responsibility to see that Jefferson was taken care of.

He is not a stranger to his son. He is still around a great deal, although he doesn't live in the house or take any responsibility. The other day I saw him changing a diaper and I couldn't believe my eyes. I told him I was shocked and appalled.

My older son, Steven, knows who the baby's father is and

they are very fond of each other. It is my hope that an equally good relationship will develop between Jefferson and his father. Everyone only focuses on the negative side when a family is split up. I see some real advantages to being a parent not in residence, especially when to be in residence means a continual battle with the other parent.

If Jefferson's father remains in the area—which I suspect he will—Jefferson will have an older man to relate to in a very healthy and happy way, without the residual guilt feelings which inevitably develop when there is tension between the parents. I have no intention of denying my son a positive relationship with his father.

*Some single mothers we have spoken to resent any interference or claims on the child by the father. Can you understand that reaction?*

Of course I can. It all depends on the situation. A divorced client of mine once explained why she wanted to deny the father any relationship with his child. After several years, when her daughter was about six, the father suddenly appeared, saying, "Hey, you know I'd really like to get to know my little girl." That made her bitter. Since the father had refused to help her at the time when she really needed help, with the drudgery of diapers and all the terribly hard work connected with raising a child from infancy, she felt justified in denying him the fruits of her labor—namely, the privilege of relating to a charming, pleasant child who had reached the age when children almost become people and are really lots of fun.

I can understand that anger and I think many women experience it. Terrible feelings also build up when children become pawns in the continuing effort to get money out of the absent parent, especially if the mother does not have sufficient economic resources to avoid the constant and tremendous drain that early child rearing represents. The social tragedy is tremendous: the child is denied a good relationship with another human being, and the parent is denied a relationship with the child.

*Many women say that with one child, combining motherhood and career is manageable. The real difficulty comes with the second child. Was that true for you?*

No. I think the great wrench comes with the first child. By the time you have a second child you've already given up any clothing that can't be put into a washing machine; you've given up those friends who invite you to a small intimate dinner party at a moment's notice and expect you to be there at six, fully made up with your clothes nicely pressed. You've gotten rid of any desire you might have had for fancy china or glasses. You've learned to appreciate the virtues of plastic. Even though plastic may represent the degradation of our cultural values, it's practical because when the baby drops a plastic cup on the floor, it doesn't break, it bounces. Most important, you've already fixed yourself in space—with children you can't move from place to place as freely—and you've fixed yourself financially. The expense of even one child is enormous. I didn't think a new baby would add any more of a burden, and he hasn't.

*How do you manage from day to day with two children, a private law practice, and your demanding job as a city supervisor?*

Okay, here's a typical day. Jefferson wakes up between five and six and quickly makes his presence known. Because of a recent back problem, I can't run up the stairs and pick him up, so someone, usually Steven, brings him down to me so I can nurse. I've been nursing Jefferson for eighteen months now. Despite my busy schedule it is not impossible for me to find time twice a day to lie down with the baby. It's not that much of a hassle, and the satisfactions far outweigh anything else.

Steven comes down about seven, and I cuddle him for a while, read him a story, chat—whatever. At seven-thirty everyone in the household is supposed to be up. We have a live-in couple, Roger and Terry, plus some tenants who help me with the children and other household needs in exchange for rent. Steven dresses himself and gets his own breakfast. Jefferson has his diaper changed and wanders around the house with a piece of bread or a banana, something relatively portable. I don't try to sit down and feed him. After the usual emergencies of the morning—the temper tantrums, the crises of not being able to find the baby's shoes or discovering that we're out of diapers—everyone is out of the house by eight-thirty.

Roger and Terry take Jefferson to his baby-sitters and Steven to his school. I am either dropped off at one of my offices on the same run, or else I hobble down to the bus stop and take the streetcar. Jefferson spends all day with a baby-sitter named Mrs. Wong, a Chinese lady in the Sunset who has been taking care of him since about a month after he was born. She has five children of her own, but he's the only baby she takes care of. Steven goes to the Gold Mountain Instilling Virtue Buddhist Elementary School, which is a bilingual Chinese-English school. I want both boys to be able to speak Chinese.

Steven stays in school until about two and then goes across the street to the Jewish Community Center, where he takes swimming lessons or plays with other children until he is picked up in the evening. Roger and Terry fix the kids' dinner, and at around seven I come home and play with the children for about an hour.

I either work at home nights or go out to various meetings. If he wants, Steven can come with me. Otherwise he stays home—but just as long as he doesn't watch television. He's allowed one hour of television a day, and even that much I don't like. One night a week I stay home and play baby-sitter. That's a typical day.

*Do you ever worry that the children are missing something by not being with you more?*

No. I think I'm with my kids enough. Children don't know or care who washes their diapers or who cooks their food. I believe it's the quality of the time spent with them, not the quantity that counts. I spend about an hour in the morning and in the evening of totally committed time. I don't answer the phone; I don't give interviews. I totally concentrate on my children whether I'm rolling around on the floor with Jefferson or teaching Steven to use his erector set which I've never been able to figure out.

When I'm not here, the children are surrounded by people familiar to them. Jefferson is as fond of Jack, who has lived in the house since the baby was a month old, as he is of me. Roger and Terry have only lived here six months, but they are very committed to the children, as were the previous baby-sitters, who still visit us frequently. Jefferson's father is a frequent visitor too. I am not the exclusive person in the children's life, and I think that is good.

*Many psychologists would argue that one, at most two, primary caretakers are preferable.*

That comes from assuming that the nuclear family is the only viable family unit. I maintain that the nuclear family of two parents and 2.75 children is an invention of the twentieth century and an experiment which has totally failed. It was created by the frontier mentality: the man would pack up his family to march off and settle the West leaving behind all the kin who traditionally took part in raising the children. Thus the multigenerational household where there is a mother and a grandmother and maybe a couple of aunts became a thing of the past. But that was a much healthier and more natural environment in which to bring up children; in that kind of setting mothers didn't go nuts trying to run a household, take care of their husbands, feed and clothe their older kids, and at the same time take care of a newborn.

Since the middle-class nuclear family cannot usually afford household help, a new mother is bound to go crazy alone with a baby unless the husband can take a maternity leave and help her out. But even then, he goes back to work after a few weeks and there she is sitting and staring at the walls, tending the baby for twenty-four hours a day, seven days a week, fifty-two weeks a year. It's a terrible situation.

A household composed of some older people, some younger people and a number of children is healthier for the kids and certainly healthier for the adults. I have seen numerous new family regrouping among my divorce clients. A woman with two children teams up with another woman with two children and they make a household together. That's a positive trend. The nuclear family is dead.

*Do you see any disadvantages for children being raised in households with members of only one sex?*

No. It doesn't matter whether the household members are male or female or both. What matters is that there is a collection of adults, whatever their sex or sexual orientation. If men and women are involved, they shouldn't be divided into the traditional male-female sex roles. Sex-role division is another outdated legacy of the frontier mentality. Then the man went out to hunt deer and make buckskin while the woman ground corn and took care of the children. Today we don't need that kind of male-female specialization. I was back at my desk two days after the baby was born while Roger, one of my male baby-sitters, took over.

I didn't have to go back to work that soon, but I wanted to do it and could do it, having arranged a support system that made it possible.

*How much does such an elaborate support system cost?*

At this point my child-care expenses are between $600 and $800 a month, and that's only for child care and schools; it doesn't include rent for the large house I need in order to accommodate live-in child care. Part of my housing costs are really child-care costs. It's a tremendous commitment of money for something for which you can see no tangible benefits and that you know will only keep growing and demanding a higher and higher percentage of your total resources.

*Are there moments when you regret having children?*

At times I feel very resentful of the constrictions on my life, of not being able to do what I want to do. Sometimes when the boys are misbehaving, I get very, very frustrated and wonder, Is it all worth it? But they don't misbehave very often and I know in my heart of hearts that it is worth it.

You can't look at children as an investment with future returns, i.e.: "When I get old, my children will support me," or "When I get old I will have the children to relate to and I won't be lonely." That's not guaranteed these days. You have to feel that the present enjoyment of children day by day makes it worth the sacrifice. For me that is certainly true.

*What are the greatest pleasures?*

That's hard to articulate because it's a feeling. Cuddling a child or cuddling a babe is just a superbly pleasurable present experience. It's kind of like sex: it has no purpose (unless you're trying to have kids), but it just *feels* good.

*Do you think you'll have more children?*

The feelings are very strong, but it's unlikely that I will. If I am to be taken seriously when I talk to other people about zero population growth and birth control, I can't be touring around the country with five or six homegrown kids, can I?

Of course, I've only had one of my own so far. If I get to the point where I have the money to afford another child before I get beyond childbearing age, I'll probably have another. But I'll be forty this year and that begins to get into the biologically dangerous zone. I may try to adopt again, but I doubt I would succeed.

*Is it difficult to adopt as a single mother?*

If you are willing to take a handicapped child or a mentally retarded child, your chances are good, but otherwise they are very, very slim. I spent four years trying before I succeeded in adopting Steven.

As soon as I began calling the adoption agencies I discovered that there were literally no adoptable children for nicely married, religiously oriented, upper-middle-class, upwardly mobile, white Anglo-Saxon couples, let alone for a single mother. There may be a thousand children a year, probably less, in the whole United States who become available for adoption, but tens of thousands of couples want to adopt.

There are numerous starving children abroad that need homes, but unfortunately, our international systems are not set up to maximize the ability of American parents to adopt them.

*How did you eventually manage to adopt Steven?*

My process, unfortunately, is not replicable by anyone else. It was achieved through blind luck on the one hand, and involved, on the other, a payment of an old debt. The woman instrumental in arranging my adoption of Steven is a high-ranking legislator in what is the equivalent of our General Assembly in the Republic of China on Taiwan. When I was at the University of Chicago, I helped her daughter to overcome the language barrier, and eventually we became best friends. This woman happened to know of a three-year-old boy in Taiwan whose father had recently been killed in a car accident and whose mother had died when he was quite small. Without that kind of connection, the adoption never would have happened.

*You were thirty-four when you adopted Steven and thirty-seven when you gave birth to Jefferson. From your experience, what are the advantages and disadvantages of being an "old" new mother?*

In the first place, although I'm almost forty now, I don't think of myself as old. My mental perception of my age is about eighteen. But undoubtedly there are advantages to being an older mother. It takes an enormous amount of sophistication to live in our complicated modern society, and my years give me a certain knowledge and experience in the world that help me get along better. For example, I know enough to be wary about what's in the food I'm feeding my children. I read the label before I buy any prepackaged, preprepared baby food. Sugar, it turns out, is the primary ingredient in most of them, and the doctors say too much sugar is bad for children. I also know how to evaluate medical insurance programs, to make a choice between Blue Cross or a Health Maintenance Organization like Kaiser. That's a very complicated decision.

Most people, unfortunately, do not have the sophistication to avoid the pitfalls of our society, but they pay for it and their children pay for it—in the junk baby food their children eat; in all the television their kids watch; in the radiation their kids are absorbing from microwave ovens. There's nothing like a microwave oven for a busy professional woman. You whip up a dish, pop it in the oven, and fifteen minutes later it's on the table. Yet how do we know what all that radiation is doing to the baby playing in the kitchen next to the oven?

The advantage of being older is that older is usually somewhat wiser and more sophisticated and more experienced. The only disadvantage I can think of is that you may be out of shape physically, and the exertions of raising kids might cause more wear and tear. On the other hand I understand that there are certain hormonal advantages related to the physical experience of having a baby which would most likely outweigh any disadvantages of age.

*What advice do you have for other women contemplating single motherhood?*

I would not encourage other people to do what I have done without the same preconditions I have set up. I would say that anyone who wants to have children, married or unmarried, should be in a living situation where the ideal ratio of children to adults is one child to four or five adults. Unless there are other people to help care for your child, you don't even have time to go to the bathroom. Even when the baby is lying in his bassinet, a million things can go wrong that are potentially harmful: something may blow into the bassinet; the baby could turn over and spill out. So I always tell people who want children that to do it yourself without sufficient support leads to insanity. To avoid the constant and continual drain on one's energy and emotional resources that child rearing necessitates, you must have other people in the household to help you.

*Most people do not have the financial resources for an elaborate support system like yours.*

The way that I have managed is not the only way to do it. I've become the head of a household in which I'm the primary wage earner. I pay the bills for all the people who live in my house and, in essence, I run the whole show. But that choice comes from my own rather particular personal needs. I have friends who are doing just as well as I am by combining two female salaries in a single household which can then support live-in baby-sitters. So everyone's economics need not be as good as mine. You might have five adults and two children, or five adults and five children.

But no matter how ample your household support, you still have to make sacrifices. The financial sacrifices may be the greatest, but there are others as well. Having children drastically limits social life for most people. For me, that's not so serious. A social affair or a dinner party is just another place where I have to put on a face, make interesting chit-chat, and be on my best behavior. Believe me, I can do without that. What I can't do without is a little time on Sunday morning to just lie around and read the newspaper. That kind of time is precious to me and I have precious little of it.

*Any final comments?*

Oh yes, there's one final precondition for having children: you really have to feel you want to. To choose to subject yourself to yowling babies and pots of dirty diapers is totally irrational. There is nothing so foul as the smell of urine that emanates from a pile of diapers that have been around for a week— festering—before you dump them into the washing machine.

So, if you don't have a very strong impulse, it's crazy to take on the mental and material expense of children. On the other hand, if the impulse is there, don't fight it. It can be done.

# EXAMINING
# THE ISSUES

What are the psychological risks for my child?

Will social stigma be a problem?

Does a child need a father in the home?

What should a child know about a father?

What will be the psychological costs to me?

Will I have special problems combining children and career?

How will being a single mother affect my relationships with men?

How do I go about getting pregnant?

Single motherhood as a life style is becoming more common, but at present it is still unusual for a career woman to decide to have a child if she is not married or living with a mate. What motivates these older women to become single mothers, and what gives them the strength to take this unconventional and often difficult step?

Among the women we spoke with, a very strong desire to have children was a precondition for their choice. For a variety of reasons—psychological, sociological, ideological, or a combination of all three—they were either unable or unwilling to have children within the traditional context of marriage. Janice Ritter wanted to get married and have children, but she couldn't find the right man. Carol Ruth Silver had strong career ambitions and doubted that she could find a man to fit into her life. Also, her work as a divorce lawyer caused her grave doubts about marriage as a viable institution. Margaret Donahue, a lesbian and radical feminist, was not at all interested in matrimony. A second important factor was the way the women viewed single motherhood itself. None thought that having a child outside the context of marriage was a deviant act. They were all aware of the skyrocketing divorce rate in the United States and the increasing number of children who consequently spend a significant amount of their youth living in homes headed by a single parent. Being a single mother in their view was not very different from what happens to many other women in the course of their more conventional lives. One single mother we talked to summed up this attitude as follows: "What I'm doing is skipping a step, that's all. Almost all my friends who married and had children are now divorced and in the same boat I'm in. But I think I'm better off because I avoided the pain and expense of divorce."

A third decisive element in the choice to become a single mother was the confidence these women had that they possessed the psychological, social and financial wherewithal to adequately care for a child. Like Donahue, Ritter and Silver, the other single mothers we interviewed had carefully assessed their resources and considered at length the possible advantages and disadvantages of single motherhood before they had their child. Yet another factor for many women was the biological clock. A number of them told us that at a younger age they would not have considered having a child on their own, but as they approached what they considered to be their deadline for reproduction, they felt they were forced to make a "now or never" decision. The choice of "now" was often facilitated by hearing about or meeting other single women who had recently had a child. Before

Margaret Donahue came to the West Coast, she never considered becoming an "unwed mother." But when she arrived in San Francisco, she met many straight and gay women (some previously married) who were successfully raising children on their own. Seeing that they could manage bolstered her confidence that she could do the same. Janice Ritter was mobilized to make her decision after hearing about a female physician who had deliberately gotten pregnant by a friend who agreed to be the father biologically only.

Even if the single-motherhood trend accelerates, however, most career women will have serious concerns about what the consequences of going it alone might be for themselves and their offspring. The undecided women we interviewed raised a host of questions that reflected their awareness of the general negative cultural stereotypes of the unmarried mother and the unfavorable views currently held by many psychologists and psychiatrists. We now examine some of their concerns in light of the thoughts and experiences of the single mothers we interviewed for our book: (1) potential consequences for the child, (2) important issues for the mother, (3) methods of getting pregnant and their social repercussions.

## POTENTIAL CONSEQUENCES FOR THE CHILD

Mental-health authorities commonly disapprove of single motherhood because they believe the situation can create an unhealthy dependency between the mother and her child. As one psychiatrist we consulted put it: "I am often disturbed that the child becomes the significant other for the woman, her *raison d'être*, her companion, everything that is significant to the self. That is an enormous burden for a child to bear. When a mother depends too much on a child to meet her needs, the child reciprocally becomes overdependent on the mother. This makes it hard for the child to separate from her and become an autonomous and independent human being."

None of the single mothers we interviewed felt they placed too heavy an emotional burden on their children, thereby creating overdependency in them, and in part this was because they all had careers. Janice Ritter enjoys the emotional support and companionship of her daughter, but her work as an artist is also of major importance in her life. She says that she is "very selfish" about her time and certainly does not spend it all on her three-year-old daughter, whom she describes as a strong and very independent little person. Another example of a single mother with many interests besides her child is Margaret Donahue. She is involved in political activities and writes for feminist newspapers and magazines. Moreover, she has a large network of friends in the gay community whom she can count upon for emotional support and child care. In order to manage her busy life as both a politician-lawyer and a mother, Carol Ruth Silver set up an elaborate system of parent surrogates for her children. She is not the exclusive person in her children's lives, and she believes that is all to the good. Any mother can become overfocused and overinvolved in her children. But women, married or not, who have many interests and commitments outside their children and who have a sufficient support system obviously minimize the chances of creating unhealthy dependencies in their children.

The issue of social stigma was raised as a concern by many undecided women, but, again, none of the single mothers we interviewed thought they were subjecting their children to this stress. Carol Ruth Silver argued that the stigma the child bears reflects society's disapproval of the unmarried mother who (according to the prevalent stereotype) irresponsibly brings children into the world. She felt that since it was already known in San Francisco that she was doing an excellent job raising her adopted son, Steven, no one would disapprove of her choice to have a child, and Jefferson would not suffer social stigma. In fact, Silver got only "positive feedback" when she publicly announced that she was going to have a baby. Janice

Ritter "legitimized" her daughter by getting the child's father to agree to sign a document acknowledging his paternity. She believes that since Maria knows her father and will have some contact with him in her life, she will see herself and be seen by others "just like a child from divorce." Margaret Donahue does not worry about stigma because in the gay community where she lives there are an increasing number of women raising children alone, and her son will therefore have the company of many other children raised in circumstances like his own.

The problem of stigma for the unmarried mother depends in large part on where she lives. The women we interviewed were all from large urban centers. The experiences of women living in small towns where even divorce is uncommon may not be similar to those described above. But attitudes are changing everywhere. One thirty-eight-year-old single mother from Los Angeles was pleasantly surprised when she took her three-year-old daughter back to her home town in Kentucky for a visit. The problems she anticipated did not materialize. Even her mother's "uptight," conservative friends were very supportive, and she concluded that this was a significant sign of social change.

Many prospective single mothers wondered if their children would be confused about their gender identity if they do not have a father in the home. Frequently they are aware that most authorities on child psychology hold that children need a parent of each sex for optimal psychological development. The primary concern of these authorities over the single-mother trend is, indeed, that children raised without a man in the house will fail to develop secure feelings of gender identity. In their view, a girl needs a father to confirm her self-concept as a female, and a boy needs a father to confirm his self-concept as a male. The controversy on this issue is great, and there are many experts who frankly admit that there haven't been enough studies to determine if this is true. Identity theorists are in agreement that a clear sense of gender identity is crucial to a child's psychological sense of well-being, but not all authorities are convinced that children must be raised with a father to develop these feelings. Some argue that one's sense of gender identity is innate: boys "know" they are boys; girls "know" they are girls, and therefore children of single mothers can confirm their gender identity through contact with the men they meet in the course of their lives. Other specialists maintain that secure feelings of gender identity are formed primarily by the *attitude* of the parent toward his or her child's sex. According to this thinking, mothers, for example, who convey conscious or unconscious strong negative feelings about men to their sons will have a negative impact on a boy's growing sense of his maleness. On the other hand, by this logic a woman with positive feelings toward men could create a secure sense of masculinity in a boy, whether or not there was a man sharing in the child rearing.

Children who are brought up without a father in the house may well not have as much exposure as other children to conventional adult sex roles. For a number of single mothers we talked to, that was seen as an advantage rather than as a disadvantage. These women explicitly reject the traditional sex-role socialization with which they grew up, and they want no part of it for their children. In Carol Ruth Silver's view, what is considered appropriate behavior should have nothing to do with one's sex. Also, the specialized division of labor by sex, she argues, is an outdated legacy of the frontier mentality. Margaret Donahue does not see why a positive father model is any different from a positive mother model. She feels that her son will have the advantage of growing up free from a narrow conception of sex-role stereotypes. For her, moreover, it doesn't matter if her son becomes gay or straight, as long as he grows up to be a decent human being with the right values about life.

Carol Klein, author of *The Single Parent Experience,* writes: "Research has shown that despite nuclear-family my-

thology, having a good relationship with one parent is healthier soil for emotional growth than growing up with two discontented parents." Many of the single mothers we spoke to
strongly agreed. Several women who had grown up with parents constantly bickering felt that it is a wonderful advantage
for themselves and their children to live in an atmosphere of
harmony and peace.

Every single mother will eventually have to deal with the
issue of what to tell a child about its father. The women we
interviewed handled this in a variety of ways, depending on
their relationship with the child's father. Carol Ruth Silver
continues to be on friendly terms with the man by whom she
became pregnant. Her son will know who his father is and will
have the opportunity to develop a relationship with him.
Janice Ritter maintains only a marginal relationship with her
child's father and does not expect him to play much of a role
in her life. But because she feels strongly that Maria should
have someone she can think of as "Daddy," she told her child
who her father was and arranged several meetings with him,
even though she knows that her decision to move soon to
another state means that they will have little contact in the
future.

Some women, of course, do not know or will not acknowledge the father. What do they tell their children? A thirty-
one-year-old accountant who got pregnant in a casual affair
without informing the man involved plans to tell her daughter that her father was killed in the Vietnam war. Because
Margaret Donahue feels that children "basically know what's
going on" and become confused if you don't tell them the
truth, she plans to take another tack and be open and direct
with her son, but tell him about the way she got pregnant in
different ways at different ages. She'll explain that she chose
artificial insemination because as a lesbian she feared the
possibility that she may one day lose him in a court custody
case.

## IMPORTANT ISSUES FOR THE MOTHER

Common sense suggests that single mothers with careers will be subject to all the stresses and strains encountered by married career women with children—and then some. Money concerns will loom larger if the woman is the sole financial support of her child or children, and if she lives alone, there will be no one to give the all-important breathers that provide necessary relief from the stress of child care. Ellen Talbot, the psychologist we interviewed for our chapter "Career and Children," said she could not endorse single motherhood for that very reason. She argued that bringing up children is a tremendous job, and single mothers get no relief: "If special problems come up with the children, a woman alone has no one to spell her, no one to talk to, and no one to share the burden." Janice Ritter understands the disadvantages of having no one to give her relief and is the first to say that taking care of an infant alone is not easy. But she feels that her maturity and her deep desire for a child helped her to cope quite well, even during the most difficult moments. Women who deliberately choose to be single parents, she believes, will perhaps cope *better* than divorced women or married women whose husbands offer little support, since they know what they're getting into from the start.

A number of single mothers we talked to stressed the idea that because they knew they would not have the "built-in" supports that marriage can provide, they were careful to make special arrangements for help and support well in advance of their child's birth. Margaret Donahue made very sure she could count on support from her friends before she made the decision to have a baby, and when her child was born, she had numerous helpers during childbirth and after. The disadvantages of single motherhood which Talbot described apply least to the women who live communally. Carol Ruth Silver emphasized in her interview that the best way to reduce the physical and emotional stress of child rearing—for single and married mothers alike—is to live in a large household ideally composed of some older people, some younger people and a number of children.

Like married women or women living with a mate, the ease or difficulty a single mother will have trying to combine children and career depends to a great extent on the flexibility she has on the factors discussed at the end of our previous chapter —the demands of the job, attitudes toward work, and beliefs about child care. If the single mother lives alone, however, the logistics of juggling the demands of children and work can be especially problematic. More advanced planning is needed, and options are usually more limited. Most married women can count on their husbands to cover for them when they are required to travel for their jobs and to give them time to work in the evenings when necessary. Janice Ritter acknowledged her difficulty working at home because of interruptions from her daughter and admits it would be nice to have a husband to share the child care. She also found that in order to support herself and her child she had to work more than full time. This meant that she had to use more day care for Maria than she liked and did not have sufficient time to search for the best day-care center available. Carol Ruth Silver manages to combine an extraordinarily demanding career with single motherhood with very little conflict. But she has the advantage of both a high income and a communal household in which the members are paid to help her with the children. Margaret Donahue does not have a career in the usual sense because she has separated her meaningful work—political activities and writing—from her factory job. Since her job is only part time, she does not anticipate that her conflict between child and her job will be that great. With friends who volunteer to baby-sit for her and the temporary assistance of welfare, she manages to keep everything afloat.

Janice Ritter's father voiced a concern of many single mothers when he told his daughter that if she had a child, she would surely jeopardize her chances for future relationships with men. The accounts of a number of single mothers we interviewed, however, made it clear that this need not be the case. At forty-one an IBM computer programmer we talked to accidentally became pregnant by her lover. Feeling that this would be her last chance to have a child, she decided to have the baby even though her lover broke off with her after she refused to get an abortion. In her seventh month of pregnancy she met another man whom she married soon after. In retrospect, she suspects her husband was initially interested in her partly because she was pregnant. He was divorced, and his ex-wife lived with their only child on the other side of the country. He missed his son a lot and wanted very much to be a parent again.

When a woman is up against the clock and longs to have a child, *not* having one can sometimes interfere with establishing a good relationship with a man. We spoke to several women who felt that because of the pressure of the biological deadline they had begun to evaluate men only in terms of their fatherhood potential. If the men didn't score high on that, they were dropped without further consideration of their virtues. A thirty-eight-year-old single mother who had been obsessed about having a child since she was thirty-two told us that she had been sent to Munich to cover the Olympics for a magazine. There she got involved with a journalist whom she described as "intelligent, kind, and charming." One evening he brought up the subject of birth control and told her she need not worry, since he had had a vasectomy. That ended the attraction right on the spot. She later regretted her action because it terminated what might have turned out to be a satisfying relationship.

Another example was a thirty-nine-year-old single professor of history who had deferred all thoughts of childbearing until she had gotten tenure at age thirty-five. She told us why her relationship with men *improved* after she began an adoption proceeding for a child: "At thirty-five I began to panic about not having a child. I was desperately trying to find a man to marry, and that was completely counterproductive in terms of my relationship with any man I met. Finally I realized that I really needed to separate the issue of a child from the issue of my relations with men. I decided to adopt. Now I am more free to deal openly and honestly with men; I no longer have a 'hidden agenda.' " For some women having a child is so gratifying that old psychic wounds heal and they are better able afterward to relate to men. Janice Ritter feels much better about herself since she had a child—stronger, more independent and self-validating than ever before. She believes that the new sense of self she achieved through having Maria makes it unlikely that she will repeat the destructive dynamics that characterized her previous relations with men.

## METHODS OF GETTING PREGNANT AND THEIR SOCIAL REPERCUSSIONS

Undecided women were interested in knowing how single mothers over thirty had gone about getting pregnant. In the group of women we interviewed, most had become pregnant by accident. Carol Ruth Silver's situation was repeated often in the stories of the single mothers we spoke with. They were pregnant by accident, and the issue they had to confront was whether to abort or to have the baby. Silver did not experience very much conflict on the matter. Although her lover voiced strong objection to her having a child, she wanted the baby so much and knew she could afford to do so on her own terms that she easily overruled his objections. Other women we spoke to who reached the same decision as Silver experienced a great deal of conflict and guilt. One filmmaker who accidentally became pregnant wanted to have a child, but her lover definitely did not. She found the situation anguishing: "I always thought that two people would make a decision about having a child, but in this case we didn't agree, and there was no way to compromise. By having the baby I was making a choice for my lover that he didn't want me to make, and I still feel guilty about it. Even if we never see each other again, he will be very affected just by knowing that he has a child somewhere, not really knowing where."

The situation for single women who *deliberately* get pregnant may be equally stressful and complex. Unless there is a willing lover on the scene, the options that remain—finding a friend or acquaintance who is willing to father a child, getting pregnant without telling the man or getting artificially inseminated—are often difficult to execute and fraught with emotional, moral and sometimes legal complications. Before Janice Ritter got involved with Tony, she considered boldly informing the next man with whom she started a relationship that she was going to have a child. A horrified male neighbor talked her out of this plan. Perhaps it was just as well, since most of the other women we met who tried that approach found that the most common answer was an adamant "No!"

Since women are usually expected to be the ones who manage contraception, it is not too difficult for a woman to choose a man to have sex with during her fertile time without informing him of her intent. Janice Ritter's male neighbor had such an experience when a girl friend got herself pregnant without his consent. He was furious that his right to determine whether or not and when he would father a child had been violated. One woman we spoke to could not sympathize at all with his outrage: "I understand the argument that when you deliberately get pregnant without telling the man you are 'using' his body. But women have had their bodies exploited in the same way since time immemorial, and even now as male legislators cut back the funds for abortion, that exploitation continues. So I can't get too upset about women getting pregnant without a man's consent." Other single women felt that two wrongs don't make a right, and that was why they would not pursue this means of getting pregnant and would rather use artificial insemination.

Janice Ritter did not consider this option because she definitely wanted to know who the father of the child was. Other women feel the opposite way. One example is Margaret Donahue. She did not want to sleep with a man, nor did she want to know the identity of the donor of the sperm she used to inseminate herself. Anonymity was of paramount importance to her because she feared that if the father were ever to press claims for the child, he might win custody in a court battle because she is a lesbian. Although several important decisions in California have recently gone in favor of lesbians keeping custody of their children, many women in Donahue's position still do not want to take any risk of losing their children. Because Donahue lives in Berkeley, she had several options open to her that women elsewhere might not have. She had access to a women's health clinic that would provide donors to unmarried women (most doctors and sperm banks are reluctant or refuse to do so), and she also had a "political friendship network" through which she found a friend willing to find a man who would donate sperm to her anonymously.

Some older single women who want to have a child do not want to bear one of their own. They would prefer to adopt. Sometimes they are successful in their efforts, but often they are not. Although the number of single mother and single father placements have risen slowly over the past several years, single mothers are still likely to encounter resistance from social agencies when trying to adopt and, when successful, are assigned only older, minority and handicapped children which the agencies are unable to place with two-parent families. Many prospective single mothers we talked to felt that adopting an older child with special needs would intensify the stress of combining career and motherhood; others did not want to face the agencies' exhaustive interviews which minutely scrutinize every aspect of the lives of potential adoptive parents—whether married or single.

We have seen from the experiences of the women interviewed that the choice to raise children out of the context of a traditional marriage can have its drawbacks and special difficulties, but raising children successfully in any context is no easy task. The high rate of divorce in this country indicates that the traditional two-parent family is in trouble, and the advantages and disadvantages of single motherhood should be assessed in light of the realities rather than the myths of the contemporary American family. Single mothers who plan their support systems carefully or live in communal settings might even find combining children and career less problematic than many career women with children in traditional marriages. While all of the women we interviewed say they made significant sacrifices raising children alone, it seems clear from the accounts of their experience that the pleasures and satisfactions they gained from their children made their sacrifices worthwhile.

# CHOOSING
# TO BE CHILDLESS

## Martha Ward

Martha Ward, a public health administrator in Berkeley, California, knew from an early age that she didn't want to have children: "My life goals were always different from those of my girl friends. I grew up in the Bible Belt, where it was expected that women would become wives and mothers and nothing more. But I always primarily wanted a career." After attending a university in Texas, she went East to a social work school, where she earned an MSW. She married soon after, at age twenty-three, but the marriage lasted only two years. In 1968 she moved to Berkeley.

While her decision not to have children had been made years before, Berkeley provided Marty with a supportive milieu for her nontraditional life choice: "The women's movement was very strong in Berkeley, and you also have to remember what it was like back in 1968. The war was still going on, the planet seemed hopelessly polluted, and even for kids coming out of college, no jobs existed. Everyone seemed to feel: 'What kind of world is this to bring up kids in? What opportunities are there?' "

Unlike women who just let their time on the clock run out until it becomes too late for them to bear children, Marty jumped ahead of the clock and—to the consternation and disapproval of many of her friends—had a tubal ligation at age thirty.

*Most women in our society grow up assuming that one day they will become mothers. At what point in your life did you realize that you would be different?*

Even as a child I felt different. To get married and have children was never a goal for me the way it was for many of my girl friends. I wasn't even that interested in dolls. If my girl friends were playing with dolls, I might join them, but my interest was only sporadic.

I preferred outdoorsy things. I was very athletic, more so than most of the girls I knew, and loved sports, especially horseback riding. The older I got, the less that was encouraged, though. Horseback riding was okay up to a certain age, but if you kept at it when you got older, people thought there was something wrong with you. I was probably interested in horses a little too long.

*As a teen-ager, did you continue to feel "different"?*

Yes and no. I was boy-crazy, like everyone else, and dated a lot. I really craved a relationship. But unlike my friends, I didn't have fantasies that my relationships would lead to marriage and kids.

*What early goals did you set for yourself?*

I wanted some kind of professional career. Who knows where I got that. My parents were from a traditional fundamentalist background and didn't push me in that direction, but they didn't discourage me either. As a teen-ager I went to a Methodist Church study group and that's where I met people who guided me toward my present career.

*You did eventually marry. Did the idea of having children come up then?*

Yes. That was the only time in my life that I ever considered having children. I felt there was something wrong with the marriage and that maybe children would make it right. But I never said, "Let's do it in a couple months." It was always something I thought we might do in a couple years. Even then I was pretty far away from making that decision.

*Some women who choose not to have children relate their choice to an unhappy childhood or to problems with their mother. Were there such factors in your background?*

I can't say that my childhood was unhappy. My sisters and I felt very, very loved. We were our parents' whole life. But interestingly, when I recently spoke to my twenty-nine-year-old sister, she said something that I have always felt, "I just don't want to duplicate my mother's life." I know exactly what she means. My mother was so bogged down with her kids that she had no life of her own. She was a nurse for the civil service and worked very hard. When I was sixteen my father had a series of disabling heart attacks that made him an invalid. He was never a strong, equal partner in their relationship, but after his heart attacks Mother had to carry the ball financially by herself. With an invalid husband and three kids to support, that wasn't easy. We were always in great financial stress.

All her life my mother was giving to others with nothing left over for herself. Nursing is a giving, draining profession, and when she came home there was us to take care of. I'd say my family background definitely relates to my not wanting to have children. Like my sister, I don't want to duplicate my mother's life.

*If you had come into a great deal of money and were positive that you would never have financial worries, would that have made a difference in your feelings about having children?*

Since my childhood made me acutely aware of the financial burden of children, having plenty of money might have made some difference in my feelings. But money would not have ultimately changed my mind. It would have opened up more options to me, more things for me to do in the world, and children might have seemed all the more burdensome. If I were rich, of course, and had an upper-class mentality, I could simply turn the kids over to a nanny. But what's the point of having children if you're going to do that?

Even at my present income level I could probably afford kids without cutting back on too many luxuries, but money isn't the point. My reasons for not wanting kids are more selfish—or what people would define as selfish: I just don't want to devote a large part of my life to raising children. That option doesn't appeal to me and it would shut me off from too many other options in life.

*Some women feel that raising children offers rewards and intrinsic pleasures that nothing else in life can equal.*

Women who feel like that should obviously have children. I don't feel like that. And it's not that I don't like kids. I do. I love developing relationships with my friends' children. I just don't want to make children a major part of my life.

I find spending short periods with children rewarding, especially if I've planned an activity that I know they like. Children are fun to be with when they are the center of attention and all activities revolve around them. But when adults want to do adult things and the children don't have anything to do, they become a real interference. I quickly get bored and impatient and don't want to be around them anymore. I turn off.

*Do you think you would have been a good mother?*

This may sound strange, but I think I would have been too good a mother. I have such a super sense of responsibility as well as a tendency to forget about my own needs that motherhood would have been a terrible trap for me, the way it was for my mother.

*Is there any part of the motherhood experience—pregnancy, childbirth, nursing—that you regret missing?*

Nursing, possibly. Pregnancy, not at all. That has never appealed to me in the least. Pregnant women have told me that it's not all it's cracked up to be and that it's often an unpleasant experience. Since I don't have a strong desire for a child, the whole thing would probably be a burden.

*Some psychological theorists claim that motherhood is a vital developmental stage in reaching full adulthood. Only by nurturing and guiding the next generation do we reach full maturity. What are your thoughts about that?*

I agree that the willingness to nurture others is an important part of an adult identity, but I don't agree that one's objects need necessarily be one's own biological offsprings. Nurturing comes very naturally to me and I do a lot of it.

I haven't told you this yet, but I have been a mother. When my sixteen-year-old sister came to live with me a few years ago, I was for all practical purposes her mother. I fell into all the traps: I was overprotective; I wanted to clear away all obstacles in her life; I did things for her she was perfectly capable of doing herself. I just couldn't let go. That caused a great deal of friction between us over the past few years. But being a "mother" to my sister was an essential learning experience in my life. I learned a great deal about myself and our relationship. Now we are extremely close.

I have also established a close relationship with a young niece. She lives in San Diego, but we correspond frequently and I occasionally pay her way to come to visit me. I find it easy to identify with young girls, and enjoy being a positive influence on their lives. I don't think of myself as an immature person, nor do I think that by choosing to be childless I am skipping a vital stage in my life development.

*Few women we've interviewed decided so early in life that they definitely did not want to have children. But even among those who did, very few wanted to have a tubal ligation. What made you decide to be sterilized instead of practicing other forms of birth control?*

I tried most of them—and didn't like any. The pill is unsafe. I took it for three years when I was very young and didn't question things, but then I began to read about all the possible dangers. There are still no definitive studies on long-term use. When I went off the pill I used an IUD for two years, but that was a horrible experience. I can't believe that I kept something so uncomfortable in my body simply because I didn't want to hassle with a diaphragm. After that I used a combination rhythm-diaphragm birth-control system, but that began to feel too risky.

In the last year before I had my tubes tied I found myself taking chances, playing chicken with my body. I was getting to feel a little too sure. The tubal was to safeguard against that.

*If you had become pregnant, would you have gotten an abortion?*

The answer is yes, absolutely. And I support the right of women to have abortions. But I didn't want to ever have one, because for me it wouldn't have been easy. There would be something alive there, and I would have felt very guilty.

So I was at a point in my life when I was greatly enjoying sex, but I was also getting careless. One month I really sweated it out—I was positive I was pregnant. When I found out I wasn't, everything seemed to crystallize in my mind. I realized that I was tired of hassling with the whole birth-control business and that I wanted to have a tubal ligation.

*How did you arrange to have a tubal ligation performed?*

I thoroughly researched the subject and found Planned Parenthood especially helpful. That surprised me, because I didn't know that they did much else besides dispense pills. The clinic I went to was run by a cooperative of women who knew all the research that has been done on the procedure and could discuss with me all the issues involved.

I am a member of the Kaiser Foundation Health Plan, and all women who want to have a ligation there are required to see a lecture-demonstration film that explains and illustrates the whole procedure. I saw that and then made an appointment to discuss the operation with a doctor. That was also mandatory.

*You were just thirty. Did the doctor try to dissuade you?*

No, he was surprisingly nonjudgmental. I didn't have to convince him of anything; he just wanted to make sure I had thought the matter over. He did say he found my decision surprising. After all his years of practice he could still remember the names of the women my age, unmarried, with no children, who had had a tubal ligation.

*Did the doctor's comments affect your resolve to be sterilized?*

Not at all, but I would have liked to think that what I was doing was slightly more socially sanctioned. I had also been clipping articles from magazines on women who were having tubal ligations. Generally the women interviewed were older than I and already had several kids. I thought, Wow, these people already have kids, and for them it's such a big decision. What am I doing? Still, it didn't make me change my mind.

*Did you have any other concerns?*

My more serious concerns were related to the surgical procedure. They use a general anaesthetic, and there are always risks involved in that. I had also read that there was a slight danger that they might burn your intestines when they cauterize the tubes. That can require extensive surgery. I had confidence in my doctor, however, so I wasn't overly worried.

*How did your friends and colleagues react to your decision to have a tubal ligation?*

Well, I talked it over with almost all the women I knew, and almost everyone was disturbed and tried to talk me out of it. One woman thought I should put it off for at least a few more years, since I might change my mind and it's still safe to have a baby into your thirties. I answered that my decision not to have children was firm and had been made a long time ago. I also told her that I would never have children past thirty because for me that was a cutoff time, not only medically but emotionally.

Another woman asked what would happen if I met a man who really wanted to have children and made that a condition for a relationship. That was the strongest argument I heard. But I answered that if having a kid was a condition for somebody wanting to be with me, that would be blackmail. Our relationship would be doomed from the start.

My young friend from San Diego wrote me a letter just a few days before the operation begging and pleading with me to change my mind. She said that she considered me one of the most positive adults she knew and she couldn't understand why I would take away from myself the option of having children. She thought it was natural to be a mother. That letter disturbed me. I hated to upset her, and I was also afraid that our friendship was threatened. But it didn't make me feel any less committed to my decision.

I was amazed at how misinformed some people were about what I was planning to do. A clerk in my office thought they were going to remove everything, like a hysterectomy.

*How did your male friends respond to your decision?*

Generally their reactions ranged from shock to playfulness. There was a lot of joking around—which is the way some men deal with things that are serious.

*Were you concerned about how your parents would respond to your having the ligation?*

Oh yes, I was concerned about my mother, but there was no indication that she was disturbed by my decision and she never said a word that wasn't supportive. I especially asked her if she would be disappointed not to have a grandchild and she said she would not. Her only misgiving was one I had heard before—that I might later meet a man I liked who wanted children. When I clarified that issue for her, she was supersupportive. That's the way she's been all my life. Whenever I've wanted to do something far-out or mold-breaking, she has said, "If Marty really wants to do it, it will come out all right."

*Did you ever have any fleeting fears that you would regret your decision?*

I felt a few pangs of uncertainty because I realized that the operation would mean the loss of an option for me, and I have always liked to keep my options open. But in discussing it with my friends and thinking it through for myself, I felt confident I could say goodbye to the option of having children.

*Tell us about your experience of the tubal ligation.*

I arrived at the hospital in the morning, put on a gown, had some blood tests and a preoperative shot. I was on a big ward with ten or twelve other women who were having tubal ligations also. The setup at Kaiser in general is very mechanized and regulated, but in this particular section all the nurses and the staff were so friendly, easygoing and personable that I didn't feel at all like in a factory.

The operation itself was painless. The only thing that hurt was the initial shot of Novocaine. They made an incision right under the navel and another one right at the hairline. They light up the area through one incision and look with a laparoscope through another. Then they cauterize the tubes with a tiny instrument—first one side and then the other. I can barely see the scars now.

Right after the operation I felt a little nauseated and dizzy and they gave me an antinausea injection. But there was no other postoperative discomfort. I was in at ten and out by four. I went home, slept straight through the night and felt fine the next day. Really, I could have gone to work the next day—it was that painless and simple.

*How did you feel emotionally after the operation?*

Like a kid in a candy store. I was light, high, liberated, and free of a great big worry. I had no feelings of sadness, regret or doubt. I wanted to tell everyone I met. When I did, however, it was like dropping a small lead bomb into the conversation. People would suddenly get quiet and wouldn't know what to say. I can understand that. What could they say? "Oh, that's nice." Since people found it disturbing, I stopped mentioning it.

*Did the operation have any effect on your relationships with men?*

Soon after I had the operation, I told a man at a party who showed a great deal of interest in me what I had just done. He said, "Oh, wow, that's too bad. I'm looking for a relationship that will lead to marriage and kids. I'm thirty-five and have waited too long as it is. I can't go out with you because I don't want to waste my time on anyone who isn't a potential mate." That took me by surprise, but I thought it was good that he was up front about what he wanted.

More serious was the strange guilt reaction I experienced when I got involved with Rick, the man I am seeing now. The deeper our involvement became, the guiltier I began to feel about my tubal ligation. It seemed to be a betrayal of him and I feared he might resent my potential freedom to be sexually active with other men. I was just as free using other contraceptives, of course, but after the operation, with the threat of pregnancy totally removed, I *felt* freer. I realize now that I was imposing a double standard on our relationship, because Rick had had a vasectomy. I guess I felt that it was okay for a man to be sexually uninhibited, but a woman shouldn't have too much freedom, too much pleasure. Actually, Rick didn't feel resentful at all. He thought that what I had done was mature and responsible. My guilt was totally irrational: Rick and I had simply done the same thing.

*Were there any other times when you had misgivings about the operation?*

Sometimes I think it would be fun to have grandchildren, but if I don't have kids, I obviously can't have grandchildren. But that really doesn't bother me. I can always relate to the children and grandchildren of my friends. I feel a real sense of family with the friends I have made in Berkeley, despite the lack of biological ties. Our relationships are interdependent, not dependent. Those are the kinds of relationships I hope to develop with people throughout my life.

I know some people think you need your own children and grandchildren as a safeguard against loneliness in old age, but I think we have to take care of that ourselves. It's a real copout to expect your kids to do that for you. My sisters and I live two thousand miles away from our parents and are available to them in only a very limited way.

*Many women we've talked to who are confronting the choice for or against motherhood express concern over the negative stereotypes our pronatalist culture confers on childless women. How has your decision affected your self-esteem?*

I know the stereotypes of the childless women: frivolous, irresponsible, promiscuous and immature—all that Protestant-ethic stuff. Sometimes I worry that people might think that of me, but no one has ever said anything like that to me directly.

In my own eyes, my self-esteem has increased. I have never attached status to having children, and I can't stand women whose children become their source of status, little ego extensions of themselves. Whenever that happens, it diminishes their standing for me. Most of my friends, whether or not they have children, are career women whose self-esteem depends more on their work identity than on the traditional female roles.

*Do you ever feel any doubts about your feminine identity?*

I have no trouble with that because I define my femininity according to my sexuality, not according to my reproductive capacity. Since the operation, in fact, I feel much more womanly, more physical than ever before.

*On the more positive side, what do you think is the biggest payoff for you in remaining childless?*

I don't think of it in terms of a payoff. Life without children seems natural to me. Since I've never had a child, *not* having one doesn't suddenly seem like a great big plus.

I think more in terms of the pitfalls I've avoided because I've thought my decision through and acted on it. So many other things I've done in life I've just let happen to me—like getting married. I didn't do that for any sane reason; it was just an impulsive reaction out of loneliness and insecurity.

This time I took control and have a strong, positive feeling about the way my life is going. I cherish my freedom of options and the mobility that I will always have.

*What are your goals for the future?*

Mostly more of the same. But I am looking into other, more creative means of supporting myself so I won't be totally dependent on my forty-hour-a-week state civil service job. I'd like to explore the business world and do a little investing to insure my financial future. I also plan to travel.

Having a deep relationship with a man is important to me. Right now Rick and I have a serious involvement, but nothing permanent will develop for at least a couple of more years. He has two boys, ages fourteen and sixteen, living with him. Their mother left them eight years ago and he's been both their mother and father. Knowing how I feel about children, we realize that it would ruin our relationship if I moved in.

Right now I'm primarily involved with my house, which I bought two and a half years ago. I love working on it, creating my own environment. The house has been a very settling experience for me—in some ways it's my baby. But it's as much responsibility and attachment as I want. Sometimes it even feels like too much for me.

*Do you know many other women who, like yourself, are making the choice not to have children?*

Everybody my age seems to be struggling with the question of whether or not to have children. A few years ago, when we were younger, the subject was easier to discuss. But I've found that once women hit thirty and their time is running out, they don't want to talk about it anymore. The issue becomes too charged. Maybe they really want to have a child but don't have anyone to have a child with, or maybe they're not sure they want to have a child at all.

My hunch is that many of these women probably won't

have a child. They're going to put it off and put it off until it's too late.

*Do you have advice for women who are struggling to make a decision?*

I would advise undecided women to seek out forums on motherhood where they can look at all sides of the issues and let other people's experiences resonate with their own feelings. I joined a group a few years ago and it helped clarify my thinking. The group was comprised of a mixture of women, some who had children and some who hadn't. Our ages ranged from mid-twenties (I was twenty-five and the youngest) to the mid-forties. We met specifically to discuss the issue of having children.

We debated all the pros and cons of having children: Are children a safeguard against loneliness in old age? Do we owe it to ourselves biologically to reproduce? Those who had kids told those who hadn't what it was like. What really surprised me was that some of the women who had children came out and said that they regretted it.

There was one woman in the group, an artist who had a four-month-old baby, who said that she would give anything if she could just send her baby back. She told us that when she turned thirty she panicked and decided that she *had* to have a baby—now or never! So even though her husband wasn't all that enthusiastic, she went ahead and got pregnant. The whole experience of motherhood was wretched for her, starting with her long and terribly painful labor. She felt utterly betrayed by the Lamaze course she had taken, and even went back to her class two months after the baby was born to warn the new women in the class that they couldn't necessarily count on everything turning out great just because they had learned to breathe right. Childbirth hurt like hell! The instructor was furious and asked her to leave. Once she had the baby, she was exhausted all the time and never found a minute for her work, even though her husband helped out a lot. Everything went downhill, including their sex life. The upshot of the whole thing was that she had herself sterilized three months after the first child.

Another woman in the group, Hope, who is now about forty-five, told us that she remembers telling herself over and over again as a child, "I don't like children. I don't ever want to have children of my own." She had a younger sister, whom she barely got along with, and she didn't like to hold babies, and she didn't like to play with dolls. But then, in the fifties, she married a man from the Midwest who wanted six children. Since everyone she knew was getting married and having lots of kids, she just went along with the rest of them and said, "Oh yeah, great! Sure—let's have half a dozen." They stopped at two, but that was bad enough. Being a mother was a miserable experience for her. She dropped out of college when she had her first child at twenty, and had to give up a lot of things she wanted to do. Now she really resents it. Hope is one of my closest friends, so I happen to know that she was a supergood mom. But even though her two kids turned out very well, she feels that for her, becoming a mother was a tragic mistake.

I had never heard women say those kinds of things before. They were giving voice to my own misgivings about children, which I had never been able to articulate before even to myself because I thought they were so bizarre and inappropriate. The group affirmed my feeling that I didn't want children. On the other hand, another woman in the group thought she did want a child, and nothing that was said made her change her mind. All the negative statements made her feel even more affirmed in her choice. About half the group left, still feeling undecided, but at least the issues were clarified for them.

So there's no doubt about it, a group can be a big help. But when it comes down to the real decision, everyone must make up her own mind, figure out what's right for her. If you are struggling with the decision whether or not to have a child, I'd say examine your reasons for wanting a child very, very carefully. Loneliness is a terrible reason. A feeling of inadequacy, not thinking you can do anything else, is a terrible reason. If you can eliminate the reasons that are either socially programmed or simply neurotic, and you are realistic about what the benefits and losses are likely to be, I'd say go ahead. You've made a rational choice, whichever way you choose. But hardly anyone does that. Most women are afraid not to have kids. My God, I won't be an adult, they think, or, My God, I won't be a woman. That simply isn't true. I am an adult. I am a woman. I have chosen not to have children and feel very good about myself and my life. So my advice would be: Really examine your motives for having children and your assumptions about what will happen to you if you don't. I allowed myself to do that, and I don't think I'll ever regret my choice.

# Barbara Cramer

Barbara Cramer, thirty-five, became a nutritional scientist by a circuitous route. She first got a bachelor's degree in psychology and then a master's degree in philosophy, both at a university in her native state, Wisconsin. After three years of part-time teaching while she was working on her doctorate, she decided against a career in academic philosophy and, at age twenty-eight, began to re-evaluate what she wanted to do with her life. By then she had married Harold, a graduate student in structural engineering at the university where Barbara had been teaching.

Barbara describes the early years of her marriage as a time of painful career crisis: "Harold and I would spend hours together as I searched through my head trying to figure out exactly what I wanted to do. I finally decided to start taking courses in anything I thought might be a possible career interest and see what followed from there." Ever since Barbara majored in psychology as an undergraduate she had been fascinated by the relation between diet and mental health. Five years later she earned her doctoral degree in nutritional science.

Soon after Barbara earned her Ph.D., the couple moved to Texas when Harold was offered a job in an engineering firm. Since job opportunities were scarce for Barbara in this section of the country, she was relieved to be offered a postdoctoral fellowship at a new medical center, even though it was situated several hours from where she and her husband lived.

Barbara's delay in finding a career commitment intensified the usual conflicts women experience who contemplate combining children with a career. No matter how much and how well she worked, Barbara always felt under the gun to make up for lost time in her professional life. By the time her new career was getting under way, she was in her mid-thirties and up against the clock. By then both she and her husband realized that they were ambivalent about adding children to their lives.

*When did you first think you might not have children?*

That's hard to say. I think we took for granted that we would have children someday; it was just that we kept pushing the decision further and further back. At some point, about two years ago, it struck me how strange it was that we always assumed we would have children, even though we obviously had serious misgivings about it. For instance, every time we were with friends who had children we would think afterward that we were glad we didn't have kids. Whenever our friends couldn't go somewhere with us because they couldn't find a baby-sitter we were happy not to have that problem. So I finally decided to try out a little mental experiment and turn things upside down. I said to Harold, "Let's change the assumption. Let's assume that we are *not* going to have children and see if countermisgivings come up." None really have.

*Did you and your husband often discuss whether or not to have children?*

We never actually sat down and had a powwow about it, but it was a running theme in our conversation, especially whenever good friends decided they were going to start a family. When we asked ourselves about the reasons for having children we found it interesting that the reasons we came up with had little to do with children themselves. Harold would say he'd love to have another little me around, and I would say I'd love to have another little Harold. Then we would realize that that's not the way it works. It wouldn't be another little me; it wouldn't be another little Harold. It might be a horrible brat who wasn't like either one of us and didn't want to be.

We also considered the idea that children might keep us from being lonely when we were older. If something happened to one of us, the children would still be there to make up for the loss. But somehow, once we began putting ourselves in the frame of mind that we might not have kids, that didn't seem a very important consideration. We both thought having children would be very hard on our marriage. We've gotten pretty settled into a rhythm of life over the past ten years, and having a child would really interfere with that.

*How, specifically, do you expect a child would disrupt your relationship?*

Oh, there'd be the crying, the mess and the million and one things that can happen that you can't control. All kinds of tension would come from the baby, and it would be hard not to direct that tension against each other. Also, Harold and I don't spend that much time together, because both of us are always working. When we take a vacation it's really important for us to go off somewhere by ourselves where we can be totally alone and get reacquainted, so to speak. You can't take vacations like that once you have kids, so just in terms of the logistics, I can imagine having children would tend to separate us from each other.

Then there's the problem of time. As it is, we both lack sufficient time in the day to do what we have to do. With children it would be impossible. My God, I can see us continually haggling over who should do what for the children and when. Harold has always said that if we do have a child, he would share equally in the work, but somehow we both know that isn't true. I would wind up doing most of it and I would resent it.

*Why don't you think your husband would share equally?*

Well, Harold has a much lower threshold for annoyance and a higher threshold for just letting things go than I have. He can walk by wilting plants for three days and not do anything about them, or leave dishes piled up in the sink and not put them in the dishwasher for four days. I'm not like that. For me, certain things take priority. If I see a wilting plant, I can't just pass it by. I have to water it, or repot it, or feed it. In the same way, I can imagine that a child's crying or needing attention would have the same pre-emptive, insistent quality for me, while Harold could just blithely ignore it. He's even acknowledged as much. Since I wouldn't be capable of neglecting a child, I would inevitably end up neglecting my work. I can see myself in terrible conflict all the time.

*Tell us more about the conflict you would anticipate between your work and a child.*

I feel that, given my make-up, I would have to choose between my work and a child. I really doubt that I could manage both. I suppose there are women who function smoothly in their career and have lots of time left over for children and the relationship with their husband. I've always marveled at that when I've seen it, but I'm not that type of person. I'm an absolute fanatic about my work; it absorbs all my energies. When I am really into my research I tend to neglect the house, neglect Harold, neglect everything. I feel guilty when I put my work above Harold's needs, but I know he understands—even if he gets angry. But you can't do that to children. They don't understand and it isn't fair. So I have always feared that something would have to give. My work or my child.

Maybe if I were ten years younger I could say, "Well, I'll cut back for five or six years so I can be with my children when they're young and then get going again on my career. You know, what's five or six years?" But at my age and at this point in my professional life, five or six years seems like a huge chunk of time that I can't afford to throw away. Don't you think that many women in my—our—generation are in the same spot? It seems to me that's why so many of my friends in their thirties are in conflict about having kids.

Back in 1965, when I graduated, it wasn't common for a woman to make a serious career commitment. I remember thinking that my female classmates who were pre-law or pre-med were a different species from me and my friends. We thought of them as some kind of latter-day nuns committing themselves to a life without love. I mean, what would happen if they got into medical school or law school and some man came along and wanted to move to another city? What would they do? I didn't want to be taken off to live in the suburbs, mind you. I intended to do something interesting with my life. But I was keeping all my options open. The idea of making a really strong, solid commitment to a career didn't occur to me until I was much older, and I didn't get my Ph.D. until I was thirty-three. Now with all the competition for jobs and grant money, I feel as if I have to keep running just to stay in place.

*What are your career plans at this point?*

It's very tricky. I've been on a postdoctoral fellowship for several years now and of course that can't go on much longer. I haven't begun to search nationally for a full-time, permanent staff position in a research institute or a hospital because I'm hoping to figure out a way I can stay in this area. See, even if I got a fabulous job offer somewhere else in the country, it would be very hard for me to uproot Harold because he's in a perfect situation here. He's now a full partner in his engineering firm and he works terrifically with everyone there. If it's really impossible for me to find something in this area, we've both decided to look elsewhere, but Harold thinks, and I tend to agree, that I should first try to find government sources to fund my own research proposals. With a research grant I could stay here, do my work and publish some good papers, so that if a permanent job were to open up in the medical center where I am now, I would be right on the spot to get it. If that's going to happen, I really have to hustle, and with that kind of pressure I don't see how I could fit a child into my life.

*Do you ever feel pressure from your parents or in-laws to have children?*

I think my parents knew even before I was married that direct pressure didn't work with me in any realm—whether it was whom I should be dating, whom I should marry, or whether I should get married at all. But once I was married they used to take all sorts of little digs at me, like my mother would ask when she was going to be a grandmother, and she would hint that I wasn't going to be fulfilled in my life unless I had kids. I don't think I felt any of that as pressure because it never occurred to me that a valid reason for having children was to satisfy my parents. In any case, I satisfy them in other ways. Even though they may regret not having grandchildren they're very proud of my being a scientist and different from my cousins who went off and became accountants or secretaries and had a bunch of kids.

Now, Harold is even more extreme than I am in having discounted his family as a source of influence over his life. His parents live in a retirement community in California. They would obviously like to have more grandchildren, but they have three from Harold's sister and they all live nearby in California. With my parents it's worse, since my brother has never even married.

*Do you ever feel pressure to have children from your friends?*

I don't know if you would call it pressure, but one couple we know is constantly rhapsodizing on the glory of having children and saying that we'll never know how wonderful it is unless we have one too. Others say not to have children unless we're sure we want them, but then, how can we be sure? Most of our friends are more reasonable. We also have friends who have admitted to us that although they really love their kids and in many ways they're glad they went ahead and had them, if they had it to do over again, maybe they wouldn't have chosen to. We've seen a number of marriages break up or nearly break up because of conflicts caused by children.

*Did the women's movement and some feminist critiques of motherhood influence your decision not to have children?*

I think an awareness of feminist issues made it possible for me to take my procrastination as a sign that maybe I really didn't want children, and it helped me to come out and say outright that most likely we won't ever have them, but I don't think critiques of motherhood influenced my feelings about motherhood itself. My ambivalence about having children was there before I even heard of the women's movement.

*You haven't spoken about your feelings toward children. Do you like them?*

I'm attracted to infants and I find five- and six-year-olds appealing, but my interest is rather intellectual and I rarely feel a yearning for one of my own. Frankly, I've always just assumed that they would be a lot of trouble. Many of my friends have children and I'm around them a lot, so if I were going to be overcome by some great maternal pull, it would already have happened. Instead I often feel uncomfortable around young children. I never did much baby-sitting as a teen-ager, and if someone hands me a baby, I feel kind of awkward with it. Let me tell you, if there is such a thing as a "maternal instinct," its phenotypic distribution is very broad and I'm out at one extreme.

*Does your husband share your feelings about children?*

No, I think Harold naturally likes children better than I do and relates to them more easily. He's the perfect uncle type, always entertaining our friends' kids and letting them climb all over him. Harold really gets a kick out of children, but only up to a certain point. Then he suddenly turns off: "Okay, that's enough. Back to your mother." I can imagine that Harold would enjoy a child much more than I as long as things were going well, but as I said, his threshold for annoyance is lower than mine.

*Do you ever worry that Harold will later change his mind and want a child?*

I have heard of situations where the husband decides he wants to have a child after his wife can't biologically have one anymore, and in some cases it has led to divorce. But I don't think this would happen to Harold and me. If our marriage broke up for other reasons, I can see him marrying somebody else and deciding that this time he wanted children. But unless something very irrational happens, like some procreative gene in him switching on out of the clear blue sky, I can't see the issue of children ever becoming a source of conflict or dissatisfaction in our marriage. All in all, I'd say we were equally ambivalent.

*Can you trace your ambivalence for children to anything in your own family life?*

Well, my relationship with my younger brother wasn't all that good, and that may have colored my view of what it would be like to have a child of my own. My mother had us four years apart, which was the fashionable separation period between kids in those days. I think that was a disaster. Four-year-olds are just starting to try out their wings and really want to be independent, but all of a sudden there's this helpless creature at home that they're supposed to want to take care of and love and they just don't want to be bothered. At least that's how I felt. I was not terribly interested in my brother when he was an infant and when he became mobile it was worse. He would follow me everywhere and bother me and my friends. He was a great big nuisance and I mostly ignored him. We have only just recently become friends.

*What sort of relationship did you have with your mother?*

That's a more complex issue. It never seemed really problematic. I never *hated* or even disliked my mother. But somehow or other, for whatever reason, I stopped taking her opinion seriously when I was quite young, and by the time I was eighteen or nineteen, I totally stopped consulting her on any of my major decisions in life.

She was very insecure as a mother, and that may have been because of her own childhood. Her mother died when she and her brother were very small, and her father remarried a woman who totally ignored them. When she and her brother were in high school, they left home and took a separate apartment. Her brother went to work, and she stayed home and kept house for him. As she tells it, he was always downgrading her and complaining about her housekeeping and cooking, making her feel totally insecure about herself as a woman and as a functioning, competent human being. Those feelings of insecurity, I imagine, rubbed off in her own marriage. You see, the role of housewife didn't come naturally to her. She didn't enjoy housekeeping and became a good cook only with a great deal of effort. Because she was different, she was constantly being put down by my father's very traditional family.

Deep down I think she hated the role. She was always denigrating the quacking, gossiping housewife types who sat around all day drinking coffee. She saw herself as somehow different, but it took her a long time to assert herself and find something more interesting in the world to do. Finally she decided to try a small business venture, and she began collecting and selling antique cooking utensils and kitchen furniture. She printed up a catalog and went around the country collecting items and selling to restaurants and hotels. It went well for about five years; then the idea sort of fizzled out. But during her heyday she would get subtle and not so subtle messages from my father that he didn't like what she was doing. I think he wanted her to be stuck and dependent without any interests outside him. He was always making comments to his family and friends that my mother spent all her time mulling over her catalog and that he was being neglected. He had to have his dinner at six o'clock sharp and have his house just so, and he resented any change in what she was supposed to do for him.

*In what way does your perception of your mother's life bear on your decision not to have children?*

I think my mother felt very guilty and ambivalent about developing her own interests, becoming a person in her own right, and sometimes, when I get very hung up and in the doldrums about having a successful career, I feel that's a legacy from her. I suffer from the classic female "fear of success," which in my case takes the form of writing blocks. Whenever I have something to write I stall getting started, put off finishing, and generally fret unnecessarily about whatever I'm doing. I sabotage myself. If I could only write more quickly and efficiently without the enormous expenditure of psychic energy it takes me to overcome my resistance, I probably wouldn't see children as such an enormous threat to my career. Maybe I'd think I could have a child and my career, too. As it is, it's a choice between one or the other, and I've chosen my career.

*Is there anything that might make you change your mind?*

Well, if I quickly got settled professionally, so I wasn't in constant anxiety about having a job, I might change my mind. The job would have to be nearby, with hours compatible with having a child, of course. Right now I have to commute two hours each way to the medical center where I work, and I spend the night away from home two or three times a week. Also, if I suddenly and miraculously became so efficient in my work that I could get all my research done and write up reports without so much agony and without its consuming every minute of my time, and if I didn't think I would want to spend all my *extra* time just enjoying life, then I might think I could go ahead and get pregnant.

But let's face it. I don't believe for a minute that those things are going to happen. Sometimes I ask myself, If we inherited lots and lots of money, would I feel differently? I decided, yes, money would help, but *only* if the above conditions were true as well—unless, of course, I had enough money to fund my own research institute. Then at least I would never have to worry about having an interesting job!

*Do you think you will later regret missing any aspect of motherhood?*

That's a hard question. I don't think I'll miss having the experience of pregnancy or even childbirth, but I think there would be some nice things about having a tiny baby, and there are some appealing aspects to my friends' four- and five-year-olds, but if I am ever going to miss not having children, I think it will be when I am older and my friends have children going to college or even later. My parents grew a great deal through me as I got older. I helped push them out of their complacent middle-class stodginess, and it would be nice if we had children to keep us up with the times. We have older friends who immensely enjoy their grown off-springs. On the other hand, Harold and I mostly neglect our parents and don't give them that much comfort and company, and it could be the same if we had children. Also, when you have an active career, you can count on keeping contact with young people through that.

Just as men don't have to physically bear babies to lead fulfilling and worthwhile lives, women don't have to either. When my work is going well, I really love it, and get a true sense of discovery and excitement from what I'm doing. I feel as though I'm looking at things in a way that nobody has before, and making some important discoveries. In my more grandiose moments I feel that my present research may be very significant with valuable clinical applications. Right now one of the things I'm studying is the effect of food additives on the behavior of children. I really believe I could make as great a contribution to the next generation of children through my work as I could if I raised my own and had to give up my career. Anyway, I get a real kick out of my work and I can't believe I would get the same kick out of taking care of a child.

*You're still biologically capable of reproducing. Is the issue of having children still salient in your life?*

I have to laugh at the way I keep pushing the clock back. First it was age twenty-five, then thirty, then thirty-five. Now that

I'm thirty-five I think of forty as the age when I should either decide to do it or forget about it completely. But mostly it's a background issue which becomes salient only from time to time. I mean, I worry periodically that maybe the fact that I'm not having children is a sign that I'm screwed up psychologically and that if I were really well adjusted, I would naturally want them and feel that I could handle children, and handle a career, and handle satisfactory relationships with Harold and friends—everything all at once. It's also possible that if I had a child to take care of and couldn't neglect, maybe I would give up my shilly-shallying about my work and suddenly become incredibly more efficient.

Sometimes I even think, Well, maybe I should have had a child when I was wandering around for a long time in graduate school the first time around. A baby couldn't have made me go any slower than I was already going, and now I would have a nine-year-old, and that would be nice. I think about that idly from time to time, but the truth of the matter is, I didn't feel like having a child when I was in graduate school any more than I do now. So, being realistic, I have to acknowledge that given the way I've been operating for the past ten or twenty years, it wouldn't have been possible for me to have a child. And although I may have regrets later on, there seems to be more wisdom in just letting the clock tick away. Basically, what I've been doing is following my feelings at the moment and in the long run I believe that's the wisest thing to do.

# Rebecca Lowenthal

At age fifty, Rebecca Lowenthal is an administrator in charge of preschool curriculum and director of special programs for the unified school district of a large East Coast city. A leader in preschool education for the past twenty-five years, she is especially known for her innovative efforts to upgrade education for culturally deprived children. Rebecca has been married nearly twenty-five years to Walter, a professional musician. By mutual agreement, the couple has remained childless.

Rebecca was born in Hartford, Connecticut, and raised in a traditional Orthodox Jewish family. The middle child in a family of three children, she has an older sister and a younger brother. Her father, an immigrant from Eastern Europe, ran a scrap-iron and metal business, and her mother took care of the house.

Rebecca was interested in child psychology from an early age and always knew she wanted to be a teacher. When it came time to enter college, however, she veered away from programs in elementary- and secondary-school education, preferring to receive training as a preschool teacher because "the preschool curriculum was much less conventional and more humanistically oriented than the standard school of education course of studies." After graduating from college, Rebecca became head teacher in a small experimental early-education program, and that was the beginning of her long and productive career.

We were interested in interviewing Rebecca for several reasons. At age fifty, she offers a long look back on her choice to be childless, thus offering a perspective which we felt would be particularly interesting to younger women considering the same option. Rebecca's position as an administrator supervising hundreds of women teachers has given her special insight into the dilemmas and choices facing young working women today. Although Rebecca describes herself as a very shy and private person, she told us that she welcomed this opportunity to review her own life choices, and to share her thoughts and experiences with women of this generation who are up against the clock.

*The decision to remain childless is still difficult for most women today. How do you explain making that decision at a time when it was generally considered "unthinkable"?*

In my day it was certainly uncommon for a married woman not to have children. I remember some women I went to school with who became very involved in a professional career and chose that over marriage, but I didn't know any married women who could have had children but chose not to. In that sense I was unique among the women I was raised with. But then, I always had the sense of being a little different from my peers. There was nothing I ever accepted as fiat, including that I needed to have a child to fulfill myself as a woman, that procreation was my responsibility or duty, or even that it was important for my generation to go on. If you are in touch with your own feelings and are also self-confident, and you don't happen to believe in something just because everyone else has accepted it for generations, it's not so hard to be a little different, to find new options for yourself.

*Why didn't you want to have children?*

I didn't want children because I didn't need to have children either to feel complete or to add another dimension to my life. I think many women have children in order to fill their lives, but mine has always felt complete. As an adult I have had three important dimensions in my life: a career that I love, an intimate relationship with my husband, and a satisfying relationship with myself. If I had added a fourth dimension, a child, it would have changed the relationship with my husband, taken away from my career, and left me very, very little time to myself.

I have a strong need to be a separate person and to lead my own life, and I knew that a child would make that impossible. Once you are raising a child, no matter how you delude yourself, your life begins to change and you are no longer really in control of it. This infant, this growing child, is taking you in a direction in which you don't necessarily want to go. I didn't want to walk to the tune of a being who was dependent on me. I have a cat, not a dog. A cat is independent. A dog is dependent. My life is very consistent around the concept of not wanting a dependent relationship that would give me less control over my life.

Another reason I could remain childless was that I had sufficient self-confidence as a woman to make it unnecessary for me to experiment. I don't know if this makes sense to you, but I think for many women having babies is experimenting, a way of seeing themselves reflected in this being they have created. Some people go into a marriage for that reason as well. But again, who I was, was whole for me. I didn't need to reproduce myself. I never needed a child to see myself back.

*What are your feelings about children?*

I like and respect children very much. I love the way a child's mind works; I like to watch children grow and develop— that's the reason I became a teacher. Even as I've gotten older I still enjoy being with children. As an administrator I'm not in regular contact with children anymore, but whenever I visit one of our schools I can sit down on the floor and work with the kids for an hour and a half with the same pleasure I got twenty years ago. I really do find children delightful, but I don't need to have a child of my own to experience the pleasure of children. That's a bonus of being in the teaching profession.

*Can you identify any specific factors in your background that may have played a role in your choice to be childless?*

I think that some part of how I feel about myself as a woman and how I feel about not wanting children must relate to my own childhood. Many people who want children have a good memory of their own childhood, and I cannot say that I did.

In Orthodox Judaism the dominance and superiority of the male are basic to the culture. Women are treated like second-class citizens. The men even sit separately from them in the synagogue. I'm sure my father cared very much for my mother and he was always sweet with her, but there was no question about it—she was mainly a caretaker for the children. In terms of equality, my father had contempt for women.

I was an articulate, argumentative female child, and that attitude was very distressing to my sense of who I was as a person. It made me question the whole basis of the religion, the unreal restrictions that were imposed on our lives. There are stories about the way I resisted going off to synagogue, resisted going to Hebrew school, resisted the whole pattern of Orthodox Jewish life. As a teen-ager I had very strong negative feelings about the way my parents related to each other, and I felt I would never let myself be treated the way my father treated my mother. I left my family as soon as I was graduated from college because their way of life negated everything I wanted to be.

I don't have negative feelings about my mother and father now—I love them very much—and I still feel culturally identified with the Jewish people, but it's not surprising that a person like me, growing up in that kind of family, would be psychologically set against having children. I had no childhood memories I wished to replicate, and of course I didn't want to be remotely like my mother.

*You rejected your mother's life as a model for your own. Did you have any source of support for going against your culture and family background?*

Indeed I did. I had Heidi. There always has to be a model. I've learned that from all my teaching experience. I met "Heidi" when I was only seven years old. I was apparently allowed to walk about the neighborhood by myself a good deal. I used to wander off and make friends with people all the time. One day I wandered into a beautiful wooded area near my home and discovered a cottage. In the cottage lived a lovely woman who wore long dresses and had her hair in a braid wrapped around her head. I had just finished reading the book *Heidi* and that's what I called her, and I called her husband Peter. Actually her name was Irene and she was a highly educated, creative woman who knew all the artists, painters and poets in the city. From about age seven through adolescence I used to visit her every Saturday. It became a kind of ritual. Partly I just wanted to get out of the house on Saturday, but partly I was fascinated by this woman. She had an enormous influence on my life.

Heidi taught in a nursery school and much of my interest in early education comes from her. But even more important, Heidi opened up my mind and helped me discover my potential, who I really was. I was a very bright child, and in a sense, I was being understimulated and undereducated at home. That wasn't anybody's fault. My parents are both very intelligent; they were just culturally displaced themselves. All first-generation kids go through the process of finding new models, and whatever the pulls were from my family life, Heidi's world pulled more strongly. She introduced me to art and to literature, and those are still my enduring interests today. The way I relax is to read. When Walter and I are on vacation in Europe, most of our time is spent in museums discovering and rediscovering the arts. Heidi also instilled in me a wish to do interesting, valuable work. Through her I glimpsed new possibilities for my life as an adult, alternatives to the traditional mother-housewife role I was raised with.

If I had not met Heidi, and if I had remained in Hartford and married within the framework of my family, I very possibly would slowly have faded out as a person. Fortunately, after I left home, I met and married Walter, a man who shares my values and my tastes, and we have moved in the Heidi direction together. Walter is a professional cellist and a very intellectual, sensitive and gifted man.

*How did your husband feel about having children?*

Children was one of the first things we discussed when we were thinking about getting married, and we both agreed we didn't want them. Maybe it was because Walter had been an only child and hadn't been raised with children, or maybe it was because he was an artist. In any case, he really felt he didn't want children, and I don't think it was an accident that we shared that predilection. I chose him and he chose me. We have been married now for twenty-five years, have a deep, close relationship, and we have never regretted our choice.

*Did your parents or peers ever question your decision?*

Peers, no, because we had a tight circle of friends and none of us had children. With our parents it was a different story. Since Walter is an only child, naturally his parents were counting on him to give them grandchildren. And my parents would make comments occasionally. But we rarely saw either side of the family—they were not part of our daily lives—so their desires didn't influence us. Eventually they stopped mentioning the subject.

That's not entirely true because just recently, in March, the subject came up again with my father. My whole family had gathered together to honor my parents on their golden wedding anniversary. My forty-five-year-old brother is a bachelor and will probably never marry and have kids, but my sister married at age twenty and has four children.

My father and I were sitting in the living room together with the whole family gathered around and he said to me, "Rebecca, just look at this wonderful family—the parents, the children, the grandchildren. Aren't you sorry you didn't have any?" Then he said to me quietly, "You can still adopt." I just smiled and said, "No, Father. That was a choice I made.

I wouldn't change that choice." He answered, "But you won't be able to sit here like us, celebrating your golden anniversary with your children." And I said, "No, we won't. We know that, but we have made the right decision for us. We are sure about it." He said, "I wouldn't be so sure."

*Your sister shared the same family background. How do you account for your different life choices?*

We were always very different people. She's a mellower, softer person than I am. From stories about us as children, I gather that I was always stronger, tougher, more critical than she, while she was friendlier, warmer with people, less cerebral than I was. She went to college for two years and then dropped out to help put her husband through rabbinical school. He has since become a Reformed rabbi. There was never any question that children would be a part of their marriage. My sister has been a very good, available mother and she just loved having kids. In fact, she had the fourth child when the others were growing up and leaving because she just didn't want the process to end. All of her kids have turned out well, and she in no way feels diminished by having taken the traditional housewife role. It was obviously the right role for her and she would not have been fulfilled if she hadn't gone in that direction, whereas I would not have been fulfilled if I had.

*Some women wonder if they will feel distressed if they do not have children because they will not have fulfilled something in their "nature." Did you ever have that concern?*

Yes, I've thought about that and I believe it's a very realistic concern to have. I have never mocked that kind of thinking. All things in nature, from every human being to everything that grows, shows the repetition, the reproduction of life. In a very elemental sense, not having children is a violation of nature. But I don't think a woman will necessarily suffer just because she does not do what every other living thing has done—that is, reproduce. We are, after all, human beings, and part of being human is to make choices, to go against the grain, to transcend nature if that is what we choose to do. There is surely enough variability in the human personality, in human nature, to accommodate a wide variety of options.

*Is there anything you think you'll miss by not having children?*

Certainly. I will miss a lot. When my father asked me if I was sorry that I didn't have children, I understood perfectly well what he was getting at. There he was on his golden anniversary, getting all this good feedback from the children he had produced. He liked the adults of his own generation, he liked his children as adults, and he liked his grandchildren. That was an extra something he had gotten out of life, and he wanted to express to me how nice it was for him and that I wouldn't have it. And of course I won't. There won't be that in my life, just as there are other things I won't have because of my choice. But people who choose to be childless know that. They balance out what they will be missing with what they get in return. Whenever you make any choice, there is always something that your choice will deny you.

I think I know what most women are after who want to have children. They want intimacy, sharing, a special closeness with another human being. In a sense we are all after intimacy, and intimacy can happen to us in lots of different ways. But the bond between parent and child is special: they can call upon each other for the rest of their lives in a way that no two unrelated people can. That biological bond is there and it matters. Even the relationship I have with my brother and sister is different from my relationship with my husband. Walter doesn't understand that because he's never had a sibling, but I do. Wherever they are, they can always call on me for help and I would never say no to them—maybe

I would superficially, but never at the gut level. We belong to one another. That belonging to the same family is what you give up if you don't have children, and that's a hard thing for a person to choose to give up. On the other hand, it keeps you quite free because nobody can make that call on you.

*Many women are concerned that without children they will feel lonely when they are older.*

In some ways, it's just the opposite. I think women who do have children are more likely to feel lonely when they are older because when the children grow up and leave home, inevitably there is a big void. Since I've never had children and don't know what it's like to be constantly socialized by another generation, that's not something I will ever miss.

In fact, if I were a little old lady in a rocking chair with a whole bunch of children sitting at my feet—which is the sentimental picture of blissful old age—I think I would be appalled. My image of older men and women is that they don't want a lot of people around them all the time. Perhaps they want someone to talk to and someone to show affection to them, but they really don't want to be with a lot of people.

The only loneliness I can anticipate is if my husband should die and I were left alone. How would I feel about that? That's a different kind of loneliness. When my father sat on the couch and said to me, "You won't have this, Rebecca, when you're old," he wasn't just talking about the pleasure of having a big family gathered around him, he was also implying something else: "When you're old and sick and in a hospital or nursing home, there will be nobody to come to see you." At other times he's said as much to me and he represents the way most people feel. He's talking about the ultimate fear of being alone, which is what dying is, of suddenly not being in control and having nobody there to help you through the process. Then maybe having children would be nice.

The counterargument, of course, is, How do you know your

children will even be there for you? How do you know you're
going to be friends with your children all your life or that they
will be nearby when you are in need? That's something you
can't count on. You don't know what you've modeled for your
children along those lines.

But even more important, I think that the loneliness-in-
old-age issue is a much different and much bigger issue than
the child issue. They are two different kettles of fish and
shouldn't be mixed up with each other. When we reach the
end of life, when we are old and infirm and ill, facing death,
we are all basically alone. That's a rough period for every
human being to have to face—whether or not they have
children.

*Did you ever experience social disapproval because you were
married and childless?*

The first social disapproval I experienced was for not getting
married until I was twenty-six. In my culture, unless you were
married off by your early twenties, people thought there must
be something wrong with you. So that was the beginning of
my experience of feeling different, the consequence of my
being unwilling to do serious things superficially in any way.
Now, of course, since I'm in the field of education, people are
always saying to me, "You must just *love* children. Why on
earth didn't you have any of your own?" Others have come
right out and asked, "Couldn't you have children?" in a tone
of voice that implied: "You *poor* thing, you must not have
been able to have children." I don't know why people feel
they have the right to ask such personal questions, but they
always do, and you just have to learn how to handle it. You
have to disconnect your personal decision from what other
people think. After all, the real decision is inside you, not
outside. Unless you have the inner strength to march to a
different tune, then you do become a neurotic person, very
split in different directions with different pulls.

At the same time, I don't think any woman should underestimate the pull, the very strong pull in two opposite directions, if she really wants to be a mother and have a career too. I was lucky in not having a maternal pull because I would have found it very difficult to be an administrator and a mother. There's no question about that. The number of meetings and conferences I have to attend is phenomenal. I'm at work usually ten hours a day minimum with very little break, and it's not unusual for lunch to be a conference and for meetings to last until midnight. This happens in administration more than in any other kind of job, I think, but anyone who wants to combine motherhood with a career should know that it takes a hell of a lot out of you. I see the strain all the time on my teachers who have babies, especially if they are putting their husbands through school and the family is dependent on their income. They don't have enough money to pay for baby-sitters often enough and they usually have to do all the housework by themselves. The teachers I have seen in those circumstances do get quite disillusioned about what they've taken on for themselves.

As an administrator I have come up with some solutions which have really helped. I believe women who are in a position to do so should help accommodate women who want to have children and also work. But even though I do as much as possible, they still have a rough time of it.

*What administrative remedies have you implemented to help teachers combine their family and professional life?*

First of all, whenever a teacher tells me she is taking off to have a baby, I never ask her when she's coming back; I simply don't believe a woman can make that decision until after her baby is born. She doesn't know what her baby will be like, whether she will need to be with her child or whether she will need to be away from it. Moreover, she doesn't know how long it will take her body to recover after the baby is born.

So I tell them not to make any promises but to wait until after the baby is born, and then decide the best way to structure a schedule.

I feel sorry for women who decide to come back to work six weeks after the baby is born because I think they are rushing the experience too much. One young teacher I remember came back to work five weeks after giving birth, and when I came to her classroom the first day to see how she was doing, she looked totally out of it. Her eyes were glazed and she wasn't feeling very well. I said, "For God's sake, June, go home. Come in and teach your classes in the morning and go right home afterward." She said, "I can't afford to work just four hours," and I said, "Oh yes, you can. Whenever you feel you can't stay the whole time, just let me know so I can account for you." I think one has the right to make decisions like that for other people in the work world. I'm fifty and she's twenty-one. She doesn't know how to rescue herself and solve her problems.

I choose very good teachers for the projects I supervise. They work hard for me and I believe in doing a good deal of bending to accommodate their needs. So if a woman goes through a period of time she wants to work only four hours but is desperate for money, I'll find some way to help her out. In the same way, if a woman wants to nurse her baby twice a day, I will try to accommodate that, too. I recommended to one woman that she arrange to have a baby-sitter close by the school and work it out with her co-worker so that she has time to nurse. As far as I'm concerned, they can even bring their babies to school to nurse, as long as they don't do it in the classroom. I walked in on Carol one day when she was nursing her baby in the classroom and asked her to stop. This is a conservative community and there are strong sexual codes that I felt she was violating; she was stepping on the rights of her students by nursing in the classroom.

Just recently Janet, one of my best teachers, called and asked if we could have a conference about reducing her hours from seven hours a day to four because she was beginning to feel like a visiting parent on weekends. I suggested meeting with the four or five others in the same boat and talking through some of the possibilities for everyone.

We did that. We got together, six of us, and talked. They all brought their babies, which was fun. I felt like a grandmother because I had known some of these women since they were twenty-two, not only as teachers but as growing women, and then as women going through the early stages of marriage. Well, they all came up with different plans, including some that weren't acceptable to me.

Finally we came up with several workable plans, based on how much and when they thought their babies needed them, which would not be at the expense of the kids they were teaching. From what I gathered, most of the women wanted to be home more when their children became mobile and were beginning to talk. That's when they felt they needed the socialization of parents. The solutions we found are working out beautifully.

*It's impressive that you've used your position of power to grant those kinds of options to the teachers who work under you. Are male administrators in your school system also progressive?*

No. In my school system, sexism exists all the way down the line. Most male administrators are sensitive to a woman's needs only if local regulations or the state education code changes require them to be by law. Even then they sometimes try to make things difficult. I was sitting in a meeting last week to discuss the issue of a woman who was asking to renew her maternity leave for a second year because she was pregnant with a second baby. The department wanted to deny her request. I was outraged. One of the men said she'd probably got herself pregnant on purpose. He meant it. He really sees the pregnancy as a manipulative way of getting to take off an extra year. That gives you an idea of what the male administrators in my school system can be like, and the difficulties for women, even in a profession many people assume is sensitive to the conflict between children and career.

*Do you have any advice for women who are trying to make up their minds about having children?*

A woman who is questioning whether or not she wants to have children probably has doubts about other important areas in her life too: the man she has married, whether she is going to stay married, the type of work she does, the way she is planning to live the rest of her life. She needs to sit down and ask herself some important questions: Why do I want a child? What effect will a child have on my life? What effect will a child have on my marriage? In what way will it enhance me? In what way will it deprive me? What will it change for me? Too many women, I'm afraid, end up having babies for sentimental reasons. Unless they go through the physiological process of childbirth, unless they actually live with a child, they fear they may not be fulfilled in life. I personally never believed that. In fact, I thought that having a child would diminish me and make my life less fulfilling, not more so. For some women, having children is gratifying, but I don't think that would be true for everyone.

A woman who doesn't feel strongly that she wants a child, but goes ahead and has one for what I call sentimental reasons, will have a hard time of it. The other woman who will get into trouble is a woman who has children because her husband wants them, or because somebody else wants them. On the other hand, if you really do feel strongly that you want a child, even if part of you doesn't, and you go ahead and have one, more than likely you'll have a good experience with it, as long as you're fairly whole inside. We can always convince ourselves that what we've done is for the best.

*Do you have any reservations about women who are choosing to become single mothers?*

A woman who chooses to have a baby on purpose, without a husband, is someone who is choosing to have another person in her life. Some women choose a man, some women choose another woman, some women choose a baby. The latter choice is going to become more and more popular, I think. Ever since the women's movement, women are less willing to relate to another adult unless they feel certain the relationship will be on equal terms. A woman who is conscious of wanting to be a full, complete person, not dominated by someone else, but who still wants to have an intimate relationship in her life, might naturally feel that the safest way would be to have a baby. The second safest way is with another woman. More and more women seem to feel that the most difficult way to accomplish it would be with a man, given the sexism in this society.

So there are going to be more and more single mothers, and for related reasons, more women will choose to be gay. In the last five years the gay population in my neighborhood has grown tremendously. Many gay couples we know have been together for a long, long time and are very happy in their relationship. We are very close to a lesbian couple who have been together for seven years and are as married as any two people I know. They are both professional women and very gifted in their individual fields. Recently they have chosen to have a baby as part of their life together. The woman who had the baby wanted to have the experience of childbirth, so she had artificial insemination.

I know people who are outraged by that sort of thing— single women having babies, gay women having babies, and so forth. They think it's going to be terrible for the children. I think that's a ridiculous attitude. I feel that any woman who wants a baby strongly and makes a conscious choice to have a child, especially if she is educated and self-aware, will do a better job of raising that child, no matter what her marriage status or sex identity, than the thousands of people who really don't choose to have a child but just mindlessly bring children into the world. There is nothing so bad for children as having parents who have babies just to have them, who have no self-awareness, no skill in rearing them—just an arbitrary, unthinking power of punishment and control. Having worked with hundreds of families in my professional career, I have seen some appalling situations in ordinary, traditional, nuclear families. So whichever way a woman chooses to have a child, as a single mother, as a gay woman, with a man—whatever —the choice itself is the important thing. That's what makes the difference.

*Any final observations about this generation of working women up against the clock?*

One of the things that impresses me about young women today is that they are more firmly, strongly sure of what they want to do, whether they choose to have a child or choose not to. A significant number of women who work with me are not having children, and many of them are not marrying. In almost all cases they live with a man and believe in having an intimate, total relationship, but they are not choosing the third part of that total, they are not choosing to have children. For my generation there was never really a choice. Your generation, women who are now in their thirties, was the first to question parenthood seriously. The coming generation, those women who are still in their twenties, are questioning it in a very different way.

Each generation of women bequeaths something to the next. Perhaps our generation of "supermoms" gave yours something to rebel against. Your generation, by formulating the questions about motherhood and sharing your conflicts and experiences, will help the younger women understand their choices and, I hope, give them wisdom to choose wisely.

Soon it will no longer be an issue of whether or not a woman should or shouldn't have children, but whether or not she wants children, whether or not she thinks she needs children. And women of the coming generation will be able to let the decision go one way or the other without feeling the doubts, the uneasiness, the anxiety so many women in your generation still suffer. They will truly have a choice.

# EXAMINING THE ISSUES

If I never have a child, will I feel incomplete as a woman?

How can I deal with social pressures?

Is motherhood a necessary stage of adult development?

Can I achieve psychological maturity if I am not a parent?

What does it mean if I don't feel a maternal instinct?

Will I regret my decision when I am old?

Women leaning toward the choice of childlessness understandably want to find out how other women came to their decision, and what it has been like for them living with it. Equally important is their need to know what these childless women felt they had gained and lost by their choice. The questions we most frequently heard from the undecided women relate to four main issues: the relation between childbearing and child rearing and the achievement of adult maturity and identity; the existence or nonexistence of a biologically based "maternal instinct"; the ways in which childless women cope with social pressures; and whether or not individuals without children are doomed to loneliness in old age. We now consider what the childless women had to say about these topics.

## MATURITY AND ADULT IDENTITY

Many of the undecided have heard women say that raising children was for them a maturing experience which made them feel more fully adult. "Being a mother has opened me up, deepened me as a human being," Anne Gibson told us. And Ellen Talbot maintained that children "satisfy the mature side of our nature, the part that wants to nourish and love." Women in doubt about whether or not to have children wonder if there are other ways to satisfy this side of their "nature," and to gain maturity besides nurturing their own biological offspring. Some said that their doubts and worries were reinforced by psychological theories which suggest that the experience of parenthood is necessary for the full development of an adult identity. Frequently Erik Erikson's concept of "generativity" came up in our discussions. Erikson, one of the world's leading authorities on child and adult development, postulates that adults who do not develop generativity, which he defines as "the concern in establishing and guiding the next generation," will suffer from a pervasive sense of stagnation. Erikson himself did not say that the only way one could be generative was through having children of one's own, but he has been widely interpreted to mean that. Several women familiar with Erikson's writings formulated their thoughts about adult maturity in his terms. Said one psychiatric social worker: "What keeps me from making a final decision not to remain childless is Erikson's concept of 'generativity.' I believe it is important to share in the development of another human being and to contribute to the next generation. Now, if the only way you can really have these experiences is by raising children of your own—I'm not sure I can give it up."

Martha Ward rejected the idea that by choosing to be childless she was skipping a vital stage in her adult development. She does believe that the willingness to nurture others is an important part of her adult identity; however, she feels that the objects of one's nurturing need not be one's own offspring. Over the years she has developed relationships with her friend's children and is especially close to one of her nieces. When her younger sister came to live with her for a year in Berkeley, she assumed the role of surrogate mother. Also, through her work at a health agency she has contacts with many families, and this gives her a welcome opportunity to relate to children and be a positive influence in their lives.

Though childless, Barbara Cramer feels that she will be able to lead a fulfilling and worthwhile life. She expects to satisfy her need to nurture others by contact with young people through her career. She believes that her contribution to the next generation will be far greater because of her scientific work in the field of nutrition than it would have been if she had focused that energy on one child. Rebecca Lowenthal based her adult identity on three dimensions: a career she loves, an intimate relationship with her husband, and a satisfying relationship with herself. She felt strongly that a child would have diminished her adult identity, not enhanced it. Though she has no biological ties to anyone in the next generation, she certainly guides the many female teachers she supervises, and affects thousands of children through her preschool curriculum planning and her educational innovations.

When we asked a childless radical feminist what she thought about the importance of having a child for one's adult identity, she answered, "If pushed to the wall on that one, I would argue that it is much more difficult for a woman to be an adult if she *does* have a child. Because if you're spending your energies on child care, seventy-five percent— and that's a conservative estimate—of your capacities will never be used. Your diaper-changing skills will greatly improve, but your other talents will probably atrophy."

What the childless women felt about the subject of adult identity can easily be summed up: nurturing other people and having a role in guiding the next generation are important and satisfying aspects of being a mature adult, but you don't have to give up these activities just because you're not a mother.

## THE "MATERNAL INSTINCT"

Some undecided women wanted to know: Is there such a thing as a maternal instinct, and if so, what would it mean if they'd never felt it? Even among the women we interviewed who had children, only one referred to a maternal instinct as the reason why she had a child. "It's like, Why do people climb mountains? Because they are there. Why do women have children? Because they have some instinct in them that says, 'I want to have a child.' " Most of the women —both the childless and those with children—rejected out of hand the notion that there was such a thing as a biologically based maternal instinct. Barbara Cramer spoke wryly on the issue: "If there is such a thing as a 'maternal instinct,' its phenotypic distribution is very broad and I'm out at one extreme." One social scientist, the mother of two, exclaimed, "I never felt such a thing—my breasts want it! My womb is asking for it! If there were such an instinct, a society would not have to have such powerful socializing mechanisms to ensure that girls were going to carry out that role. All women would just want to have children 'naturally.' " There may be no biological instinct, but for many women there is a strong "push from within." Many mothers we interviewed told us they had had a deep desire to have a child, but were unclear themselves as to whether this was rooted in deep psychological needs or instilled in them through sex-role socialization.

None of the three women included in this chapter had experienced a maternal pull, and none of them considered themselves in any way abnormal. However, Rebecca Lowenthal could understand why a woman who did not have such feelings might still be concerned. But she pointed out that women who do not reproduce will not necessarily suffer.

Human beings are distinguished from animals by the capacity *not* to "obey nature," but rather to transcend it.

There was a wide range of sentiment among the childless women we spoke to about giving up the unique "womanly" experiences of pregnancy, childbirth and nursing. Some were relieved that they wouldn't have to go through any of it. "There's nothing about the actual experience of being pregnant that I find attractive or interesting or anything else," a business executive told us. "It would be hard to sleep, hard to get around, and unattractive. And childbirth, I think, would hurt enormously." But other women expressed regret that they would not have these experiences. "My uterus has never been distended with a child. My breasts have never produced milk. I am thirty-six and I have in some ways an immature female body. I don't feel terrible about this, but I do feel I've missed out on something important."

Most of the women who did want the experience of pregnancy or childbirth, or both, settled the matter for themselves by accepting that when you make a choice not to be a mother, you do in fact have to give up some things. A forty-year-old city planner who wished she had experienced childbirth stated the obvious: "I think it would be wonderful to have the experience of giving birth to a child just because I would love to have that use of my body and understand all its possibilities. But I do not have that option. I've noticed that there's a product to childbirth—a baby comes out that you've got to do something with for the rest of your life. When I made the decision not to have a child, I made the decision not to have that experience. And I can live with it."

Most childless women were aware of the stereotypic belief held by some Americans that "nonparenthood" indicates a lack of femininity in women and masculinity in men. Several of the women who had not yet made up their minds about motherhood indicated through their comments and questions a concern that they might come to feel and/or be perceived as less of a woman if they never had a child. But none of the women who had actually made that decision felt that their femininity had in any way been diminished by not having children. On that point there was absolute consensus. For them, femininity was tied to sexuality, not reproduction. And that is why Martha Ward, for example, felt that since she had a tubal ligation, which allowed her to be more sexual, she felt more womanly than ever before.

## SOCIAL PRESSURES

Social pressure to have children takes many forms. Probably the least serious for childless women, though it is nevertheless annoying, comes from strangers or casual acquaintances who make remarks. Many married childless women we spoke to said that they were used to being asked questions that had to do with "Why not?" or "What's wrong?" Women like Rebecca Lowenthal who work in some way with children, in fields such as education or child psychology, seem more likely than the others to be bombarded with such questions. Most of the childless women said they wanted to answer that it was nobody's business, but only a few did that in fact. Most came up with one excuse or another that would get them momentarily off the hook. One woman told us, "When I talked to my parents' friends or people I didn't know very well, I would use the argument about what kind of a world is this to bring children into, and the population explosion, and the environmentalist critique. It's true I'm concerned about those things, but they certainly weren't my real reasons for not having children. It's just that I thought they would be a good justification that other people would accept." And another woman told us that her way of dealing with people was to imply that there was an infertility problem. Precisely what was said didn't seem to matter. What was most important was how the women felt. Rebecca Lowenthal's comment and advice on the issue are relevant here: "I don't know why people feel that they have the right to ask such personal questions, but they always do, and you just have to learn to handle it. You have to disconnect your personal decision from what other people think. After all, the real decision is inside you, not outside."

We did not encounter any undecided women who felt they were being pressured into childbearing by their husbands. Like most of the childless women we interviewed, their mates either felt the same way about children as they did, or else were willing to go along with whatever their wives decided to do. Still, a lot of women who had not yet made up their minds worried that if they did not have a child, they might later on feel that they had denied their men something which they had really wanted and to which they had a right. To many married women, motherhood felt like a mandate; to refuse to carry it out engendered guilt.

We found in our interviews that the women who had children for that reason later regretted their choice. Marlene Heldmann had never been interested in having children and was not attracted to them emotionally or intellectually. Yet she went ahead and had one, partly in response to the desire of her husband. Martha Ward told the story of an older woman in her "motherhood group" who had felt very strongly, even as a child, that she never wanted children of her own. But when she married a man who wanted six, she dropped out of college to become a mother. Even though, according to Ward, this woman was a "supermother" and her son and daughter turned out just fine, the woman herself considered motherhood a miserable experience and a "tragic mistake." These two examples prove Rebecca Lowenthal right: "A woman who has a child because her husband or anybody else wants it will probably get into trouble."

Pressure from parents and in-laws was a great concern of many undecided women. They worried that if they didn't do what was expected of them as daughters, they would end up feeling selfish. One television producer gave "a sense of family obligation" as the main reason she had not made a final decision to remain childless, although she was certain that is what she wanted to do. "I don't feel what you'd exactly call 'pressure.' I'm in conflict because I feel a sense of family obligation. I'm very close to my family and I'm the only daughter, and the only married child. My father has a severe heart condition, and he just turned seventy-two. He teases me a lot about having children and I know he and my mom would love it if I did. I'll probably end up *not* having any, but I'm going to feel that I've been selfish, I'm sure."

Even when parents no longer mentioned their wish to have grandchildren, many women felt a lingering guilt about depriving their parents of what could be perhaps the most important source of satisfaction and pleasure in their old age. In some cases, the main conflict for their parents was not their lack of grandchildren, but rather how they would explain things to their friends. According to one woman, "The biggest problem for my mother was how she could tell other people. It wasn't so much that she or my father questioned me as that they were always being questioned. And they felt that my not wanting to have children reflected badly on them. They worried that their friends would think to themselves that if I had had a happy childhood, I would certainly want to have a child of my own. I remember when I was about twenty-five and had been married for about three years, I attended a party my mother gave for some of her friends. One woman whom I'd known for many, many years came over and asked me when we were going to have children. I told her that we probably never would. And she said, 'If I didn't know you better, Mary, I would think that you had had an unhappy childhood.' Later I overheard my mother taking this woman aside and saying, 'Well, you see, it's like this: Dr. Todd, our family doctor, told me recently that Mary can't get pregnant.' I was livid when I heard that, as it wasn't true, but then I realized in a flash that my choice to be childless had a lot of consequences for her."

Did the childless women whose accounts are in this chapter have such problems, and if so, how did they manage them? Before she had her tubal ligation, Martha Ward worried about denying her mother a grandchild, but she didn't have to suffer guilt because her mother was very supportive of her decision, and if she had any regret about grandchildren, she didn't let her daughter know it. But Martha recognized that many people would find one of her most important reasons for not having children—that they would shut off too many options in her life—as selfish, and she even applied that term to herself. This did not disturb her, however, because she firmly believed that she had a right to be selfish about what she did with her life. Barbara Cramer got pressure in the form of little digs from her parents to produce grandchildren. But these, she said, were easily discounted because neither she nor her husband allowed their families to be a source of influence over their lives, and neither believed that a valid reason to have children was to satisfy their parents. In any case, Barbara feels that she is satisfying her parents in another way. There's a trade-off, she thinks. They may regret not having grandchildren, but they take a lot of pride in having their daughter be a scientist. Rebecca Lowenthal also discounted the pressure from her family, although she did not lightly dismiss what her father had to say. The lesson from her interview would seem to be: You've got to take responsibility for the consequences of your choice, but when it comes to motherhood, you certainly have the right to make any choice you wish.

## LONELINESS IN OLD AGE

For a number of undecided women, the fear of loneliness in old age was the deepest source of their ambivalence about not having children. Confident that they would benefit from being childless when they were young, they worried about the warning they had heard so often: "If you don't have children now, you're going to regret it when you're old."

Barbara Cramer is not sure that later in life she will *not* miss children. But she knows that if she had children, there would be no guarantee of contact, since she and her husband neglect their parents. Martha Ward has some regret that she will not have grandchildren, but that isn't of great concern. She intends to develop lasting non-kin networks of friends as a safeguard against loneliness in old age. In Berkeley she has been able to gain a sense of family despite the lack of biological ties, and she can see no reason why the same won't hold true throughout her life.

Rebecca Lowenthal gave thoughtful and complex answers to our questions regarding childlessness in old age. Her father had let her know how much his children and grandchildren mean to him now that he is old, and how much he thinks his daughter will regret not having the same. Rebecca agrees that she will lose something important by not having the special bond that exists between a parent and a child, but she points out that the special bond that comes from the biological tie is not necessarily a protection against loneliness in old age. She speculates that, contrary to what most people think, women who *do* have children might be more lonely when they're older because of the void left when the children grow up and leave home. Besides, there's no guarantee that one's child will be nearby when one is most in need.

The few studies that exist on childlessness and well-being in old age do not support the assumption that older people with children are always better off. Christine Bachrach, a researcher at the Kennedy Institute's Center for Population Research, examined data from the 1974 Harris Organization survey "The Myth and Reality of Aging in America" to compare the risk of social isolation between childless men and women over sixty-five with men and women of the same age who were also parents. She found that in the middle class, those who lived alone (and the childless were more likely to do so) had similar levels of social contact regardless of whether or not they had children, as long as they remained in good health. They compensated in their social life for not having children by having more contact with friends and relatives. Children made an important difference in their risk of social isolation, however, when their health was poor. In the sample Bachrach studied, the childless who reported serious health problems were three times as likely to be isolated than those with one or more children.

Less social contact does not necessarily mean that older people will have greater feelings of loneliness. This was demonstrated by J. Tunstall in his 1966 study of loneliness among the elderly in England. He found that although those who were childless were more likely to live alone and be socially isolated, they were no more likely to *feel* lonely than were those individuals who had children. In fact, the childless were less likely to feel lonely than were those who had not recently seen their children.

In our interviews with childless women we focused on the issues which most preoccupy women who are faced with the decision of motherhood. In addition, however, we were interested in learning from the childless women which reasons they believed had been the most important in their decision. In answering this question, they raised an additional set of issues: their experiences of childhood, particularly the relationship toward their mother; their feelings and attitudes toward children; the quality of the relationship they wanted with a man; and the constraints imposed on their lives by their work and the degree of their commitment to it.

## CHILDHOOD EXPERIENCES

One theme which ran consistently through our interviews with the women who had children as well as those who did not was the importance of one's childhood experience for the motherhood choice. Ellen Talbot, whom we interviewed for the "Children and Career" chapter, emphasized that she had had a happy childhood and came from a close, loving family and wanted to replicate it. For women who choose to be childless, we found the opposite was also frequently true. An unhappy childhood and unhappy family led some women in our sample to avoid having a family of their own. In fact, in our interviews with childless women we heard Rebecca Lowenthal's comment "I had no childhood memories I wished to replicate" repeated often. For these women the most decisive aspect of childhood which related to their later choice was their perception of and relationship with their own mothers.

A large number of childless women experienced a troubled relationship with their own mothers. They saw their mothers as having been victimized by others, sometimes including themselves, and in turn some felt they had been their mothers' victims. Choosing to be childless for them was a way of defending against a too close identification. It established, once and for all, that they would not become like their own mothers. Their strong desire to dis-identify did not necessarily mean there was hostility or lack of love between them. What Margaret Donahue believed about lesbians who did not want children was true for many other women as well. They had seen their mothers suffer from the responsibility of bringing up children, and they hoped that by not having any of their own, they would avoid that oppression in their lives.

Martha Ward, for example, loved her mother very much, and both she and her sister felt loved in turn. But their perception of their mother as "so bogged down with her kids that she had no life for herself" was an important factor in their decision to remain childless. Both stated they did not want to replicate their mother's life. Barbara Cramer saw her mother as an insecure woman thwarted by her husband in her attempts to assert herself and do something interesting in her life. Deep down she thinks her mother hated the housewife role. Rebecca Lowenthal related her wish to remain childless to her perception of her mother as someone oppressed by the

Orthodox Jewish culture, in which women were treated as second-class citizens.

A feminist therapist we spoke with, who had a tubal ligation at age thirty-four, felt she received the brunt of her mother's frustration at being caught in the maternal role. "She was the mother of two little girls, and she was terrible in that role. She hated it. This was a woman who had tremendous creative energy and nowhere for it to go. Like so many women who have no other access to power, she took out her rage and frustrations on her children." Women who felt they had been their mothers' victims often expressed a great deal of hostility toward them. For some of these women, the decision not to have children consciously represented to them an act of rebellion and retaliation. One social worker expressed a sentiment we heard from a number of other women: "Part of me wants to wait until my mother dies, and then I'll have kids. That way I won't have to give her the satisfaction of having grandchildren."

Women who felt they got inadequate mothering often worried that they might be unable to mother well themselves. For one woman, a professional chef, the most important reason she did not become a mother was that her own had been so unnurturing. "She did nothing for us. She was just not there as a mother. Deep down I fear that I might be the same way, that I wouldn't be capable of releasing the love that I might have for my child." Another woman, whose mother was psychotic, feared that if she became a mother, she might inflict on her own child the same damage she had experienced herself. The belief that mothering would be difficult brought these two women additional fears: first, that they would tend to overcompensate for their inadequacy by doing everything for their child; and second, because of all the energy and effort they would have to put into being a good mother, they would become overwhelmed. As the chef explained: "I would have to give up so much if I became a mother. I know I would overcompensate for the feeling that I was inadequate by trying to become a 'supermom,' and probably I would put a whole lot of energy into some sort of therapy so I could learn to be adequate with my child. If I did all that, how would I have time for the other things that mean so much to me?"

## FEELINGS AND ATTITUDES TOWARD CHILDREN

The childless women we interviewed were quite articulate when it came to the subject of their childhood, and we found surprising consensus: their negative experiences at home had disposed them toward not wanting to become mothers. Their feelings and attitudes about children, however, were in far less accord, and the relationship of these sentiments to their later choice was less clear.

In our mothers' generation, a married woman was much less likely to acknowledge, and certainly to express, a dislike or lack of interest in children. In any case, because of social pressures and unreliable birth control, such feelings about motherhood would probably not have affected the outcome, i.e., whether she had children or not. But now the taboo against expressions of negative feelings about children is weakening. Women are now asking themselves such questions as "Do I really like kids at all?" If so, "Would I actually enjoy them all the way from babyhood to adolescence?" "Am I willing to spend my time on the kinds of activities that being a mother entails?" We came across a number of women who had decided to remain childfree because of their negative answers to one or more of the above questions.

There were some women, like the magazine editor quoted here, who disliked babies and children intensely and wanted to have nothing to do with them: "I don't like children and I especially don't like babies. I don't coo over them. I don't play with them. Last week my husband and I went to see his cousin, who had just had a new baby. She came running up to me and thrust this infant in my arms, and I thought, What the hell is she doing assuming that I would want to hold her baby! So I just said "No thanks" and handed it over to my husband so that he would experience what it was like to be a woman and have everyone assume that you love little babies."

More frequently, women who said they had chosen not to have children because they were not very attracted to them qualified their negative feelings. Like Martha Ward, they found short periods with children quite rewarding. But after a while they got bored and impatient with them and turned off. Other women, though they did have a good deal of affection for children, decided against motherhood because they did not want to involve themselves in the world of a child or the routines of child care. A thirty-two-year-old filmmaker commented: "I like children very much. But I didn't think I could stand being a mother. I just don't want to have to tend to the quite legitimate needs a child would have, like being involved with their school, chauffeuring them around to their activities, having their friends over at the house, or thinking up how to keep them entertained."

Once women begin to scrutinize their feelings toward children, more and more subtle distinctions emerge. Few childless women described their feelings toward children as either-/or. Their attitudes depended on the specific ages and stages of the child, and they were attracted to them in different ways. Barbara Cramer said she was drawn to infants, and found five- and six-year-olds appealing, but her interest in them was "rather intellectual," and she rarely felt a yearning for one of her own.

Some women liked the toddler stage but couldn't stand adolescence. Others expressed just the opposite reaction. The two women quoted below anticipated that they would enjoy children who were in a particular stage of development. However, they had chosen to remain childless because they didn't think that the rewards they would get from their children during these limited periods of time would compensate for what they would have to put up with for the rest of their lives.

One woman said she could not tolerate small children but "they do get better when they're older. During the stage of latency, kids are more interesting and then, of course, they become adolescents. That's when almost everyone else hates them, and that's when I like them the best. But frankly, I can't see having a child and having to wait about fifteen years until I would enjoy it." Another woman had just the opposite attraction to children: "I love cuddling and playing with toddlers. I really enjoy it enormously. But that kind of mothering doesn't last very long—it changes as the kids grow up. By the time they are teen-agers, the pleasure is completely over."

Part of the feminine mystique that dominated American culture for so long was that all women "naturally" love children. As we have seen, this is decidedly not true. An equally interesting discovery in our interviews was that for many women, loving and enjoying children was no longer sufficient reason to have one of their own.

## THE QUALITY OF THE RELATIONSHIP WITH A MAN

A major reason many women gave for not adding children to their lives was the wish to preserve the quality of the relationship with their husband or lover. They said they valued too greatly the intellectual and emotional closeness they had found with their mate to take a major risk.

The traditional view of the family holds that children make marriage worthwhile, and without them the unit is incomplete. The views of these women challenge the assumption that there is an advantage to the package deal. Indeed, most of them strongly believed that children would interfere with their relationship and change them for the worse. They knew from their friends, even those who thought their children a blessing, that kids are likely to bring stress and strain. Even when the childless women did not expect the effects to be drastic, they feared that what Marlene Heldmann had experienced—the child driving a wedge between them—might happen to them. Barbara Cramer believed that children would distance or separate her from her husband, and that the tensions generated when one combines a child with two careers would inevitably become directed toward each other. Rebecca Lowenthal was certain that a child would have taken away a great deal not only from the intimacy she had with her husband but also from her work, and from the relationship she has with herself.

When both partners in a relationship have demanding careers, it is often difficult for them to find enough time to spend together. Barbara Cramer's comment that she and her husband don't see a lot of each other because they are always working was frequently repeated by other women. With lives so dominated by work, vacations are often seen as essential to rejuvenating and preserving the relationship. Some women felt they would have to relinquish this special opportunity to be alone with their mate if they had a child, and they concluded that this sacrifice wouldn't be worth it. As one of them put it, "Our marriage totally depends on our long summer vacations because we're so busy with work that we live almost like roommates the rest of the year. Vacations are our 'refalling-in-love period.' I don't want to give them up for a child."

These career women had generally invested a great deal of time and energy into working out nontraditional domestic roles with their mate. For a number of them, it had been a struggle over a long period of time to get things to the point where their lives ran smoothly. Children, they knew, would upset this routine, and that meant that the process of negotiation and accommodation would have to begin all over again. One physician discussed this point at length. It had taken some time for her and her husband to learn to cooperate fully in areas like housework, planning trips and planning how they were going to spend their time together. If they had children, they would want to divide the tasks of child care evenly, and they believed this would be very difficult. "Both of us would have to make a lot of changes and accommodations. It would challenge our relationship in ways that could be positive but might also be negative. I don't want to take the risk."

There were women who articulated more specifically the risks they felt they would be taking. A common theme: "I'm afraid that if we had children, we would revert to the traditional sex roles and the traditional division of household labor." No woman we interviewed who wanted a child very much decided not to have one because of her mate's unwillingness to share equally in child care. But for many women who had been ambivalent about motherhood, this factor had tipped the balance of their choice. For example, Barbara Cramer pointed out that even though her husband said that if they had a child he would share equally in its care, they both knew it wasn't true. Since he has a higher threshold for just letting things go, she felt that she would wind up doing most of the child care, neglecting her work and being in a constant state of conflict. Another woman, who was being pressured by her husband to have a child, said that if he would rearrange his work life so that he could share child care equally, she would go along with his desire. As he made no attempt to change his ways, she drew the line and said, "No children— if it's not going to be a fifty-fifty proposition, I'm not going along with it."

To sum up the thinking of these particular childless women: Why risk a known good thing—the present happy and satisfying relationship—for the unpredictable rewards and the predictable stress of a child?

## ATTITUDE AND INVOLVEMENT IN ONE'S WORK

The effect of one's career on the choice of motherhood is one of the themes which runs throughout this book. Some of the childless women in our sample, like Martha Ward, said that career was of no importance in their decision not to become a mother. For others it was a major consideration, and for some it was the most important factor of all. We met women who had always intended to pursue demanding careers and had never seriously considered having children for that reason. Their commitment to work was so intense and sustained that even in a previous era when there were fewer career options available to women, they probably would have been the exceptions.

The other childless women who gave work as a primary reason for the choice can be divided into three groups. First were those who had previously assumed that one day they would have children, but who wanted first to establish themselves in a career. As time went on, it became clear to them that they would not achieve that goal until past the point they considered advisable for them to have a child. Barbara Cramer is an example. Her decision was clearly related to many things, such as her attitudes toward children and her relationship with her mother. But she feels that if she had managed to become established in her work and secure in a job she would, despite her doubts and ambivalence, have had children by now.

A second group of women who gave work as the primary reason they did not choose to have a child explained that they had become so caught up in the demands of a high-pressure career that they did not see how they could manage both. The interviews in Chapter 2 present some of the potential difficulties women may have in combining children and career, and it is understandable why some women might decide not to do so. Gail Gordon had been certain until a few years ago that she would have children and also a profession. But the higher she climbed on the professional ladder as a corporate lawyer, the less likely it appeared that she could have both. The rigid rules of her work place, a career structure that does not allow its practitioners to move easily "in and out," and what she considers to be the intrinsic demands of the work made her doubt that it would be possible for her to be both a good lawyer and a good mother.

We interviewed one woman who was the vice president of production at a major Hollywood studio. Even though she had always assumed that one day she would have children, she was letting her time on the clock tick away without apparent anguish. She couldn't even imagine how a child could fit into her schedule. "The name of the game at this studio is 'being here.' People around here jockey around to see who can get here first in the morning and leave here last at night. If you want to advance in this business, you'd better be here at seven eating breakfast and reading the 'trades.' Whenever I leave this place before six or seven in the evening for some other commitment, everyone is shocked. Imagine what it would be like if I always had to get home to my child."

A third group of successful career women who had been interested in becoming mothers when they themselves were younger and had not yet progressed in their career lost their interest in having a child somewhere along the way. The more ego gratification and identity they gained from their work, the more their career-and-work role competed with the potential role of mother. Though they had gained flexibility in their job, and high enough pay to comfortably combine children and career, they still chose not to. One novelist who published a book which was widely acclaimed just at the time that she was trying to make up her mind whether or not to have a child spoke of how success in her work had resolved her motherhood dilemma: "I thought to myself, 'Well, it looks like I'm really very good at this. I should devote all my energies to writing and not have a child.'"

Given that we are writing on the choice to have children in 1978, we are interested in assessing how the feminist ideas about motherhood had influenced the women who had chosen to be childless. No one said that her negative or ambivalent attitudes toward domesticity and the maternal role were created by what they had read or heard. Rather, the women's movement had given them the additional needed support to acknowledge and express their feelings, and validated their right to make a choice.

Barbara Cramer stated that her ambivalence about children was there long before she had heard of the women's movement. However, her awareness of the issues raised by some feminists made it possible for her to take her procrastination as a sign that maybe she didn't really want children, and it helped her to come out and say that she most likely never would. In the tolerant milieu of Berkeley and in a network of feminist friends, Martha Ward, who did not like children and never wanted her own, felt supported in her decision at age thirty to be sterilized. Similarly, one active feminist who chose not to have children for "very personal and psychological reasons" attributes her ability to *stand* by her decision, despite the contrary wishes of her husband, to the women's movement: "It supported me in who I am as a person and made me feel that I do not have to define myself by the roles society hands me—wife and mother."

# Making Up
# Our Minds

Women contemplating motherhood are sometimes unaware that their state of indecision takes its toll. When all options are left open, there is likely to be considerable anxiety. And in addition, it may be difficult to make important decisions in other areas of life before resolving the motherhood dilemma. In the course of our research we often heard comments similar to this: "As long as I'm struggling with the motherhood dilemma, I feel stalled in my career. I can't take on any long-term projects because I just don't know if there is going to be a child in my life in the next year or two." A number of women told us that they only realized how much of a drain their indecision had been after they made up their minds, and experienced a mobilization of their energies and a sense of creative release.

Individuals and couples often deal with their indecision about parenthood by ignoring the subject. We were surprised to discover how many women and men who say they are very concerned about whether or not to have children did not discuss the pros and cons of either choice with their mate, their friends, or anyone else. A Los Angeles artist told us that even though the issue is of great importance to her, she and the man with whom she has been living for six years have never discussed it. Even when she got pregnant and after she had had an abortion, they never directly confronted the question of when, if ever, they were going to have a child because the subject "was just too hot to handle." Another woman commented that most of her close friends feel the same as she and her husband, but whenever they try to bring up the subject of children in hopes of a serious discussion, her friends either "clam up or make jokes about it." Martha Ward pointed out that everyone her age seems to be struggling with the motherhood dilemma. A few years ago, when they were all younger, the subject was easier to discuss. "Once women hit thirty and their time is running out, they don't want to talk about it anymore. The issue becomes too charged. Maybe they really want to have a child, but don't have anyone to have a child with. Or maybe they're not sure they want to have a child at all. My hunch is that many of these women probably won't have a child. They're going to put it off and put it off until it's too late."

If Martha Ward had told her hunch to Charles F. Westoff, director of Princeton University's Office of Population Research, he would have agreed. Westoff recently predicted that if current demographic trends in this country continue, 20 to 25 percent of women now in their twenties will remain childless for the rest of their lives. Unexpected fertility problems, discovered when it is too late to do anything about them, will no doubt be the source for part of this childlessness. But equally important may be the simple fact of "drift." Sociologists Ronald Rindfuss and Larry Bumpass have pointed out that older couples are likely to remain childless because of social as well as physiological factors. The older the woman is, the more likely she is to be immersed in other ego-involving activities that consume a great amount of time and energy and seriously compete with her interest in the maternal role. Also, pronatal pressures from family and friends diminish as the couples grow older and are no longer as subject to the social forces influencing many younger couples to have children.

Some women who have been postponing making a decision are jolted into action when they approach their biological deadline. When the jolt prompts reflection and careful assessment of how much they want to be a mother and how a child would fit into their lives, that's all to the good. However, when the ticking of the clock leads to panic, that is not conducive to making a wise choice and the outcome is often negative.

According to a clinical psychologist we consulted, a woman up against the clock may be vulnerable to making a precipitous marriage and having what she describes as a "symbolic child": "There are some women who at thirty-five rush into marriage with anyone who has the qualification that he can father a child, because they're terrified of missing out on an important experience of life—childbearing. Often they are women who hadn't married before because no man had been good enough to please them—one wasn't tall enough, one wasn't smart enough, the other wasn't rich enough and another one was from the wrong social set. Then, when they've just enough time to slip under the wire they marry the first Joe Shmoe they can get. They are pregnant within the first year with what is usually their one and only 'symbolic child.' The child is symbolic because the real purpose for which it was brought into the world was to attest to the fact that its mother had a womb. It's not surprising that these marriages often don't last very long. And neither does their interest in their child."

Difficult as the choice of motherhood may be, it should be confronted head-on. Clearly, it is better to reach an enlightened decision by grappling with the complex problems involved than to risk finding oneself childless by "default" or in a "panic pregnancy." Voices of Experience can be very helpful to undecided women by bringing key issues into sharper focus, and by offering insights into the consequences of living with each choice. But they cannot answer the most important question a woman must ask herself before she makes her choice: *How much do I really want to have a child?* In this final chapter we suggest some tools and techniques that may help a woman assess her needs, wishes and desires about parenthood and examine her motives for wanting or not wanting to become a mother. We also suggest some practical matters which should be considered before a woman comes to a final decision.

## PSYCHOTHERAPY

Some women who feel the desire to become a mother are confused about the source of their feelings. Do they arise from a strong feeling from within or are their feelings of "want" really feelings of "should" imposed upon them by culture through sex-role socialization? Two women, Beth Hall and Mary Paley, discovered through psychotherapy that the feeling they had interpreted as an intense desire to bear and care for children was masking a deeper need to nurture themselves. When they gained this insight, their "maternal desire" dissipated. Beth Hall reached a decision to always remain childless; Mary Paley plans to have a child but will wait another few years. Hall explained how therapy worked for her:

"Whenever I used to hold a tiny baby, I would burst out crying. I felt so much love for this little thing, and I assumed that meant that I desperately wanted to be a mother. I went into therapy for other reasons, but eventually this topic came up. Over time I explored those emotions rather fully, and I came to recognize that holding that baby was symbolically really holding me, taking care of me, accepting me. I got very little nurturing when I was a child. So holding a baby was all of those things—being my mother, accepting the love from my mother, being able to give it to myself, and being able to give it to my mother. When I disconnected the feeling of loving to hold the baby from the social meaning I had attached to it—reading this feeling as evidence that I wanted to become a mother—I realized that nurturing a baby was a very indirect and not very effective way of doing what I really needed to do, nurture myself. I decided to take care of myself directly, and I'm sure that's a better choice for me and for the child that would have been."

Mary Paley's wish for a child became greater and greater as the pressure in her work increased. She entered therapy to analyze the source and nature of this desire. One day her therapist asked her to visualize herself as a little girl and imagine how she was treated, who was taking care of her, and what they were doing. Exploring her fantasies, she realized that she wanted a child primarily as an excuse to take time off from her work and have fun. She, like Beth Hall, really wanted and needed to take care of herself, but she was unable to give herself permission to do it: "With that insight, the intensity of my wish for a child diminished, and the issue was put in its proper place. I do want to have a child one day, but now is not the right time for many reasons. In the immediate future I plan to take more time off from work and take better care of myself, and I know I don't have to have a child as an excuse to do that."

Therapy can also be useful to a woman whose troubled past or present relationship with her mother interferes with her ability to make her own decision about having children. One woman was worried that the "bad mothering" she got as a child destined her to be an inadequate mother herself. She found out in therapy that the issue of whether or not she *could* be a good mother was preventing her from grappling with the question of whether she *wanted* to be a mother at all: "Only after I dealt with the issue of adequacy could I begin to directly confront the issue of choice."

One female New York analyst who had a special interest in the subject of motherhood told us that she thought therapy could be very useful to a woman who did not have a positive identification with her mother: "I think that many women have a secret fear that having a child will mean fusion or merger with the mother. And this fear hinders them from even considering what it would be like if they had a child. In therapy they can confront that issue, and try to work out their inhibitions and gain confidence that they can be a mother and a separate person at the same time." However, a San Francisco psychologist points out the goal of therapy for women considering motherhood is certainly not always to help them resolve all the issues so they can have children: "When the need for disidentification with the mother is tremendous, sometimes it's just as well left alone. The struggle isn't worth it. Why should these women make themselves miserable just because most women have children?"

## COUPLE THERAPY

There are many good reasons why women who think therapy will help them might consider counseling together with their mate. The most obvious reason is that having a child has enormous impact on the lives of both parents and on their relationship. Before making this decision, couples should explore their feelings, needs and desires. Often when a couple is undecided, it's because neither partner knows what he or she wants. Many couples are locked into a seesaw of ambivalence with their mate. Each ambivalent partner adopts a firm position on the question: militant yes and militant no. From time to time one person bends and begins to see things from the perspective of the other. But when that happens, the partner suddenly and emphatically switches sides. Therapy can help some couples get off the seesaw by giving both people the opportunity to explore fully their feelings on both sides of the question. As long as they maintain a hard-line position, it is unlikely that either will really find out the full range of their feelings about parenthood.

Often a couple's indecision masks a lot of their other problems. One psychiatric social worker who counsels couples considering parenthood spoke about her first session with a couple whom she considered typical of many others: "The first five minutes was about 'we can't decide whether or not to have a baby.' The next fifty-five minutes was about—there are a lot of things I do not like about this person, but in our relationship we're not allowed to talk about them. Once they felt they were in a 'safe' situation, they allowed their resentments to come out. As is the case with many couples, their indecision about a child was related only secondarily to the other problems they were struggling with in their relationship. There were issues of control—I love the power of making this guy who always takes power over me wait until I'm good and ready to make up my mind.' And there were fears: 'If we have a child, he'll turn into a male chauvinist pig; if we have a child, she'll become a freeloader.' In my experience, once couples work through the problems between them they find that the decision about a child is not so hard to make."

Another reason why parenthood counseling for couples might be useful is what Los Angeles writer Patricia E. Raley calls the "dynastic imperative." According to Raley, "There are men who never wanted children when they were younger who begin to question their previous decision once they get into their late forties and early fifties. They begin to think about who is going to carry on their name and wonder if they shouldn't have established a 'dynasty' when they were younger so that there would be children to care for them in old age and give them a sense of immortality. Some of them decide that it still isn't too late. If the Dynastic Imperative asserts itself after the wife has passed childbearing age, the consequences can be tragic." A man who feels he participates in the decision rather than just "go along" with the wishes of his wife may be less likely to act out on this impulse, should it ever arise.

Groups for couples considering parenthood led by a trained therapist is another new option available in a number of cities. Leah Potts, a psychiatric social worker, started the first of such groups in Berkeley. She stresses that the goal of the group is not to reach a decision in eight weeks. Rather, members can expect to gain a clearer understanding of why it is hard to make a decision. She describes the agenda of her groups: "We use discussion, written exercises and optional reading to explore the following topics: our life goals and how children do or do not fit into the things we want to accomplish; how we use time now and how its use would be modified if we had a child; our relationships and how they would be affected by the presence of a child; our childhood experience of growing up and of being parented. We also talk about how we would like to raise children. Then we look at what children need and what strengths and weaknesses we have in meeting those needs. Finally, after looking at how we would live our lives if we had children, we also think about what we would do with our lives if we decided not to have children."

### GETTING MORE EXPOSURE TO CHILDREN

Marlene Heldmann pointed out that many career women have not spent much time around children. Before they find themselves tied to one for at least eighteen years, she thinks they ought to find a way to gain some experience with children in order to "find out what they're getting into." Beth Hall, who reached her final decision to be childless through therapy, had also explored a concrete way to test her feelings about children by volunteering at a day-care center. She learned quickly how she liked being in the company of preschoolers: "Terrible, terrible, it was terrible. The noise level was just unbelievable, because the kids would never stop banging on their little blocks. When I couldn't stand it anymore, I would stand up and just scream, saying, 'Shut up, shut up, all you nasty little children.' All those little faces would look up at me and I felt dreadful. It was a very difficult experience, but I feel I learned a good lesson."

Several of the women we interviewed had borrowed a child from a relative or a friend to see if that would bring them useful insights. Each felt she had gained something from caring for someone else's child, although few women believed it was a valid test of how they might feel about one of their own. One woman kept a friend's toddler one day each week over a period of several months. She said this experience was well worth the effort because it revealed just how a child would fit into her life: "Nowhere, nowhere." It also suggested the ways in which she and her husband might not be good parents: "A child would be very lonely living with us. We're very quiet people. We read a lot and do a lot of nonverbal things. It would be a very isolated kind of environment for a child." Despite the feeling that she had learned a lot, this woman doubts it was a fair test of what her life would really be like with a child because they had created an "artificial environment" for the little visitor. The time they spent on this child—undivided attention as long as he was there—was not the kind of time she felt that she and her husband would put in with their own child, who would be integrated into the rest of the structure of their lives. Also, she added, "If you get bored with someone else's child, you can never be sure that you'd be as bored if it was your own."

Another undecided woman borrowed a friend's three-month-old baby for only one day and she made sure the environment was *not* artificial. She felt the experiences of the day were a good test of both her parenting skills and how well she and her husband might like to take care of a baby: "My husband and I took him to a semipublic screening of a movie, and we got a good dose of a common reaction people often have to parents who bring along their child: 'Why didn't you leave the baby at home?' Later, when we were still with other people, the baby cried a lot and became quite difficult. Neither of us got upset. In fact, we were both pleased by the way we handled the matter. After that experience both my husband and I felt more positive about parenthood."

Borrowing a child or children can bring unexpected insights. When Peg Morrison, a businesswoman, was trying to make up her mind, she invited her two nieces, ages seven and ten, who lived nearby to come to her house and spend occasional weekends. She thought this would give both her and her husband a chance to find out how well they could tolerate round-the-clock child care. Her biggest discovery, which came as quite a shock, was how children affected her egalitarian relationship with her husband. "Every time the kids were visiting I fell right into the traditional woman's role and became the chief cook and bottle washer. My husband would entertain the girls or just relax and take it easy while I assumed the mindless, unrewarding 'organizer's' role—planning meals, getting them on the table, cleaning up, arranging the children's activities. It began to echo my own family situation and that made me nervous as hell. I struggled long and hard to get my husband to share equally with the housework and I saw in a flash that children would take us back to base one. I would never have known how the division of labor between us was going to fall if the children hadn't come over. Now, if we do have kids, at least I know something of the struggle in store for me."

## INSIGHTS FROM THE IMAGINATION

Barbara Cramer and her husband demonstrate well how using a little imagination can help clarify one's feelings and reach a final decision. They devised what they called a "little mental experiment" which helped them resolve their ambivalence. They changed their previous assumption that one day children would enter their lives, and started to assume that they would not. They waited for countermisgivings to arise, but none ever did, and thus the decision to remain childless was finally made. Leah Potts uses a special technique in her "Considering Parenthood" groups which also draws on the imagination. On an arbitrary basis some group members are told to live with the decision during the following week that they will never have a child; the others are to act as if they will. She reports that this approach, in which a person must pretend a firm decision has been made, helps people who deal with their conflicts about parenthood primarily in an intellectual way, to get in touch with their "gut level" emotions.

Fantasies and dreams can also give clues about one's feelings and desires to have or not to have children. An astute and introspective observer may be able to gain some insight from following the wanderings of her mind into various states of consciousness. One woman who thought a child might interfere with her career believed that her fantasies were important indications of a very deep maternal desire, and in making her final decision, she realized she wanted to take that into account. "I have fantasies of having children at all different stages of their lives. They started around five years ago, when I turned thirty, and I have them more and more each year. I have fantasies that I've just gotten pregnant, that I'm five months pregnant, that I'm delivering a baby, that I've got a little baby, that I'm nursing a baby, that there's a child upstairs, that kids are running in and out of the house. I am sure these fantasies tell me that though I am in conflict about motherhood because of my work, I really do *want* to have a baby very much."

Another undecided woman who felt enormous social pressure to have a child had the following dream: "In the first part of the dream I ran around showing my new baby to several older women. The first said, 'Why are you showing that to me? Of course I expected you to have a child.' The second just looked at me coldly and said, 'Oh, I see.' To my surprise and great sadness no one gave me any indication that I had done something 'good.' In the second part of the dream I was on a train and I said to the person sitting next to me, 'Well, I can get off anytime, there are plenty of stops on the way.' And she said, 'No, you cannot. You must stay on till the end of the line. No one gets off till the end.' I was terrified and was trying to decide if I should jump off of the train when I woke up."

She felt she didn't need a psychiatrist to explain the meaning. "That dream made me aware that a lot of my positive feelings about having a baby were really efforts to please others and that this effort was going to get me nowhere. My terror of having to go to the end of the line is symbolic of my fear of making the irrevocable decision of having a child. The fact that I so desperately wanted to get off the train in the dream got me in touch with my very strong negative feelings about having a child which hadn't been brought to consciousness before."

The tools and techniques considered so far may help the undecided woman examine the internal factors affecting her ability to make a choice. External factors, however, should bear on the decision as well. If a woman has decided that she definitely wants to have a child, her next question should be: Is having a child feasible? Some women wonder how much money they need to have before going ahead. There is no simple answer to this question. Janice Ritter, for example, does not earn a great deal of money, and Margaret Donahue earns even less, but both think they can manage quite well. Still, the price tag for raising a child should be considered when trying to make up one's mind. Population economists have tried to figure out how much it costs to raise a child from birth through college. The estimates which appeared in the media in the years 1974 and 1975 ranged from $70,000 through $150,000 for the "direct costs" of one child. In March 1974, *Esquire* magazine came up with an estimate for one "high quality child" (meaning a child from an urban upper-middle-class family who was treated to such things as summer camp, braces for the teeth and private schools) at over $200,000. These figures increase considerably when you add on as "opportunity costs" the potential earnings of a woman who stays at home with her child. The higher the mother's pay, the more the child costs her when she takes off unpaid leaves from her job. With the cost of living rising each year by about 10 percent, those estimates must be revised substantially upwards to reflect the actual costs today. How much is "too much" to pay for having a child is impossible to say. It all depends on what a child means to the individual as well as one's priorities in life.

The importance of a support system was a persistent theme raised by women who had children. And by "support system" they didn't just mean baby-sitters and household help. Anne Gibson stressed that mothers need emotional support as well: "Every person has dependency needs, and I know that the ability to care for those who are dependent on you is related to how well you're able to get your own needs met." The mothers we spoke to were clear: undecided women should carefully assess their resources in terms of the people who will help them, their own reserves of time and energy, and their financial status.

The Voices of Experience had a lot to say about what kind of support is needed by a woman who wants to combine children with her career, and how one can set up a viable system. And the point should be stressed that the kind of support system one needs has a lot to do with the constraints and demands of one's work. And here, Anne Gibson's advice to undecided women bears reiteration: ". . . analyze your work situation and consider what might be changed to help you manage a career and family. Push for paid maternity leave of the kind they have in most enlightened countries. . . . Push for flexibility in your working hours, for optional part-time work or whatever you feel is necessary. But don't wait until you're pregnant to try to get the rules changed. Start planning ahead."

Even with the interviews, the special tools and techniques and consideration of some of the practical matters involved in having children, the new choice of motherhood is likely to remain difficult for many women. This is due partly to the inherent features of the choice—it is irrevocable and the consequences are ultimately unknowable. Also, the choice is difficult because external circumstances—such as the constraints and opportunities of a career and the needs and wishes of other people (particularly a mate) may impinge on the choice by making the consequences more or less difficult to live with.

It may be helpful for the undecided woman to keep in mind that the decision to have children or to remain childless is usually not made all at once. Of course there are some women who do make a firm decision on motherhood early in life, and regardless of later circumstances do not alter their position. But for a great many career women today, the decision crystallizes slowly over time, through a long process in which they analyze the issues over and over again, and evaluate the advantages and disadvantages of either choice in light of the changing circumstances of their lives. Sensitivity to the issues, self-awareness and information are the key ingredients which can make the choice easier.

Finally, there is one last point which we feel is especially appropriate to make in concluding the book: important as the choice of motherhood may be, it should obviously not be considered the one choice which determines the quality of the rest of one's life. As we've learned through the interviews with women who combined children and career, the outcome of their choice was affected by a number of factors, both internal and external. Some degree of conflict and strain was encountered by all. However, the extent of it was influenced by their decisions concerning work and child care which were made after children were added to their lives. Similarly, the consequences of being childless emerge from all the other choices one makes after deciding against motherhood. Whether or not one is lonely in old age depends on the quality of the bonds forged with other people throughout a lifetime. Self-enrichment through generativity depends on the projects a woman sets for herself and on the kinds of relationships she establishes with children or young people. Self-esteem as a childless woman or as a mother will be enhanced or diminished according to all the other decisions and actions of a lifetime.

The choice for *or* against motherhood marks a beginning —not an end.

# Appendix

# THE
# BIOLOGICAL
# CLOCK

Undecided women are very concerned about how much time they have left on their reproductive time clocks, and the biological consequences of late childbearing. Commonly women have a vague feeling that deferring childbearing past thirty increases the likelihood of complications during pregnancy, labor and delivery, and the possibility of birth defects in their children, but rarely do they have the facts. In order to get some perspective on these issues, we consulted physicians and other health professionals and discussed with them the most important problems that women who defer childbearing into their thirties and beyond might encounter. All in all, the news is good. There is growing consensus among health professionals that the medical risks to both the older mother and her baby have been exaggerated, and that healthy women of any childbearing age who have access to fine medical care can look forward to a normal pregnancy and a healthy baby. These optimistic conclusions, however, should not be taken to mean that there are no drawbacks, from a medical standpoint, of postponing children. In the opinion of a great many medical authorities, the *optimal* time for a woman to have her first child is between the ages of twenty-five and twenty-nine. Before considering what the specialists we spoke to had to say about the biological consequences of deferring, we'll call attention to a potential problem few women think about—the possibility of having trouble getting their pregnancies started. Infertility may be the greatest problem these women will face, and often it is the most unexpected.

## INFERTILITY

For the female, the years between fifteen and forty-four are considered the "reproductive life span," although the average age of the onset of menstruation in this country is thirteen, and many women have not reached menopause by age fifty. As a woman approaches menopause, however, her fertility declines. Experts are not in full agreement as to what extent age, in and of itself, accounts for the decline and how much it is due to other factors. Dr. Robert Glass, director of the University of California's Fertility Clinic in San Francisco, points out that one reason it is difficult to assess the reproductive capacities of women in different age groups is that most fertility studies do not take the rate of sexual intercourse into account. "There are data to demonstrate that couples at age thirty-eight are less fertile as a group than those age twenty-eight," commented Dr. Glass, "but that may partially reflect a decreasing rate of intercourse."

Most fertility specialists concur that many women in their late thirties begin to ovulate less frequently, and there is evidence to suggest that the eggs remaining in the ovaries become less fertilizable with age. Age also increases the likelihood that a woman will develop a pelvic condition that may interfere with her ability to conceive or sustain a pregnancy. About 40 percent of women over age forty have fibroid tumors—benign growths attached to the uterine wall. As long as these remain small, they do not interfere with fertility. However, if they grow large, which they tend to do with age, they can cause problems. Endometriosis—a condition in which the cells of the lining of the uterus become lodged on the reproductive organs outside the uterus or on the ligaments in the pelvic cavity—is also strongly associated with both age and infertility. And the longer a woman defers childbearing, the greater the likelihood is that she will develop this disorder. Pelvic infections, due, for example, to venereal disease, can lead to scarring of the reproductive organs and cause infertility and even sterility. Again, the older a woman is before she attempts to conceive, the more time she will have had to incur an infection. Also, there is speculation that a number of systemic diseases, some drugs and possibly environmental factors such as radiation and chemicals can negatively affect a woman's ability to reproduce. The longer she lives, of course, the more exposure she will have to their effects.

All of these factors add up to a long list of potential problems, but according to the specialists we consulted, the vast majority of women, at least until age forty, will be able to conceive without difficulty. For those who do plan to defer, there is a final important factor to keep in mind. Men, too, have a reproductive time clock, though it ticks more slowly than a woman's. They are exposed to the same potentially damaging environmental influences, and men over fifty produce fewer and less active sperm. Even a man in his forties does not have the same reproductive potential as a man in his twenties. If the reproductive system of both partners has become substantially less efficient with age, fertility problems are compounded.

Can a woman planning to defer childbearing predict whether or not she will have fertility problems later on, and take any measures to prevent them? Unfortunately, the only sure test of fertility for a woman is pregnancy itself. A woman who has scanty or irregular periods, or has had a serious pelvic infection or a diagnosed touch of endometriosis, should anticipate that she may encounter difficulty conceiving later on. If, due to the conditions mentioned above, she has been subfertile in her twenties, her fertility will probably drop off more rapidly after age thirty. However, a woman who has *not* had these difficulties and plans to defer past thirty-five would not be considered by most gynecologists to be running a special fertility risk.

Women who plan to defer childbearing would be well advised to seek counseling from their gynecologists or other fertility counselors about the risks and benefits of various methods of birth control, and their possible effects on fertility. Dr. Glass maintains that although there are many good reasons to fear the pill, its potential for depressing fertility has been exaggerated. Recent large studies have demonstrated that within two years after stopping the pill, users, as a group, regained the same level of fertility as nonusers. The IUD is now considered to be a more serious threat to a woman's fertility because the risk of tubal damage through infection is three to ten times greater than is found in the general population. As a result, many physicians now counsel patients who do not have children but plan to someday not to use the IUD. The diaphragm, properly used, is considered to be both an effective and innocuous means of contraception.

The consensus of the health professionals we consulted was that regular pelvic examinations are the best safeguard against unexpectedly discovering fertility problems later on.

## BIRTH DEFECTS

Only one birth defect, Down's syndrome, or mongolism, has been definitely proven to be associated with advanced maternal age. Down's syndrome is the single most common cause of mental retardation in the United States. Approximately 1 in 600 babies born each year is so afflicted. Though it is often referred to as a genetic disorder, it is rarely hereditary. Only in an estimated 3 percent of the cases is the disorder passed down through the generations. In the remaining 97 percent of the cases, it is caused by the presence of an extra chromosome in the fetus; instead of the normal 46, there are 47. The disorder is clearly associated with maternal age. For a woman under age twenty, the risk of having a mongoloid baby is only about 1 in 2,500. Throughout her twenties the risk remains very low—about 1 in 1,500. Between the ages of thirty and thirty-four, the risk is about 1 in 750. In the years between thirty-five and thirty-nine the risk increases to 1 in 280. After forty, the risk is 1 in 100, and after forty-five it is 1 in 40.

Fortunately, all recognized chromosomal disorders, of which Down's syndrome is the most common, can now be detected during early pregnancy by means of amniocentesis. In this procedure a sample of amniotic fluid is withdrawn from a pregnant woman's uterus sometime between the thirteenth and sixteenth week of gestation. The fetal cells in the fluid are then cultured and analyzed. By examining the cells under a microscope, technicians can spot abnormalities in the chromosomal pattern. If the fetus is afflicted with mongolism or another chromosomal disorder, the woman can decide whether or not she wants to terminate her pregnancy. In about 98 percent of the women who have amniocentesis performed it turns out that the baby does not have a defect present. The analysis can also detect nearly seventy inherited biochemical disorders which are not related to maternal age, and it will also identify the baby's sex.

When done by a highly trained physician, amniocentesis is accurate in diagnosing chromosomal and genetic abnormalities, and the risk to the mother and fetus is very small. At the University of California's Prenatal Detection Center, where more amniocenteses are performed than at any other center in the world (over a thousand a year), Director Dr. Mitchell Golbus reports that the risk of complications is less than one half of 1 percent. But in inexperienced hands the risks to the mother, such as infection or bleeding, and the risks to the fetus, such as fetal puncture or induced abortion, substantially increase. In recognition of this fact, the National Foundation—March of Dimes, which funds most of the genetic service programs in this country, has formulated a clear position regarding the conditions under which amniocentesis should and should not be performed. According to Dr. Arthur

Salisbury, Vice President for Medical Services: "The procedure should only be done in a hospital (on an inpatient or on an outpatient basis) and only by an experienced obstetrician who performs the procedure at least weekly, at the very minimum. It must be done in close collaboration with the medical geneticist at the hospital or medical school, and only if ultrasound is available immediately prior to the procedure so that the physician can locate the placenta and fetus."

At most centers in the United States where amniocentesis is performed, only women thirty-five years or older are eligible to use the service, if the only suspected disorder is Down's syndrome. If a woman is at risk of having a baby with an hereditary disorder, however, she is eligible for the procedure at any age. Most experts concur that the incidence of mongolism or other serious chromosomal defects under age thirty-five is not high enough to warrant the procedure. In Dr. Golbus' opinion, however, that cutoff point is as much an administrative decision as a medical one. He pointed out that "there is no magical age, say thirty-five, where a woman is suddenly at risk. The incidence of chromosomal abnormalities does not abruptly take off at some specific age; it rises on a curve. But if we lower the age to under thirty-five, we would not have the facilities to accommodate the needs of women over thirty-five who are statistically at greater risk."

Though the number of amnioceuteses performed in this country has doubled in the past two years (an estimated 15,000–18,000 in 1978) the demand exceeds the services available, and it may be a long time until every woman who wants to have the procedure performed will be able to do so. Almost all of the approximately seventy-five centers where amnioceuteses are currently performed are in the major urban centers. Besides the limited availability of trained physicians and technicians, cost may be an obstacle to some women. Average fees in 1978 ranged from $350 to $450.

A woman interested in locating the center nearest her should first consult her obstetrician. If she does not get the answers she needs there, she can write to the National Foundation—March of Dimes, P.O. Box 2000, White Plains, New York 10605, and request the names of program directors of the centers in her geographic area. The National Foundation also publishes *International Directory of Genetic Services,* which lists hundreds of genetic counseling units associated with hospitals, medical schools and research institutes. Many medical authorities recommend that women having their first child over age thirty-five seek genetic counseling. A professionally trained counselor can help an individual woman or a couple assess their risk of having a baby with a hereditary or an age-related disorder, and make the decision whether or not to seek an amniocentesis.

## PREGNANCY, LABOR AND DELIVERY

The Council of the International Federation of Obstetricians and Gynecologists calls a first-time mother age thirty-five or older an "elderly primapara" and places her in the "high risk" category, indicating that she should be treated with special care. However, medical authorities are unable to say with certainty at this time to what extent (if at all) a *healthy* first-time mother of thirty-five, thirty-eight or forty runs a greater risk of problems during childbearing than a healthy woman ten years her junior. Some physicians we consulted felt that age in and of itself does not dispose a first-time older mother to any greater difficulties; others believed that a woman over thirty-five, even in good health, would be somewhat more prone to complications during pregnancy, labor and delivery. They pointed out that cervical dilation may proceed more slowly in older women, and that women over thirty often have less muscle tone and therefore weaker contractions. Uterine fibroids, as we have noted before, tend to develop and grow with age. In addition to interfering with fertility, they can cause complications during labor. The specialists we spoke to concurred, however, that the most important fact for deferring women to keep in mind is that as middle age approaches, one is more likely to develop medical problems such as diabetes, hypertension, and kidney and heart diseases which can interfere with maternal-fetal interaction and jeopardize the health of the mother and the baby.

Dr. Robert Neff, a clinical instructor at the University of California Medical Center and a practicing obstetrician-gynecologist in Berkeley, is one of many specialists who feel that age in and of itself does not place a woman or her baby at greater risk: "If a woman asks me, 'Can I wait to have a baby until I'm thirty-five?' I say, 'Sure.' 'Forty?' 'Sure.' You can have a baby as long as you can get pregnant. In our office, we do not feel that older mothers are at greater risk—unless, of course, they begin their pregnancies with pre-existing medical illnesses. Even then we can be reassuring. With modern obstetrical tools and a greater understanding of physiology, we're able to handle the problems which may arise much better now than ever before. So, even for women who are at greater risk because of their medical problems, we can almost always expect a positive outcome."

Dr. Maida Taylor, an obstetrician on the staff of Children's Hospital in San Francisco, states that all things considered, there's a trade-off for "old" new mothers. Although they may be somewhat more disposed to medical problems, women who defer childbearing because of careers are likely to have an *advantage* over younger, less mature women: "The woman who waits to have her child until she feels emotionally mature, financially secure and sufficiently established in her work gains an advantage which will no doubt positively affect the outcome of her pregnancy. Psychological stability, as we know, has a profound effect on physical well-being. Personally, I would rather take care of a mature, well-nourished thirty-five-year-old woman who has deferred until such time that pregnancy really fits into her life than a twenty-two-year-old who is ambivalent about the pregnancy. Even though the older woman might have more medical problems, her motivation, devotion and commitment to her pregnancy will hopefully enable her to cope with whatever problems come along."

Part of coping with the problems may involve accepting restrictions such as extended periods of bed rest, increased testing and monitoring, and a drug regime, should complications arise during pregnancy. Also, an older woman's options for the place of childbirth and the mode of delivery may be more limited. Most obstetricians feel strongly that older women especially should labor in a hospital where advanced facilities are available. Women of all ages in this country are more likely than ever before to have operative rather than vaginal deliveries. According to a recent hospital-record study, in the period between 1971 and 1976, the number of Caesareans performed rose almost 87 percent. Older first-time mothers are the most likely of all women to have Caesarean sections. Almost always, as Dr. Neff points out, this is done on behalf of the fetus, not the mother. "Every time a woman goes into labor there is a risk to her and the fetus. When it's an older woman, and there is a chance that this is the only child that she will ever have, you want to make sure that it is alive and well. So I call a halt to the risk-taking much earlier through surgical intervention." He added that in his middle-class practice, patients tolerated the surgery very well. However, women should be aware that the risk of every complication incurred with vaginal deliveries increases when a woman has an operative delivery. Older mothers are already at greater risk of vascular complications, such as thrombophlebitis, pulmonary emboli and cerebrovascular accidents because of their age, and there are many physicians, like Dr. Taylor, who believe that "when you do a C-section on women over thirty-five, you're giving them a 'double whammy.' "

The best prevention for complications of pregnancy, labor and delivery later are regular medical checkups and the basic practices of maintaining good health—proper diet, sufficient rest and exercise. Every pregnant woman should consult her obstetrician during her first trimester. For the women over thirty-five this is especially important, since the early visit will give her physician time to arrange an amniocentesis (should she request it), which must be done between the thirteenth and sixteenth week of gestation. Unless unexpected complications arise during pregnancy, a woman over thirty-five can expect that her prenatal care will be the same as that of a younger woman: visits once a month until thirty-two weeks, then visits every other week until thirty-six weeks, and after that, weekly visits until delivery.

We suggest that pregnant women over thirty find a physician or other health provider who is not alarmist, but at the same time is aware of the attendant risks to older new mothers and is willing to discuss them fully with the patient. Both sides need to be informed of the options for such things as amniocentesis, different modes of delivery, the use of anaesthesia and labor-stimulating drugs. If good lines of communication have been laid and trust is developed early, when things happen most rapidly, which is usually in labor, decisions that have been mutually agreed upon can effectively be made.

#### SUGGESTIONS FOR FURTHER READING
#### ON THE SUBJECT OF DEFERRED PREGNANCY

Apgar, Virginia, M.D., M.P.H., and Beck, Joan. *Is My Baby All Right?* (New York: Pocket Books, 1974). Gives a highly informative and detailed discussion of birth defects and the mechanisms of heredity.

Boston Women's Health Collective. *Our Bodies, Ourselves* (New York: Simon and Schuster, 1977). A comprehensive guide to women's health which contains several chapters on pregnancy and childbirth.

Price, Jane. *You're Not Too Old to Have a Baby* (New York: Farrar, Straus and Giroux, 1977). Informative discussion of the biological, psychological and social aspects of late motherhood.

# WHAT ABOUT ADOPTION?

If a career woman's time on the biological clock runs out, what are her chances of adopting? If she is willing to adopt an older child or one with physical or emotional handicaps, her chances are good. However, married or not, the likelihood of her adopting a healthy infant or even a child under two years of age through a private or public agency is very, very slim. As most people are aware, the number of infants available for adoption in the United States has greatly declined, whereas the number wishing to adopt has not. As a result, agencies can now be extremely picky about whom they select as adoptive parents. Although most agencies do not have a policy which sets age limits for prospective adopters, in practice successful applicants almost always fall within the range usual for biological parents—between twenty-five and thirty-five years of age. An older woman who intends to pursue her career will be at a special disadvantage. Although she would not automatically be turned down by most agencies as long as she could provide adequate child care, in practice babies are almost always placed with nonworking mothers. Even younger couples with nonworking wives who pass all the agency eligibility requirements with flying colors can expect a waiting period of from three to four years for a healthy infant. A married career woman in her forties with a full or even a part-time job would probably have to wait forever.

Because of the few babies available and the restrictions which make it so difficult to adopt through private or public agencies, some couples are turning to independent adoption. In this nonagency procedure, often referred to as the "gray market," an adoption lawyer who is in contact with a pregnant woman handles the transaction. In exchange for the pregnant woman's medical expenses and the lawyer's fee, the couple acquires a baby. Since most states have laws which permit parents to place a child for adoption with a family of their choice, the process is legal. Unfortunately, however, lawyers who specialize in this procedure are often reputed to exploit the desire of childless couples for children by charging exorbitant fees. Recent estimates range from $3,000 to more than $25,000. Even at these prices there are few babies available on the gray market.

While there is a great shortage of healthy infants, there are thousands of older children and children with handicaps who need homes, and recently adoption agencies have begun to focus most of their energies on finding parents for them. The standards, rules and procedures for adopting the "hard to place" child have become increasingly more flexible to allow more people who want to to adopt. Thus, if an older career woman, married or single, can demonstrate that she can take care of such a child and that she fits the needs of a particular child, her chances of adopting are good. Regional computerized exchange systems are now being set up all over the country to facilitate the process of matching "waiting" children with potential adoptive parents. More couples and individuals who are unable to adopt infants are now taking advantage of the option to become parents of older children or children with special needs. Several books on the subject suggest that there are unique satisfactions to be gained by those who accept the challenge these children offer.

## BOOKS OF INTEREST FOR WOMEN
## WHO WISH TO ADOPT OLDER OR SPECIAL CHILDREN

Anderson, David C. *Children of Special Value* (New York: St. Martin's Press, 1971).

Kadushin, Alfred. *Adopting Older Children* (New York: Columbia University Press, 1970).

McNamara, Joan. *Adoptions Adviser* (New York: Hawthorn Books, 1975).

Rondell, Florence, and Murray, Anne-Marie. *New Dimensions in Adoption* (New York: Crown, 1974).

## About the Authors

MARILYN FABE attended Northwestern University and received her Ph. D. in English Literature from the University of California, Berkeley.

NORMA WIKLER did undergraduate work at the University of Michigan and the Sorbonne in Paris. She received her Ph. D. in sociology from the University of California, Berkeley.

Both authors now live in Berkeley.